About the Author

Dr George Blair-West is a medical doctor, psychiatrist and a lover of entrancing tales like those of King Arthur. Sub-specialising in three areas only: relationship therapy, obesity and trauma therapy, his experience in the latter has taken him to confronting the very limits of human tragedy, distress and pain.

Taught by the greatest teachers of all, his patients, he has been deeply inspired and instructed on how to not just rise above adversity, but to appreciate its inherent teachings. This has led him to a therapeutic focus of helping people find meaning and purpose in their life. Moreover, his work with the obese has highlighted the research findings of a strong link between a lack of purpose and obesity. Without an alternative, eating and food can become the most meaningful part of a person's day.

With the power of story-telling and metaphor, he weaves what he has learnt from working with many, many people over twenty-five years into this tale of great minds and big hearts as this world clashes with the next. The Way of the Quest is his third book. He has a son and a daughter and lives in Brisbane, Australia, with his wife of twenty-four years and a labradoodle.

For more information on his work and recent writings, visit his blog site: dr.blair-west.com

Published by Alclare Pty Ltd
4b/80 Stamford Rd, Indooroopilly, Qld 4068, Australia
P: +61 (0)7 3878 1222
www.thewayofthequest.com

Jacket image design - Stuart Fraser
Jacket design – Marija Vilotijevic

Copyright © 2012 - George W Blair-West

All rights reserved. No part of this book may be reproduced or transmitted in any form or by any means, electronic or mechanical, including photocopying, recording, or by any information storage and retrieval system, without the written permission of the publisher, except where permitted by law.

DISTRIBUTORS

AUSTRALIA: DENNIS JONES & ASSOC PTY LTD
1/10 Melrich Road, Bayswater, VICTORIA 3153
P: +61 (0)3 9762 9100
E: theoffice@dennisjones.com.au

INTERNATIONAL: LIGHTNING SOURCE INC. (US)
1246 Heil Quaker Blvd
La Vergne, TN USA 37086
P: +1 615 213 5815
E: inquiry@lightningsource.com

*"**This magnificent and magical tale**, while taking me to far off lands, helped me back into my own heart and soul. This is a captivating and delicious reminder that we, like the Knights of old, have the right to defend the truth of our own being with courage, honour, love and wisdom. This story will light your journey with some long forgotten truths about who we are, what we are capable of, the importance of finding our meaning and the immense and adventurous journey that life is supposed to be."*
– Krista Fuller, Writer & Editor

*"**Dr George hooks the reader with the perfect blend of absorbing history and witty asides as he weaves an epic tale.** While it is rare for me to reread, I have read this thoroughly enjoyable book twice and then dipped into it again. It is powerfully uplifting to be reminded, as we deal with life's challenges, how to look for the signposts to guide us back to what gives our life meaning and purpose. The backstory on Francis Bacon and Shakespeare was equally fascinating."*
– Jennifer Saggers, Education Advisor

*"**A wondrous adventure to places, within yourself and beyond!** This multi-dimensional tale takes you into a fascinating history touched by fantasy and great legends. The challenges of finding one's meaning is intricately woven with ancient wisdom and intrigue – sparking our inner worlds with a revelatory light. With story-telling magic Dr George has crafted a book that entertains at the same time as it provokes and astonishes."*
– Kathryn Brimblecombe-Fox,
Artist & Author of 'For Everyone'

The Way of The Quest

*A young Shakespeare's search
for life's meaning & purpose*

Dr George Blair-West

DENNIS JONES & ASSOC
MELBOURNE AUSTRALIA

*f*or my Mother

Your incisive mind, your knowledge of modern history and
your preparedness for patient debate has
honed this story into an even more
rigorous and complete work.
More than anything else, I thank
you for your eternal faith in me. I only wish
that every child was given such a precious gift.

With thanks to

Jenny Saggers, for your informed feedback, historical
contribution and eternal enthusiasm for this entire project.
Andrew Matthews, for your deep wisdom – which appears at a
couple of points in this book – your advice, support and laughs.
My long-suffering wife and love of my life – I so value
your attention to detail, your patience in re-reading
ideas you have heard too many times over,
and your putting up with my less than
excited responses to your always
constructive criticism!

CONTENTS

Foreword 13

I	708 A.D.	19
II	1560 A.D.	27
III	1577 A.D. Francis at 16	34
IV	The Dream	46
V	Mont Tombe	53
VI	The True Chevaliers	68
VII	Diablo	74
VIII	Catherine	79
IX	The Duke	89
X	Marguerite	101
XI	A Better Question	109
XII	The First Master	113
XIII	The Templar	125
XIV	A Bed for the Night	142
XV	The Code of Chivalry	146
XVI	The Grand Rue	158
XVII	The Question	168
XVIII	The Greatest Weapon of All	170
XIX	The Letter	180
XX	The Bishop	183
XXI	Focus	196
XXII	The Church's Great Secret	209
XXIII	The Answer	216
XXIV	The Meeting	235
XXV	True Love	246

XXVI	The Importance of Evil	264
XXVII	Alchemy	271
XXVIII	Dear Francis	286
	Epilogue	291
	Afterword - The Backstory	292
	The Shakespeare Authorship Question	298

These quotations and those at the beginning of each chapter are all by Sir Francis Bacon

A witty conceit is oftentimes a conveyor of a truth not so well ferried over.

Reading maketh a full person, conference a ready person, and writing an exact person.

Some books are to be tasted, others to be swallowed and some few to be chewed and digested.

FOREWORD

(Do not read this now – jump straight into the story –
I recommend reading it after chapter five - GBW)

*Imagination was given to man
to compensate him for what he is not;
a sense of humour to console him for what he is.*

This medieval tale, first and foremost, is an exploration of the importance of the personal quest of making sense of one's life. Why am I here? What is meaningful for me? How does this awareness help me to pursue my purpose in life? Why should I work out my purpose in life? What will make my life happy and rewarding?

These are the questions this book explores in the context of an unfolding drama of a young man starting out on his adult life. It was no coincidence that I began writing it as my two teenage children were grappling with the almost unreasonable task of making life-changing career decisions as they finished high school.

The focus of this book reflects my work over the last twenty-five years as a psychiatrist with a particular interest in helping people make sense of just these questions and their underlying issues. I specialise in treating just three areas: trauma, relationship problems and obesity. Specialising in the management of severe trauma (e.g. childhood sexual abuse, attempted murder, witnessing violent deaths of loved ones) in particular, has given me a potent insight into the human mind.

I have been honoured to participate in, and to appreciate, just how the human mind can make sense of, and heal from, the worst kinds of human experiences. Through this work, I came to appreciate the critical role of meaning and purpose in our lives in making sense of adversity. Along the way, I have also had insights into the minds of perpetrators who might be considered the more 'evil' among us.

The central male character in this book is an historical figure who influenced the very world we all live in – Francis Bacon. When I was at medical school, he was first introduced to me as the 'Father of Modern Science.' As it turns out, he was so much more. Amongst other initiatives and writings, his call for collaborative, critical evaluation became the basis of modern scientific research.

Relax, this story will not be a history lesson – no more than the tales of Merlin or King Arthur are history lessons. It is the tale of a young man, who runs away from his responsibilities, meets a woman and has to deal with life's challenges as he tries to make sense of this thing called 'life'. My point here is simply to introduce you to the young man you are about to meet and some of the rather extraordinary mysteries that encircle his life.

If our male protagonist seems a little too clever and knowledgeable (not so much with the ladies), the reality is that in real life, he was probably much smarter again. Growing up in an intellectual home, it is a fact that he attended Cambridge University from the tender age of twelve. At sixteen, after commencing his law studies, he was sent to France as the assistant to Queen Elizabeth's Ambassador to the French Court.

Why choose Francis Bacon? For over a decade, I have been researching the interface between power, politics and religion. Part of this research has focussed on the authorship and evolution of the Bible. (For the record, I am not a supporter of any particular religion – although I do see myself as a spiritual individual.) In my research I came across just one line that resulted in Francis Bacon becoming the protagonist of the book you are about to read.

I was reading about the editing of what would become the Authorised King James Bible and what happened when the appointed editors presented it to their King. The line? 'It was self-evident that James was not competent to check their work and edit it, so he passed the manuscripts on to the greatest genius of all time ... Sir Francis Bacon' (WFC Wigston, *Bacon and the Rosicrucians,* 1888). As well as senior advisor to the King, as Lord Chancellor, this man of many talents was head of the English justice system.

Francis Bacon's wide breadth of knowledge and influence is such that I had incorrectly assumed he was a physician. Technically, he was a lawyer. So how does history evaluate Francis Bacon? He ranks twelfth in McWhirter's top 100 legal minds of all time. He is ahead of Aristotle (21), Franklin D. Roosevelt (41), Ghandi (49) and Martin Luther King Jr (52).

Francis Bacon was a particular kind of genius, he was a polymath. A polymath is defined by Mirriam-Webster as 'a person of encyclopaedic learning.' They are experts in a wide range of fields in both the arts and sciences. Wikipedia lists examples of the great polymaths as follows: 'Leonardo da Vinci, Michelangelo, Galileo Galilei, Copernicus and Francis Bacon.' The breadth and depth of his writings are hard to grasp. He published over thirty books and detailed essays on philosophy, the law, science, history, natural history, botany, biblical issues, medicine and music.

In Michael Hart's book *The 100: A Ranking of the Most Influential Persons in History* (2000), Francis Bacon comes in at 90 (in the 1992 edition he ranked 78). He is ahead of people like Mikhail Gorbachev (for bringing communism to an end), Henry Ford (for mass production), Queen Elizabeth, Leonardo da Vinci and Gandhi.

I have always been intrigued and captivated by great minds. It is why I love reading biographies and researching people's lives. Three eternal questions for me are: What inspired them? How much of greatness comes from experiences in their formative years? How did they manage meaning and purpose in their lives? I have no doubt that I became a psychiatrist, in part, because of my natural fascination with how it was that people became who they become.

In working as a trauma therapist you can spend a long time working with people, especially victims of gross childhood abuse.

After many hours of exploration, over many months, the pattern inevitably emerges. An internal consistency becomes clear such that later adult behaviours can be readily understood in terms of formative year experiences. The human mind is not so complicated. It just takes time to understand. So, to bring Francis Bacon (back) to life, I read all I could about the boy and the man.

A couple of years into working on this book, on a trip to the United Kingdom to promote my first book, I was able to take some time to further research the life of Francis Bacon and fill in some gaps. It was a singular experience to visit the ruins of Old Gorhambury House where he grew up and then St Albans, the town that he lived in (more on this in the Afterword at the end of this book). I also visited the huge British Library in London and it was here that I found the books asserting that Francis Bacon was the son of Queen Elizabeth. In the end, I found no less than six books on the subject (listed in the Afterword).

The two controversial mysteries that this book plays with – the authorship of Shakespeare's works and Francis Bacon's mother being Queen Elizabeth – were not initially intended to be a part of the story. In researching the life of Francis Bacon and the people around him, however, these issues came up again and again – creating a story just begging to be told. In the end, I gave in. I was particularly interested in repeated accounts of Queen Elizabeth taking an ongoing interest in the young Francis Bacon and his precocious intellect. How many boys gain the respect and attention of a Queen? She referred to him as 'my young Lord Keeper.'

You may or may not be aware of the longstanding debates around who was the real author of Shakespeare's works. To summarise, I think it is not unreasonable to observe that the debate is at the point where, on the balance of probabilities, it is highly unlikely that the author was the actor from Stratford, known as 'Shakespeare' by the masses. As part of my research for this book, I also researched all that I could find on the man from Stratford. In the Afterword I go into this research in greater depth. Certainly more attention has been given to, and more books written on, the question: Who was the real author?

A key aspect of the argument is that to write Shakespeare, as well as being a naturally gifted writer, the author must be highly educated and unusually knowledgeable of many fields – a polymath in fact – and worldly in his travels and personal experience. Things that the actor from Stratford, by all accounts, lacked in spectacular degree. In particular, the author, to write plays like Macbeth and Richard III, needed to be intimate with life at court. This is something that we know that the actor from Stratford was definitely not.

There is much written about the characters at the courts of Queen Elizabeth and King James. Nobody tries to argue that the actor from Stratford was amongst them. Francis Bacon was entrenched at both – starting at a very young age.

Accordingly, the other part of this book that I researched extensively, and is factually correct, is the cultural and intellectual environment in which Francis Bacon grew up. Of particular interest was Anne Bacon's advanced education and superior intellect. I see this as pivotal in identifying the author of Shakespeare's works. I believe that the most powerful argument is that given that the writer of Shakespeare's works was clearly a genius and a polymath, we just need to look for the geniuses of the time – it was not a long list … (For interested readers I have gone into much greater detail on all of these issues in the backstory in the Afterword.)

The book that you are about to read covers a few months in the life of young Francis. The contextual history of England and France of this time is factual, as are each of the main characters at Elizabeth's court and in Francis' circle of friends and family. So too are the histories of the Chevaliers of Mont St Michel, Robert of Torigni, the Templars, and the deliberations of the Ecumenical Councils. The rumours in the French and Spanish courts about her pregnancy, the surprising interactions between Queen Elizabeth and her French Ambassador around it and Francis Bacon's parentage, are all based on the accounts of other historical writers. The legends portrayed in the first chapter and later, about the donkey that became a wolf, are all retold legends of The Mont.

However, the events of his life once he arrives at Mont St Michel depart from history and are fictional. While in France, it is true that Francis Bacon met and became enamoured by Marguerite de Valois, Queen of Navarre. However, they met at the French court, not on Mont St Michel.

The setting was inspired by my visit to the truly legendary Mont Saint Michel as it sits around two thousand metres off the coast of France. To this day, I can clearly recall the majesty of its appearance when I first glimpsed it over the trees along an otherwise somewhat unremarkable coastline.

I came to understand why The Mont became the alternative to Jerusalem as a place of pilgrimage. I could not help but wonder at the stories it could tell if its walls could talk. I was not disappointed. As I went looking for the history of The Mont I found legends, strange happenings, great people and accounts of heroes and their great battles – I have included most of these, almost word for word, in this story you are about to read.

The quotes at the beginning of each chapter are all those of Francis Bacon. The Sonnets in the text are attributed to Shakespeare – who I strongly suspect was Francis Bacon. Finally, I ask the women readers to forgive the male-centric viewpoint presented in Francis Bacon's quotes. Despite his forward thinking and his respect for the women of his time e.g. Anne Bacon and Queen Elizabeth, he was nevertheless a product of his age.

I 708 A.D.

Every man should be quick to hear,
slow to speak, and slow to anger.

His long, exquisitely tailored, purple and white velvet robes swished as he strode along the ornate cloisters. For Bishop Aubert, it was just another perfect day. Life was good. Try as they might, no one could have convinced him that within the hour he would sport a hole in his skull the size of a man's finger.

As the most powerful man in the region which surrounded the thriving town of Avranches of Normandy, on the west coast of France, he enjoyed a life of wealth and luxury. A life of abundance. No pleasure was out of his reach. He had almost forgotten the dreams he had had on each of the last two full moons. While they had seemed disturbingly real, Aubert was not a man so interested in the spiritual side of his work. He knew the biblical texts as well as the next Bishop, but he was a quick learner with a superb memory, rather than a diehard devotee of the faith. He was interested in the power 'the faith' gave him. Having faith he would leave to the masses.

He understood the masses. He knew, better than they did, what they needed at any point in time. From his lofty height, he could look down his eagle beak nose at all of them. He was easily the tallest man in the diocese. It was in his fourteenth year that he grew to be the tallest in his village. Initially his height was an embarrassment, but in time, the young Aubert learnt to use it to his own ends.

As if people were demonstrating their formidable powers of observation and enlightening him to the incredible news, they would utter inanities like, 'You are a tall boy are you not?' Initially he humoured them with a smile, but this was not his nature. Over time, he found himself responding with a comment like, 'Only at one end,' which confused them nicely. As his boredom mounted, he responded with lines like 'No, I suspect you are shrinking to your true size.'

It was not long after his fifteenth birthday that he noticed that people seem to listen to him and pay him respect. Initially, he was not sure why, but as he realised that his height had something to do with it, he puffed out his chest and pushed his shoulders back. It was his proud mother who pointed out that people 'looked up to him'. He found this phrase amusing.

He came realise that when people had to look up at you, they looked up to you. Especially when you were lean and strong as well as tall. Tall, fat people did not seem to enjoy the same respect. Aubert asked his father, the tax collector, if he could work his uncle's farm. It was not that he liked hard work. He detested it, but he wanted to add muscle to his height. While he could take no credit for the height God had given him, he intended to make the most of it. After all, presumably God saw him as worthy of such a gift. Besides, he liked people looking up to him.

After two summers, he never went back into the field as his father's bribes to the then Bishop gained him entrance to the hallowed halls of the monastery.

Over time, Aubert perfected his 'commanding presence,' as he liked to think of it. During scripture study, he had observed his peers when they got anxious and saw how they rushed their words when questioned by the monks. Not only were they more likely to say something they might regret, he noticed that people in authority knew that rushed, ill-thought-out responses were a sign of insecurity and lesser intelligence. He learnt that if he responded to questions by hesitating as if thinking deeply, then responding slowly, as if he was measuring his words, his authority was greater.

In reality, speaking slowly allowed him to recall from his prodigious memory the words of great thinkers that he had read. Original thought was not something Aubert pursued. Why bother when others had done the thinking for him? This strategy, along with some well-placed bribes, had made him the youngest Bishop in France. Now he applied this energy to the younger widows in his bishopric to whom he often gave solace and comfort. Indeed, he had just left his private chapel after some hours of 'comfort-giving' to a rather attractive, well-bosomed, young parishioner. She had, oh so sadly, been recently widowed after a terrible accident had befallen her husband. Who better than the Bishop to comfort her at every level?

So, as the sun was setting on yet another glorious day of his charmed life, he was surprised to find the lone figure leaning against the wall as he returned from the chapel. This should not be. This was a locked-off section of the cathedral that no one but he had access to. The man seemed strangely familiar. And there was something else about him – he did not move. He stood perfectly still, seeming to shimmer in the soft evening light.

However, it was his sheer size that impressed. While he faced away from the Bishop, it was obvious that he towered over the Bishop by a head. His cascading, wavy blonde hair fell down over his coat. His dark red leather coat, in turn, ran to his ankles. His powerful shoulders were more than an axe handle across. The fit of his exquisite coat, inlaid with a fine pattern of precious stones, narrowed to his slim hips. The Bishop had met enough warriors to know one from a distance, but he could not recall a warrior in such finery who carried himself like a king.

'Wh-who are you? How did you get in here?' the Bishop demanded with less confidence than he was used to wielding.

Slowly the man turned. The Bishop could not help but notice the sword at the man's waist as it came into view. It reached from his stomach to his ankles. Even sheathed, the sword lit its scabbard. It glowed as if linked ethereally to the very sun. Its light shone upwards from the mouth of the scabbard, bouncing off the diamonds and precious stones inlaid into its elaborate, foot-long handle. No mortal could wield such a weapon effectively.

'Do you not remember me?' The voice was deep, but menacingly quiet.

The Bishop faltered. His hand went to the balustrade to support himself. The being before him was all too familiar. His image was to be found throughout the cathedrals of Christendom. The Bishop's dreams from the nights of the full moons returned to him.

As the great warrior turned to fully face him, his face was aglow, as if lit by the same inner luminescence as his sword. Aubert's memory gave up its name – the Sword of Truth. His hands and wrists glowed alike. His features were fine, the jaw-line strong. He was irresistibly beautiful. In the Bishop's dreams, it had been clear to him who this was, but this was no dream.

He prostrated himself before the being. If he had not been a true Bishop of the faith, in that moment he became one.

'Commander of the Great Celestial Army of our Holy Father, I beseech your forgiveness.' The words came out in a hoarse whisper. From his prostrate position, he could only see the Archangel's knee-high leather boots in front of him. It took a moment for his mind to register, as Archangel Michael turned and stepped closer, that the heels of the boots made no sound on the paved floor. The Bishop's mind raced to make sense of what was happening.

'Rise, Aubert.'

Slowly he found his feet.

'Walk with me.'

His feet were slow to respond. He sensed displeasure from the Archangel.

'Why have you not done as I asked?'

'I am sorry, My Lord. I thought they were just dreams.'

'I am displeased. You are rather slow on the uptake. If you were any slower, you would walk backwards.'

The Bishop went to object …

'Do not waste your breath. You will never be the man your mother was. Pay attention. If I, or my brethren, ever appear in a dream with specific instructions, it is never "just a dream." Especially the second time. So now I must waste my time visiting you in this heavy flesh. This is only one of many realms that I have to oversee and while there are many in this dimension that I have time for, that is a list you do not rate a mention on.'

Aubert blanched at the rebuke. 'I should have known My Lord. Please forgive me. Again, I beseech you. I am but your humble servant.'

'Humility is not your strong point Aubert. Indeed, it is not even a weak one for you.'

The Bishop did not even think of arguing. He was acutely aware that only one pair of steps echoed off the stonewalls as they walked.

'Believe me when I say that if I could deal with another, I would. However, Mont Tombe is in your Bishopric. In your physical world, there are few places its equal when it comes to spiritual significance. Here the separation between our worlds is at it thinnest. It is however, much more than a gateway. Your world needs a safe, defendable place that can be a storehouse, a repository of wisdom and great knowledge. This wisdom will be found both in those who will go there, as much as in its stonewalled repository.

'Your world needs a hallowed place of teaching, with a great library, that can be readily defended by but a handful of devout warriors. In the millennia to come, long after your never-too-early demise, it will hold true. As great wars rage across this earth, as man attacks man from the skies and from under the oceans, its great library and underground repository will endure.

'Humankind will need such places, as few sites will be able to withstand the forces of destruction that man will bring to warfare in time. Moreover, it sits outside of what will become the great cities of your world. It will be largely overlooked by marauders.

'As I have told you in your dreams, you need to build an oratory on it as a start. You need to mark it with my sign. In this way, my fallen brother Lucifer, will think twice before motivating men to march on it. Nevertheless, he will persist. But he will not prevail.'

As if to change tack, Archangel Michael asked a question. 'Have you not taken note of the stories that the Mont's monks are served by a donkey that travels the Forest alone and without harm. Have you not wondered about such a thing?'

'I suppose I did not think too deeply about it My Lord,' the Bishop mumbled.

'Hmm, I suppose your flock and I should give grateful thanks that you think at all!'

The Archangel did not wait for a response, nor was the Bishop going to risk giving one.

'Soon, the donkey will be replaced by a more unusual pack animal. This will be a sign. When this occurs, you are to start construction of the oratory. A boy will show you precisely where.

'You will generously and irrevocably cede land for farming and rental to support a clergy of twelve you will dedicate to preserve The Mont. They will be twelve of your wisest and most dedicated clergymen. You will help them in any way they might need. Ceding the land will be the more important of your tasks as this land will allow the growth of The Mont in the centuries to come. It will become a centre of special pilgrimage. It will provide to those who seek a higher truth. Indeed, it will hold the very secret to alchemy.'

'As you command, My Lord.'

'And just so you are not inclined to see this as a dream that you can ignore, I leave you with a reminder.'

Faster than his eyes could see, the Archangel disappeared from beside him and appeared ten steps in front of the Bishop. This time he was not standing on the ground. The great being floated knee high above the pavement. But this was not what astonished the Bishop.

The Archangel's wings were extended in their breathtaking glory. Each wing was as high as the Bishop and more than both his outstretched arms in width. The Archangel filled the entire width and height of the wide cloister they had walked along. The wings appeared to be made of the finest, whitest feathers. The feathers on the outer edge, that framed the pure white, were the most lustrous emerald green. The wings emanated a brilliance that required the Bishop to shield his eyes. The effect struck awe in Aubert. Involuntarily he bowed his head as he dropped to his knees.

The Sword of Truth was unsheathed, as it usually was in graven images of the mighty warrior who vanquished the fallen Archangel Lucifer. This was the last image the Bishop had as his bowed head felt the touch of the Archangel. Whether it was from the Archangel's sword or his finger, he knew not – as he lost consciousness. The last thing he heard was an invocation.

'May the Light flow through you.'

***

The Bishop awoke in his bed. His physician was by his side. Behind him Father Vincent, his long-time colleague, was ringing his hands. He reached up and felt his head to find it heavily bandaged. There was no pain.

'It is good to see you awake, Your Grace,' the physician said with some relief.

'Our Dear God, in the name of all that is Holy, what happened to you?' Father Vincent asked.

'How long has it been?' the Bishop asked, ignoring the Priest.

'You were found in the cloister between the private chapel and the cathedral the evening before last,' the physician replied.

'What is wrong with my head?' Bishop Aubert fingered his bandages.

'You have a most unusual wound. You have a hole the size of your ring finger through your skull. Amazingly, your brain cavity was not breached. There was no bleeding, as if the wound had been made with a hot poker. It is clean. I have never seen such a wound or sore.' The physician paused, the question asked by Father Vincent hung in the air.

'It began with a dream I had, and then another, that I should have paid more attention to ...' Slowly, the Bishop told his story. He needed to tell it.

When he finished his account, there was a long pause. The Bishop could see the disbelief and confusion in their eyes – which then went to his head. He knew, that if not for the unusual hole in his head, they would see his story as the ranting of a madman.

As if to enthuse them, The Bishop added, 'The secret of alchemy. The ancients have written of it. The making of gold from next to nothing ... the very secrets of wealth and happiness ... and it is coming to our Mont.'

Father Vincent's thinning, grey hair and fleshy, wrinkled face belied the wisdom of his years. While he hid it well from his Bishop, he knew the man to be a fool – too much of a fool to make up such a story.

The old priest was less than excited by the prospect of what he had just heard. If nearby Mont Tombe was to become a repository of great knowledge, it would also become a target for power-hungry, rampaging kings. Moreover, he knew that where there was the promise of easy wealth – and alchemy was the greatest promise of all – it would attract the greatest evil. With a weary heart, the tired priest took his eyes from the bandaged head of the Bishop and quietly bowed his head in prayer. Dear Lord, please do not let me live to see the day ...

II 1560 A.D.

It is impossible to be in love and to be wise.

The afternoon summer sun wandered warmly through the ceiling-high windows into the sitting room where it found the fine porcelain tea set. The two women watched a pair of swallows swoop and skim the waters of the large pond surrounding the elaborate marble fountain. Queen Elizabeth took tea and enjoyed a private moment with her favourite Lady-in-Waiting.

The relaxed scene belied the storm brewing across the channel in the courts of France and Spain, and indeed the small squalls occurring not far from their exquisitely furnished room. For these secret meetings, all but the most trusted servants had been dismissed.

After sipping her tea, she put the cup down, sank back into the lounging chair and sighed. Elizabeth always found Lady Anne Bacon a soothing presence in her times of trouble – which were promising to be more than even she was used to weathering.

'Now we have decided on the witnesses to your marriage, I think all the plans are in place.' Anne remarked as she sipped her tea.

'Yes and it was gracious of Lord Pembroke to provide this grand house for the occasion. This is one of the few places where I can escape the madness of court,' agreed the Queen.

The witnesses to the marriage of the Queen and her husband-to-be, Lord Robert Dudley, would be two of the most powerful men in England. The Lord Keeper of the Great Seal, Sir Nicholas Bacon was to stand beside her Secretary of State and Chief Minister, William Cecil. The party would be completed by their wives: Anne and her sister, Mildred, wife of William Cecil. The wedding needed to occur for the oldest of reasons.

Moreover, it needed to be kept secret until the political impact was clear. The men were all, each in their own way, dear to the Queen and could be trusted. However, few really appreciated the enduring link between these three women. Their bonds were established in their childhoods, when Anne and Elizabeth began their lifelong friendship.

There was a knock at the door and, after the Queen bade entrance, a messenger appeared. 'The Chief minister wishes to speak with you on a matter of urgency, your Majesty. He is on his way and said you will see him should you wish to or not.' The young man delivered the message nervously, as if he might be punished for Cecil's gall.

She dismissed the knave with a wave and turned to Anne. 'It would seem that your brother-in-law is somewhat perturbed.'

'Would you prefer I leave?'

'No Anne, I value your counsel and I suspect that it has to do with matters that will involve you.'

At age 32, she was five years the Queen's senior. Anne was more of an older sister to Elizabeth than Queen Mary, her older half-sister, had ever been. Seventeen years older than Elizabeth, Mary's jealousy of her gifted, articulate, younger sib had been barely concealed.

The more intelligent of his two daughters by far, Elizabeth had also inherited Henry VIII's musical aptitude. If anything, Mary had been more of an unforgiving mother-figure, than a sister. Their relationship reached its lowest ebb when Mary, as Queen, imprisoned the then Princess Elizabeth in the Tower of London for suspected treason. The growing popularity of her half-sister had not only made it impossible to execute Elizabeth, it had cemented Mary's resentment of her clever sibling. She took that resentment to her grave.

Anne's ruffled white collar sat stiffly under her chin, hiding her long neck. Her dark brown eyes missed nothing. She wore her dark hair pulled back severely from her face. While creating an unfair harshness to her features, it did convey her puritan values. Anne had a cool head, a quick mind and a reluctance to quickly form opinions.

Once formed, however, they were invariably astute opinions. Her thoughtful composure and dignified self-possession were the perfect foils to her Queen's fiery spirit. Often, a momentary, steadying look from Anne was all the Queen required to reground her during conflicted and heated interactions. More than once in her reign would Lady Anne save the Queen from her very self.

The Queen was wise enough to recognise that Anne's true value lay in the very differences in their personalities. Elizabeth, a keen observer of her father's, brother's and sister's reigns, had clearly seen how useless it was to surround oneself with eternally-agreeing, sycophantic advisors with no voice to their own minds. Indeed, it was much worse than useless. It was foolhardy and dangerous to deny oneself access to the best minds at one's disposal ... provided they could be trusted.

Notwithstanding their contrasting personalities, the two women connected at two, deep levels. They shared hungry and ferocious intellects and a commitment to something greater than themselves. For Elizabeth it was her country. For Anne it was her God.

Anne was one of the few women, or men, who lived above the glamour and intrigues of life at court – a world she had lived in since childhood. She was the daughter of the learned Sir Anthony Cooke, tutor to Henry VIII's only son Edward. Upon Henry's death Elizabeth's younger (by four years) half-brother, was crowned, only to die six years later at age fifteen. While Edward was tutored, Elizabeth would often pass the time with Anne. Sometimes they sat in on Edward's classes – and so the lifelong friendship developed.

There were few whom Elizabeth could trust to value her for herself, rather than for the exalted power she held. A simple test was a loyal and trusted friendship that existed before her ascension to the throne. This test created a short list. Anne was first on this list. Her loyalty and genuine concern for her Majesty was never in doubt. The Queen's betrothed, Dudley, was next on the list.

Anne's father, Sir Anthony, gave each of his five daughters the greatest gift he had to offer – particularly for the women of his time – an education. Indeed, it was an education worthy of a future king. Anne mastered Greek, Latin, French and Italian. Not only could she speak French like a native, she had an intimate knowledge of the Scriptures. At twenty-two, she not only translated, but published, Ochino's Sermons from the Italian. It was said that Elizabeth, who could write Greek, Latin, French and Italian, was the best-educated woman of her time. Out of respect, her leading Lady-in-Waiting was quietly overlooked for this honour. In any event, there were few, if any, other women their intellectual equals.

'Anne, we need to discuss the arrangements for the care of this child. Have you discussed it fully with Nicholas? Is he agreed?'

'We are as one. It would be our greatest honour to be the foster-parents of your child, my Queen.'

'Of course you need not make any provision for him in your wills. I will ensure that my child is well provided for. Cecil will see to it.'

'Thank you, Your Majesty. We have made it known that I am with child. The date is set around that of your expectation.'

The Queen smiled in satisfaction. The plan was coming together. 'We need to design some frocks that allow us both to hide our shape - my bump and your lack thereof. We need a bodice that balloons out from just below the bosom. I will have the Royal Dressmaker style attire that each of my ladies-in-waiting and myself will wear.'

'It will become the fashion for the while. Your Highness will set a much-followed trend.'

'The is-there-a-baby-or-is-there-not?-fashion.' This made them both giggle like young wenches.

Their amusement was cut short by the door being thrown open. Cecil strode into the room. From his dark face, no wit was required to see that he was verily troubled. The messenger had had good reason to be agitated by the Chief Minister.

Cecil bowed briefly. 'Your Majesty, Lady Anne.'

'Some wedding this is turning out to be! Cecil, why this intrusion?' Her toleration of his manner reflected her respect for him.

'This is never going to work your Majesty. It is sheer, unadulterated folly.'

'How so my dear Cecil? Anne, Nicholas and I have everything well in hand.'

'Well in hand! Is my majesty deluded? Has your love for Dudley addled your mind?! I should never have agreed to this madness.' Cecil was almost yelling as spittle flew out with his words. 'You should never have made him your Master of the Horse and allowed him to share the chambers adjoining yours. The death of his wife, by falling down the stairs, only two months past, followed months of rumours that he wished to poison her so he could marry you. A Queen cannot be associated with such matters as these. I should have resigned when first I realised the fickleness of your heart.'

No one, other than her trusted advisor, could have spoken this way to Elizabeth and escaped the rack! If there was anyone she needed by her side now more than Anne, it was Cecil – yet no one was indispensable. 'That is enough Cecil.' She stood and advanced towards him. Her good humour now evaporated. 'Quiet your tongue or I will gladly have it removed and you may holiday in the Tower.'

'If the Lords hear of it, their distrust of Dudley is such that we will all end up in the Tower. There are still those who question your right to the throne. Those who question the validity of the marriage of your late father to your mother, Anne Boleyn.' Cecil sat and cradled his head in his hands. 'What a mess,' he sighed with resignation.

'I have survived my sister trying to execute me and those who would keep me from the throne. I will survive this too!'

'I did not tell you before, but upon my recent return from Scotland, I was informed that Mother Dowe of Brentwood in Essex has openly asserted that you are with child by Dudley.'

'Well silence her.'

'It has already been done. We can control what people say here your Majesty, but it is within the Courts of France and Spain that the rot is harder to manage. We are powerless to stop the rumours – and rumours there well are.'

'How can you be so sure?' the Queen demanded.

'My spies have copied despatches that Bishop De Quadra has sent back to Spain. He suspects that not only are you married, or soon will be, but that you are with child. That is not all. I have Ambassador Throckmorton's envoy, Secretary Jones, downstairs. Apparently, Throckmorton felt that even a cipher message might not leave the French court and reach us safely. He confirms that both the French and Spanish courts have documented reports from their Ambassadors that you are expecting.'

It was the Queen's turn to take a seat.

Anne finally broke the silence.

'We are where we are. Anger and recrimination will not advance this matter. The marriage we can keep secret. We will make it known that Elizabeth is the Virgin Queen. The child ... well leave that to me. If the Queen has no child, the rumours will inevitably appear to be simply that. For the last six weeks of her confinement she will be taken ill with a minor but troubling ailment and will not hold court. This can be done. It will be done.'

With Anne's words, the steel returned to Elizabeth's voice. 'Bid Jones to reassure Throckmorton that nothing will damage the position and power of my court and my country. Let it be known that I am still looking for a suitor of means. For as long as it continues to serve me, I will keep the world guessing as to my intentions. I will prevail.'

'Indeed, your Highness.' Cecil stood to take his leave. He would serve his Queen. It was not in his nature to do otherwise.

As he took his leave, he reflected on the two women in the room. A child of either woman would be endowed with a great mind and an unsurpassed education. However, he did not envy a child who came under the tutelage and demands of both of them.

As he approached the door, the Queen made a final comment. 'The work on matters of state will tax you and I am appreciative that you will handle it effectively. As of January next year, you will also take the office of Master of the Court of Wards and Liveries.'

This was a lucrative position that promised to ensure Cecil's wealth. It was not lost on him that this was when she was due to give birth – January 1561. 'Your Highness is most generous. One last question if I may?'

'Yes, Cecil?'

'Having gone to all this trouble to ensure that the heir to the throne is not a bastard, when were you planning to register the marriage? Without an official record, the point is lost. As discussed, I will keep the record with the crown jewels.'

'Do not worry yourself Cecil, the marriage will be registered before the birth.'

POSTSCRIPT

In the end, the Queen cut it rather finely. The marriage at the House of Lord Pembroke was finally recorded in official, but unreleased documents, as occurring on 21 January 1561. The birth of her son, Francis, was registered the next day to Lord and Lady Bacon.

History was not surprised to find that while raised as the son of Lord and Lady Bacon, Francis Bacon was to be the only child who was never entered into the official lineage records of the Bacon family genealogy. For the same reasons, although Sir Nicolas Bacon, as the most powerful lawyer in the land, would die a wealthy man with a detailed will for his biological children, he was to leave nothing to Francis. While he loved Francis as his own, ultimately the son of the Queen was not his responsibility...

III 1577 A.D. FRANCIS AT 16

Seek ye first the good things of the mind,
and the rest will either be supplied or its loss will not be felt.

He had been in Paris for only a few months and now he was leaving. As he listened to the clip-clop of the horses and the creak of the coach, Francis was confused and angry. His dark thoughts bounced around his mind as the carriage rocked on its springs. I will be damned if I am going to be a diplomat, he thought. I am sick of life at court with its fake flattery, its pomp and endless, meaningless gossip. No one has asked me what I want to do, what I want to be! Why should I do what that queen bitch wants? His thought caused him pause. He was surprised to find he could think of his previously beloved Queen with such venom.

The bearded Frenchman sitting opposite could not help but be intrigued by the scowling youth before him. The two of them were the only passengers that day. In cultured tones behind his surprisingly good French, he had introduced himself to the Frenchman as Francis Bacon. Pierre Clost introduced himself with a handshake. In their brief interaction, Francis explained that he was in the employ of the English Ambassador and on his way to Mont Saint Michel to meet the great Duke and Chevalier who trained knights there. In return, Pierre Clost explained that he was a physician on his way to visit a colleague at 'The Mont of Legends' as he called it.

Any other time Francis would have pressed him on the Mont, but today he was preoccupied. He was about to defy his Queen. He was not going to remain in Paris. I will be damned if I will let her come from nowhere into my life and start telling me what I must do, Francis thought.

The English Ambassador to France, Sir Amyas, sympathetic to his charge's plight, had agreed he could briefly visit Mont St Michel and meet the great Duke. The Ambassador could see that Francis was not settling into Paris and needed some time on his own. A life of negotiating had made Amyas Paulet a wiser soul. He knew precisely how far he could push a man before he reacted and pushed back, often violently. He knew that now was not the time to push Francis. He let him go.

However, for Francis it would not be a brief visit. The letter from Sir Amyas was ambiguous, mainly because Francis himself had drafted it for the Ambassador's signature. As his aide, this was not unusual. Ambassador Paulet had quickly recognised Francis' abilities with both words and pen. Francis knew he could use this talent to get into their knight-training program. He was sick of being pushed around, his life being the plaything of others. He was going to be a great knight, a warrior that no one would dare trifle with.

Francis was thankful for Sir Amyas' support. He was a tough man who could face down a foreign King at court while arguing for his Queen. Nevertheless, he had a softer, nurturing side that Francis had come to know and respect. He behaved as if he knew Francis well and was kindly towards him. To Francis he seemed like a kindly uncle. As he signed the letter Francis had penned, he had remarked 'There is no hurry for you to become a man troubled with the burdens of responsibility. Take your time. Your youth will end sooner than you think.' The last was said with a sadder, reflective tone. Francis suspected that responsibility had come to Sir Amyas too early. Did he realise it was Francis' intention to stay longer? Maybe, Francis pondered.

Since their introduction, the young English gentleman had been lost in thought. This gave Dr Clost the opportunity to study him. Sitting before the physician was a young man with dark hair, smooth, pale and surprisingly, given his youth, unblemished skin,. He was not a short lad, which against his slim frame, left him with a lanky appearance. His fine clothes were those of the upper class. He was exquisitely dressed in a silk lined, tailored coat with gold buttons. His shoes were of the finest leather. However, it was his eyes behind his finely boned, slightly feminine face, that drew the attention. It was not so much their hazel colour, as their alert intensity, suggesting a keen intelligence. Pierre studied him intently. Understanding the human mind was his forte, the part of medicine few of his colleagues were interested in – but which fascinated him.

Dr Clost realised there was something behind the young man's scowl. It was not just the rebellion of overly-confidant, hot, young blood. No. He turned over their brief discussion in his mind. Out of habit, Pierre had noticed the young man's facial expression change with his words. Many years of experience had taught the older man that either words or facial expression alone meant little, but put them together and deep truths were communicated. If they conflicted, the facial expressions were the more revealing. Around that angry scowl, was another emotion. It was in his eyes. That was it; behind the anger was the sadness of hurt ... of loss.

As the coach rattled on the cobblestones, the smells of Paris drifted in through the open window. It was a clear, crisp, sunny morning. The patisseries had finished their first bake of the day and were wafting their enticing aromas onto the street. The leafless trees by the Seine had been powdered overnight by a light fall of early snow. The crystal leaves of white sparkled in the morning sun while the droplets from the melt glistened in the light. The worst of winter was over and spring was not too far off.

As pretty as the scene was, Francis' mind was back in England. It seemed a lifetime ago, instead of just a few months, that his life as he knew it, had ended. In many ways, his new life, with all its problems, made more sense to him. All his life he had felt different from his four older brothers – even allowing for the fact that the first three were born to his father's first wife. Deep down, he had wondered if he was adopted. 'Many children go through that phase,' his father had told him dismissively.

To distract himself from these thoughts, Francis turned to his travelling companion, 'So tell me doctor, is there an area of medicine you have a particular interest in?'

'That would be the mind. How it works intrigues me. I am convinced that the mind is responsible for some maladies of the body.'

'What makes you believe so?' Francis asked.

'Too often have I treated a patient for an illness that lasted many months, only to find that, despite all my efforts, it would only improve when they became happier,' the physician replied.

'Maybe you should have worked more to make them laugh,' Francis suggested dryly.

'Actually, that is very true. Indeed, I have found that people do not laugh because they are happy, they are happy because they laugh. So, yes, I find ways to encourage people to laugh more, but the benefit is only there while they are in good spirits. My real interest is in how to keep people in good spirits for longer.'

'And how do you do that?'

'I help them to find a reason to live for. Most people die in their early twenties, it just takes a few decades before we get around to burying the body. You would be surprised how many people have no real reason to live. They just go through the motions of life. Most of my patients are of this kind. They are just filling time until death takes them. Those that do not need my services are much more likely to have a reason to live.'

'So how do you work out who has a reason to live and who is going through the motion?'

'There are many ways. Dreams are of particular import. Dreams are like a window into the soul. They are the simplest way of knowing what concerns the deeper levels of our mind.'

It sounded much like witchcraft to Francis, but he kept his thoughts to himself. He simply nodded and looked out the window. He remembered a dream that he was trying hard to forget. He certainly was not going to share it with this physician, a total stranger. If there was ever a fateful night, that night, in August a half year earlier, was such a night. It had begun with a dream. Unlike most of his dreams, this one had stuck with him, the fear embedding it in his mind.

Francis was in a large manor house with many rooms. His footsteps echoed on the wooden floors up to the high ceilings atop the panelled walls. No one else was around. As he moved quietly from room to room, he noticed that each one was different. Some were lounging rooms, dining rooms and others were bedchambers, but that was not it. It was not their use that made them different, nor their furnishings. After a while, it came to him – they felt different. The feelings did not necessarily match the room or its furnishings. A part of him told him to pay close attention to the feelings. A particular feeling was calling him. He was moving more quickly now.

It was like that game he had played as a child. 'Hotter, hotter ... no, colder...,' as his older brother Anthony would direct him to the hidden wooden toy he had teasingly taken from Francis. He came to heavily-timbered double doors. The feeling around them was strong. He threw them open. It was a huge library. A feeling of awe and fascination washed over him. It was delicious.

In front of him books were stacked on shelves from floor to ceiling. The room was three stories high. Francis stood in wonder. He had never seen so many books in the one place. So much knowledge, so much wisdom. As he walked into the library, he felt himself drawn to a writing table. On it lay an elaborate quill pen. It was made from the most exotic, lustrous, emerald green feather. A leather-bound book with blank pages was open on the table. An ink well sat to the right.

There was one sentence on the page. In elaborate penmanship it read, 'Grant me the gift of insight to know my truest ability.' It took up but a quarter of the page. The rest was blank. It was waiting to be added to.

With great anticipation Francis reached for the quill. He dipped it in the ink, but just as he was to set the quill to the paper, a demonic hiss came from behind him with the words, 'Now you are mine.' In an instant his feeling of deep pleasure evaporated. The hair on the back of his neck stood on end as a shiver lit up his spine. His fear rose in his throat as he dropped the quill and ran. He did not look back. He had never been more scared. The demon's ghoulish laughter followed close behind. He ran as fast as he could. He awoke in a sweat, his fear still with him as his heart thudded in his chest.

To wake himself up, as he had not wanted to return to that dream, he went downstairs for a drink. As he approached his father's study, he was surprised to hear voices coming through the door. The door was slightly ajar. His father was talking with another. At this late hour, the men had not expected to be overheard. 'The Queen wishes that her son begin to learn the ways of diplomacy.' Francis had heard the other say. 'His father has spoken to the French Ambassador. It is being arranged for Francis to leave with Ambassador Paulet for Paris.'

In these two sentences and in less time than it took to breathe out, Francis' world changed forever. He had not been eavesdropping, that was not his way. What was being said did not make any sense. The Queen's son ... Francis ... him? How could this be? It could not be him they were talking about ... could it?

In Sir Nicholas' response, the question was answered. 'But he has not turned 16 and has only just started his study of the law at Gray's Inn. It has been hard enough for him having been pulled out of Cambridge before he could take his degree. Why did she do that?'

'The Queen did not want to draw further attention to his precocious intellect. People were starting to wonder who this boy was that was performing so much better than not just his peers, but boys many years his senior. Did you know that since Cambridge was founded 350 years ago, Francis has done better than any fourteen year old who ever attended? Never before has one questioned and argued against Aristotle so articulately. We cannot afford to have too much attention on him. The stable sovereignty of the state depends on it ...'

As he heard this exchange, it felt like the very air around him had disappeared as he fought to breathe. He did not walk on because, quite simply, he was incapable of doing so. The wind was taken out of him. The other man, his voice sounded familiar, had said 'His father has spoken to the French Ambassador,' but was not Sir Nicholas his father!? The man he had known as his father, spoke again.

'What has brought all this about?' said Sir Nicholas gravely. Francis could hear the concern in his voice. While they were not openly affectionate, like so many fathers and sons of that age, he respected and looked up to this man and sensed kindliness from him.

There was no response. 'Good God, Cecil. Out with it!'

His name was like a blow to his stomach. If he had any doubts as to the credibility of the other man, they were lost in that moment. Baron William Cecil Burghley, the Queen's most trusted advisor and the Lord High Treasurer – her Chief Minister. She relied on him as she relied on no one else. When she would not take a decision, for which she was becoming increasingly famous, her most loyal counsellor would. The wiser observers said this was not because she could not decide, but because there were some decisions she needed to distance herself from.

Few people other than the Queen, referred to him as just 'Cecil'. Since he had become Lord Burghley in 1571 and Lord High Treasurer a year later, his visits to their home were less frequent. As the most powerful man in the kingdom, his father often spoke of his good friend and brother-in-law. Lord Burghley was married to Mildred, the sister of his mother – or at least the woman he had called his mother up until this very moment. It was all very confusing. Francis knew him well. In the years before Cambridge, he had attended for tutoring at the Burghley mansion with Lord Burghley's son, Robert Cecil, and a couple of other privileged children. Robert Cecil, his cousin, had always behaved spitefully towards Francis, for reasons he never understood.

With Sir Nicholas' urging, Lord Burghley continued, 'There is too much attention on Francis at the moment. Now, more than ever, she needs to keep her marriage and son a secret. By keeping the Spanish hopeful of a marriage, she has cleverly kept war off the agenda. The Spanish fear her Protestant leaning. Those Catholics will stop at nothing to reassert their faith if we give them reason. The French may even join with them. We need more time to build our military and financial power, a war now would be catastrophic.'

Resignation crept into Sir Nicholas' voice. 'His father has organised it, you say?'

'Yes. He will leave soon. He is off to the court of King Henry the Third.'

Francis was overwhelmed by the news of who his real mother was. He felt totally discombobulated. As his thoughts slowly fell into place, his mind turned to the other news – the identity of his father. He knew whom they were talking about. Lord Robert Dudley, the Earl of Leicester. Francis knew the Earl well from Court. He had always been kind to Francis. Rumours that he and the Queen were lovers had been around for as long as Francis had been old enough to appreciate such matters. Rumours that he had his first wife murdered to make way for marriage to the Queen, painted a less honourable picture.

'And Francis has made things worse. He has drawn even more dangerous attention to himself and this matter.' Lord Burghley went on.

'Why? What could he possibly have done to annoy her majesty?

'Do you know of the incident at Court between one of the maids-in-waiting and the Queen this last week?'

'I heard there was a scuffle.'

Francis knew exactly what Lord Burghley was talking about. He felt ill to think of it.

'Well there was a little more to it. My son, Robert, seems to have mentioned to some of the ladies of the Court that Francis is the Queen's son. It was out of line and he and I have had words on the matter. Anyway, the Queen then overheard Lady Scales speaking of the matter and started to physically discipline her. Francis apparently intervened. It was impetuous and inappropriate on his part.'

Francis remembered it well. Lady Scales refused to defend herself, her only option with the Queen, and was being beaten horribly. He could not stand by and allow it to continue. From across the Court, quite involuntarily, he had found himself stepping in to protect the woman. The Queen then turned her wrath on him. He presumed it was just because he had defended the poor woman. Until this moment he had no idea that the entire incident was about him.

'Her Majesty is not happy with Francis. Truth be told, she is probably just as angry with herself for reacting as she did – the matter should not have been dealt with openly at Court in such a manner. Either way, Francis is now off to France. We need to remove him and allow things to settle. While she is not happy with him, she still respects his sharp mind and quick wit. Besides, the Queen needs some ears in France that she can trust.'

Then things went from bad to worst. Francis heard a few quick steps and the door to the drawing room was flung open. 'It would appear he has the ears for the job!'

Francis cowered in fear as Lord Burghley's frame filled the doorway. The large man grabbed him by the neck and threw him into the room.

The loud whinny of their carriage's lead horse brought him back to the present. 'Easy there you crazy colt,' drifted back from the driver good-humouredly, as he soothed the frisky horse. Francis understood French almost as well as his native tongue.

Before he had left the white cliffs of Dover behind, he had met with the Queen. It was not the first time. He had met her often throughout his childhood and then at Cambridge not long after his thirteenth birthday. There had been several more occasions since. He heard that he had made an impression on her and that she apparently referred to him as 'the young Lord Keeper.' His foster-father (as he now had to think of him), Sir Nicholas, as the Lord Keeper of the Great Seal of England, held the highest legal position in the land.

Francis had been chuffed about the Queen's interest in him. But the fact that the Queen took such an abiding interest was not lost on him. Nevertheless, he had not given the matter much thought ... until, that night.

His meeting with the Queen had not gone well. There had been no grand meeting in the public forum of the court. Wined, dined and celebrated, he was not. Unlike his many other visits to Court, this time he had been hustled into a room near her chambers late on the night before he left for France.

Whitehall Palace, or York Place, as it was originally known, had been greatly expanded by Elizabeth's father, Henry VIII. Despite its grandeur with almost a thousand rooms covering twenty acres, it felt dark, unwelcoming and forbidding.

The meeting had been brief, her tone official. It did not get off to a good start. Francis found himself wishing that his heritage was that of Lady Anne and not this haughty woman whose blood seemed as cold as the castle walls around them. 'So you were eavesdropping young man.' Francis knew that even if he had an argument that could convince her otherwise, it was a statement not a question. One could only speak to the Queen in response to a direct question. While he thought he had managed to convince Sir Nicholas and Lord Burghley that he had not been spying that night, the Queen obviously had not heard it that way.

Even though she had dismissed all her attendants and they were alone, it was not in his nature to be insolent. He stood quietly with his head bowed.

After a pregnant pause, she fortunately decided to move on. 'Yes it is true. You are my own son, but you, though truly royal, of enquiring mind and masterly spirit, shall rule not England nor your mother, nor reign over my subjects.

'I have already declared that I will be the Virgin Queen. Mind you it still does not stop them from petitioning me every couple of years to marry a Spaniard! That will never happen ...'

This last comment, almost an afterthought, seemed to be more for her own benefit than Francis'. He heard something in her voice, a reflective tone. Was it sadness? A life as a mother and wife lost? For a brief moment he saw the woman behind the crown. He saw – dare he think it – his mother? His very flesh and blood. The words had stopped. He looked up. He looked into her eyes. He wanted to see his mother. For a moment she held his gaze and then they both looked away. He sensed she wanted to reach out to him. Was he imagining it?

The moment passed. The mother gone, the Queen was back. 'In Paris you will learn the ways of their court. Sir Amyas Paulet will teach you matters of diplomacy, but your real reason for being there is somewhat different. I want you to use that brilliant mind you have to notice the things that Sir Amyas, in his official role, will not be privy to. With your youth, people will let their guard down. I then want you to come up with a cipher, a coded way of getting information back to me.'

Francis was familiar with ciphers. He had become fascinated with them in his time at Trinity College.

'We have a very fragile relationship with the French. While I have allowed discussions to occur about my marriage to King Henry's brother, nothing could disgust me more. Their mother, Catherine de Medici, is evil incarnate. I hold her personally responsible for the Saint Bartholomew's Day massacre of thousands of innocent Protestants. On top of this that black Queen nurtured my greatest enemy.'

Francis realised he was being given a brief understanding of his mother's political relationship with the French. However, the last statement was lost on him. He wanted to clarify this, but as he went to speak, she raised her hand and he dutifully remained silent.

'Right now England needs time to grow and establish its own identity. To achieve this I need stability for years to come. That is my goal – to nurture and ready this country so it can go on to become the greatest empire in the history of the world.' At that she stood and turned to walk away. Their meeting was over, but there was a parting shot.

'And one last thing. Do not cross me. You may be my son, but if you declare it, I will deny it and you will find yourself in The Tower for treason. I will not intervene in the inevitable outcome of that charge. While you are my blood and born of the purple, the State will always be my most precious child. Unless things change drastically, I will leave the crown, as it would fall by blood, to James of Scotland, which will unite our two countries. I have thought long and hard about this and for either country to survive we must unite – it is our only way forward. I will protect it at any cost.'

As the carriage rattled along, it was not the warning that Francis' mind turned to. His mind went to the tender moment they had shared where, ever so briefly, they were almost mother and son. As he thought of it, his eyes felt unreasonably moist.

IV THE DREAM

A wise man will make more opportunities than he finds.

They had been travelling for many hours. Francis was bored. The carriage seemed intent on rattling his bones from their joints as it jerked its way along the rutted road. The doctor seemed quite comfortable. There was a peace about him, a quiet comfort. Despite his earlier decision, Francis decided to risk it.

'I had a dream,' Francis began tentatively.

Pierre Clost nodded encouragingly, 'Go on.'

While his green eyes were quite intense, there was a kindness to them that Francis found reassuring. He told the physician the dream that had awoken him that fateful night. When he was finished, he waited expectantly.

There was a long pause as Dr Clost gently tugged his beard, obviously in thought. 'First, let me say that the best interpretation of the meaning of a dream can only come from a knowing of the teller. However, while I do not know you, as it turns out this dream has some images in it that are as old as humankind. I have come across elements of this dream often enough to know that they hold true for most who dream of such things.'

Francis leant forward, now that his dream was out he was impatient to know its message, 'So what does it mean?'

'Houses in dreams, particularly when we are searching them and when we are alone, relate to our own minds. You are searching yourself, looking within. This is the ultimate journey that you have begun – the journey of contemplation. You are looking for who you really are and what you came here to do.

'To really understand a dream you need to look to the feelings. As the feelings unfold so too does the meaning of the dream. What did you notice about your feelings in the dream?'

Francis reflected back, 'I noticed that as I moved through the house that different rooms made me feel different things.'

'But there was more to it than that. What were the feelings doing? Try to remember ...'

Francis closed his eyes. 'They were guiding me.'

'Aha! Très bon. You have been shown an ancient truth in a very powerful way.'

While the Frenchman was excited, Francis was not sure why. 'I am not sure I understand. Feelings can be a guide?'

'Not *a guide*. They are the *ultimate guide*. Our thoughts can mislead us easily, indeed they mislead themselves. But once we learn to be guided by our feelings we have the very power of the sun at our disposal.'

'So you mean, if I really want to buy something I should buy it if I am excited by it?'

'Maybe.'

'But I thought you just said that we should be guided by our feelings.'

'No. I said *once we learn to be guided* by our feelings we have the very power of the sun at our disposal. The first, and most important lesson, is to give our feelings time to confirm themselves. If a few weeks later you are still excited to buy the item, then indeed you should.'

'So what were my feelings guiding me to in this dream?'

'Let me ask you Master Bacon, are you unsure of what to do with your life? Not that it would be a crime for one so young. Have you changed course recently?'

'It seems that is all I have been doing. I was studying at Cambridge, then I had to move to Gray's Inn where I started reading law, then I was told I had to go to Paris and now ... I know not.'

'Aah, people have thought it a luxury to be able to choose one's job or purpose in life,' the physician said. 'Now I see it differently. People who learn how to be guided by their feelings are not only the happiest that I have met, but they are invariably in better health than those around them. This is another part of what I spoke of earlier. Your confusion from chopping and changing is a great gift.'

'It is? It feels like I am the plaything of others.'

'Maybe, but the chopping and changing will allow you to learn how to listen to your feeling guides. Without the contrast of different experiences, it is very difficult to learn what your feelings are saying to you.'

'So the first lesson is to allow our feelings to confirm themselves over time, so we can allow them to guide us. Is there a second?'

'The second lesson is to become expert at working out what they tell us we do not want to do. A simple, but important lesson. By knowing what we do not wish to do, we are forced to focus on the things we might wish to do. In time, we cannot help but work it out. Never will your feeling guides be clearer than when you stop and reflect on different work that you have done. If you simply stop and listen, your feelings will tell you if you should do more of it, or less of it. If it is not clear initially, it will become so over time.''

'But does that mean I should not do my chores because my feelings tell me I should do less of them?'

Dr Clost responded with a laugh, 'No, there are many things that we will not feel like doing that we must do. In time, however, we can set our life up to do less of them. Often when we do what we are meant to do, we find the wherewithal to pay others to do those chores for us. Until then, we need to do them ourselves. So, back to your dream, 'How did you feel as you walked into the library?'

'I felt wonderful.'

'Why? Think about it.'

'I am not sure ... I do enjoy reading ... some authors,' he added.

'But why?' Pierre pushed.

Francis paused. 'It is because I sense that buried amongst these writings, are truly wonderful words to behold that have been crafted by people of great wisdom. People whom otherwise are difficult to find in real life.'

'That is because they are often dead. Making it a good deal harder to chat with them,' the physician said with a wry smile. 'And how did you feel as you picked up the quill?'

'Well that was pure fear. That was when the demon appeared.'

'No. Take your mind back to just before then, when you reached for the quill. What was the feeling?'

Francis thought carefully. 'I ... I was excited. It was like this beautiful quill was wanting me to connect with it. Like together we could do something special. But what about the demon? Was it the devil who came to visit me?'

'No, not directly. That was a friend we all have, our very own personal demon.' For a moment, the physician appeared lost in his own thoughts.'

'It did not feel at all like a friend.' Francis prompted.

'Think of him as the friend you do not like to have around, but in the end he makes it all worthwhile. You see, he is a guide too. Lesson three, while negative feelings like boredom, disgust, unease and fear tell us that we are going down the wrong path, there is one negative emotion, a kind of fear, that is different.'

'How many kinds of fear are there?' Francis asked.

'Several, but it is the fear of failure that I am talking about. Failure fear, as I think of it, tells us that we need to confront something important. Fear often has nothing to do with whether or not we should do something. There is no courage if there is no fear. If there is no courage, there is no real achievement. So, if there is no failure fear, there is no real achievement.'

Now Francis was confused. 'Dr Clost, in simple words; who, or what was that demon?'

'That was your fear of failing son. The fear of reaching for your highest dream. We need to learn how this fear feels so we know when it is in the room. What did he say to you when you picked up the quill?'

'Now you are mine,' Francis could not get those words out of his mind.

'With great dreams come great fears. It is as simple as that. What is left if you try to do what you came here to do and you fail? This is why so many people live without pursuing their purpose, without listening to their feelings. It is the greatest of all fears. People will forgo true happiness so as to avoid the ultimate failure. One day you will toast your demon and thank him for helping you to see the way. Indeed, next time you meet him in your dreams, if you can control your fear and not run from him, your demon has much of value to say to you.'

Francis could not imagine doing this. The fear was still very much alive. 'But what did he mean by "now you are mine?"'

'He had you through your fear. By running you gave yourself up and over to him. He did not need to catch you. When we are running scared we are lost. We are lost until we turn and confront our fear. In fact, his words were designed to frighten you, but they were not true. You were not his, unless you gave into the fear, which you did and then it became true.'

Francis turned this over in his mind. It made sense. 'So the first lesson is to allow my feelings, when they persist over time, to guide me. The second is to take notice of the things that do not feel right and notice what we do not want to do in life. Except, when that feeling is the fear of failure – the third lesson. If it's failure fear then I should be confronting it?'

'You have it. For most people the fear is so great they do not even begin the journey. People will drink themselves to death rather than risk trying and failing. If we are not trying to work out what is meaningful for us, and pursue this, then we are not living, we are slowly dying.'

'So the words "Grant me the gift of insight to know my truest ability" are ...'

'The ultimate wish. The basis of all the great quests.'

'But what about the quest of finding true love, as the minstrels sing of it?'

'Aah, true love. Well the bad news is that if you are lucky enough to find true love but then fail to find out who you are and what you do, even true love will wither and fail. You need to love yourself first before anyone else can love you.'

'Yes I have heard it said, but I never quite understood what it meant.' Francis confessed.

'What most do not realise is that to love oneself is all about discovering oneself. To discover yourself, to embrace it and give it expression. Your dream is all about the need to discover who you are and what you do – to be the author of your own life. It is a dream and a quest that has existed from the beginning. It was why Adam and Eve were always going to leave Eden.'

'Could a dream be about so much?'

'Only you can decide. A dream is only interpreted accurately if the dreamer feels it to be so. If it does not feel right, it is not.'

'You are talking about being guided by your feelings again, are you not?' Francis, was not sure if believed everything he had just heard, but it gave him pause for thought.

Pierre nodded as Francis returned to his own counsel. With satisfaction, the physician noted that the young man's anger had settled, for the moment. He liked his work.

V MONT TOMBE

God's first creature, which was light.

The Big Man spoke slowly and carefully. He was a natural storyteller. As he spoke, the two younger children found themselves entranced. Even the teenaged Francis found himself drawn to listen. 'This has always been a place of wonders and miracles. Holy people have lived here on The Mont from even before Archangel Michael put a hole in Bishop Aubert's skull to get him to pay attention!' He paused, leaning forward to make sure he had their attention. 'They received their food and supplies in a rather unusual way.'

The fire crackled beside them as the four sat around after the evening meal. Catherine, The Big Man's wife, had just served them a hearty dish of onion soup followed by baked fish. However, the red wine with the food was what had surprised Francis. With a warm, pleasant fuzziness in his head, he nursed the last few mouthfuls of his second cup of the glorious nectar.

His letter of introduction from the English Ambassador had done its job. The Big Man, the head of the local Gendarmerie at The Mont, had welcomed him like a long lost son. He had insisted that Francis board with him and his lovely wife Catherine until he found his own lodgings. He later discovered that their own two boys were grown-up and working a farm with their grandfather. The couple clearly enjoyed having a younger person to take under their warm wings. I am going to like it here, he thought contentedly. This feeling, mixed with the effects of the wine, took him back to his first experience of The Mont on the evening his coach had arrived from Paris.

Indeed, when he first caught a glimpse of Mont St Michel through a gap in the forest from the carriage, he had been enthralled. It looked like a cross between a great cathedral and a majestic palace. It carried the aura of a mystical place. It was only as the carriage emerged from the forest that one appreciated how The Mont sat apart from the mainland. The Mont was the island and the island was The Mont with its fortified walls extending to its very limits.

They had missed the last guided crossing for the day as the tide was in. After eating at the tavern with its attached stables, he took a stroll to the water's edge. As he walked past the last tree and looked out towards The Mont, he had reason to pause.

The full moon had risen and the sky was clear, the wind was still and the water was a mirror. The fires and torches on The Mont were alight. The moonlight seemed unusually bright. The Abbey atop The Mont, and the buildings below, reflected in the water in exact duplicate. It was like heaven and earth – as above, so below. Francis looked on entranced. It evoked a strange feeling in him. At some deep level, he felt nurtured by it. He knew not how long he stood there.

The Big Man's voice jolted him back to the present. Catherine had retired to read, leaving her husband to tell his stories by the fire. Josephine and her recently arrived cousin Pieter lived next door. Her parents were good friends with The Big Man and his wife. Josephine had pleaded with her mother to come over after their supper so The Big Man could tell Pieter, some of his stories. The young girl was proud of her Mont and wanted Pieter to know its legends from the best storyteller on the island. It gave Francis a welcome introduction to his new home as well.

The Big Man was big in every way. He had a big voice that would suddenly soften at certain points in his stories. His arms were almost as big as Francis' thighs. For many of the doorways, he needed to duck to avoid hitting his head. Even his moustache was big! It carried bits of his last meal and as a result, there were bits of fish swimming in the froth from his ale.

'The holy men who lived here when this island was simply known as Mont Tombe received their supplies by donkey. "That's not strange" I hear you say. It would not have been so strange except for one thing.' At this point The Big Man lowered his voice to a whisper. 'You see, the Donkey travelled alone.'

'It was loaded up by the merchants in the town on the other side of the Scissy Forest. As it walked through the town, people would add what they could to its saddlebags. Alone the Donkey travelled the forest and then the salt marshes. As it approached the seashore, it would wait. On low tide, it walked out to the island. Never once did it sink into the quicksand. Somehow, it knew the way around those fatal sinks.

Once loaded by the holy men with whatever simple offerings they could give back to the merchants, every full moon it made its journey back to town. The townsfolk knew the Donkey well. It radiated calm and brought happiness wherever it went. Young children would dance and skip along behind it.'

'How did it know where to go? Did someone train it?' Josephine asked. At age ten she was only a year older than her cousin Pieter. She had heard the legends of The Mont many times, but she never tired of them – at least not when The Big Man was doing the telling.

With Josephine feeding him the question at just the right time, The Big Man continued in a soft voice. 'It is said that the Donkey always travelled alone. The hand of God guided it. And so it had for the Merchant's father and his father before him. No one knew if it was the same donkey or if it was of many generations. But no one saw it with its young.'

'But the Donkey was in danger,' prompted Josephine with excitement, for she knew the twist in the legend.

'Indeed it was, young Josephine. It was in grave danger. While it was no ordinary donkey, it was still of the flesh. In time, it attracted the wrong attention. You see, Mont Tombe was not just another small rocky island off the coast of France. It has been a place of battle between the forces of Truth and the forces of the Lie since time began. Indeed the greatest battle of heaven and earth was played out here.'

55

With a twinkle, he turned his lively eyes on Pieter and asked him, 'Do you know why this place was originally called Mt Tombe?'

Pieter shook his head. He could not take his eyes off those of The Big Man. Never before had he heard such stories. The Big Man spoke of events of another world – a world of mystery, danger and forces beyond the usual.

'In the old language of Latin it is said as "tumba," meaning "burial mound". You see, since far back in the very origins of time, this island has been a sacred place. This has been the point of connection between this world and the next.' The Big Man said the last five words with slow weight. They were not lost on Pieter. His eyes wide, he swallowed in unison with The Big Man as he took another sip of his ale. The fire warmed the room as it flickered and illustrated the stone walls. The sun was well set and The Big Man, on his third tankard and like a great actor, was becoming one with his story.

'Many people have passed over from here. To be buried here you had to be someone of import. By being buried here, it is said, your Judgement Day would be brought forward. Following your burial you would be forced to see your life, your true self and all your deeds with total clarity. You would be assisted in this evaluation by your personal angel or spiritual guide.

'You would then judge yourself and go to either the Lord of the Light or the Lord of the Dark. Both Lords also knew the fullness of who you were. Whom you would choose to join was about whom you felt you had the right to be with. With full self-knowledge, you could not get it wrong. The Lords of the Light and of the Dark received their followers as they departed this material world at the rock atop Mont Tombe.

What an interesting idea, Francis thought, Judgement Day was really about '*self*-judgement.'

It was Pieter who spoke up. 'Who is the Lord of the Dark?'

'The Lord of the Dark was previously of The Light. Few know that the name "Lucifer" actually means the "light bringer". He was the most glorious of angels. Then he was thrown from heaven by our very same Archangel Michael and left the warmth of the light. If we have time, I will come back to that great story.

'So it was inevitable that the Dark Lord, on a visit to Mont Tombe to collect another soul, would notice the journey of the Donkey. The Donkey represented all that the Lord of the Dark despised. The Donkey walked in the Light. Its journey between the holy men and the Merchant and the people of the town was a walk of love. This was no trade, at least not in the usual sense. The Merchant and the people loaded the Donkey with gifts, not because they had to, but because they chose to. Somewhere along the way, the people of the town had come to truly accept the idea of simply giving, with no need for a return favour. They had discovered the most powerful reward for giving. They gave themselves a precious, soul-uplifting feeling – the one that only comes from giving.

'Nothing annoys the Dark Lord more than people behaving out of love. Just before he left Mont Tombe one stormy night, he went into the forest and found the pack of wolves that lived there. Lucifer chose a big black wolf and vested it with an evil task. "Take that donkey and feast on it. Feed yourself and your family well." The wolves had always left the donkey alone, as they sensed there was something different about it. But they could not ignore a direction from the Dark Lord.'

'That next night, as the Donkey made its way through the forest, the townsfolk heard its brayed scream cut short mid-breath as the beasts attacked. The next morning the Merchant organised a search party and went into the forest. On the forest floor, they found the place of attack. They could clearly see the footprints of the wolf and the remains of the Donkey. They could not believe what had happened. The men in the search party cried as they remembered the

Donkey from when they were children – from when their fathers had taken them by the hand and told them of its sacred journey.'

'How could God allow his Donkey to die? Why did he not protect it? What did it do to deserve death?' Pieter burst out, his voice tinged with sadness and anger in equal parts.

'Ahhh, young Pieter, your emotion and your three questions are based on a simple presumption. You presume that death is a bad thing.'

'But of course it is!' Francis added, feeling the need to support the boy. 'This is why death is used as the ultimate punishment.'

'What if it is not?' asked The Big Man quizzically. 'Death is behind the very nature of all living things. Take the magnificent blooms of spring. If they did not die, if they were with us all year round, would we pay them a second glance? In your time here you will meet people, wise people, who see life and death very differently.'

Pieter sat quietly, mourning the Donkey and all it represented. The Big Man saw things differently from most.

'It was bad for the Donkey,' Francis argued. 'A flower may not know it is dying, but the Donkey felt pain.'

'You think more deeply than most of your age. You will fit in here very well. But who said pain was a bad thing?' asked The Big Man.

Of course pain is a bad thing, Francis thought, but there was something in The Big Man's eyes that suggested he had thought more deeply about these issues than had Francis. He responded more carefully. His four years studying the classics had taught him how to respond when on less sure ground. 'What are the good aspects of pain?'

'Pain, if the cause of it does not kill us, tells us there is something we need to learn. It is a flag. It might be as simple as "do not touch the hot stove," but there is always a lesson. Different lessons for different people. When memories of traumatic events come back to haunt us it means there is something yet to learn. Even long term pain, like from a bad back, can teach us to make the most of times when the pain is less.'

'But what about when the pain is great and the lesson, as with the Donkey, is "You are about to die,"' Francis pointed out, a little too smugly. 'Is it not then a bad thing to feel?'

The Big Man was not put out by Francis' tone. He went on patiently, 'The moment that any pain exceeds what we can cope with, our mind steps in to protect us. It numbs the pain. Spend time on a battlefield and you will see what I mean. The men who continue to scream are usually not under immediate threat of death. Those who are will usually speak to you with an eerie calm. In the same way a horse with a broken leg or mortal injury will often be quiet and placid as it awaits its end.'

Francis was silent. He was now out of his depth. The Big Man clearly spoke from first-hand experience.

Josephine got them back on track. She knew that the story was not yet at an end. Death was not yet a subject that interested her. 'Go on, please Mr Big Man,' she said.

The Big Man smiled at the nickname she had given him. She had first used it when she was four. He must have looked very big to her then. It had stuck and now most people called him The Big Man. He thought it strange how nicknames were picked up when other times they were not, but he did not mind his. 'Yes, the story is not over with the death of the Donkey. The Light was paying attention. It sent the Lord of the Light, bearing the Sword of Truth, to earth to make amends. And who is the Lord of the Light, Josephine?'

Josephine clapped with delight. 'Saint Michel!'

'The very one after whom this place – Mont St Michel – is named and for whom it was built. The Britons know him as Archangel Michael in their Christian writings. He was the second angel created.

The much less well known Saklataboth was the first angel created while Gabriel was the third.

'All religions know Saint Michel as a great archangel. In the Koran, the followers of Islam call him Mikal. They know him as the Chief Angel of Blessings. As Muhammad lay dying he said that Gabriel would be the first and Michael the second to pray over him.

'Saint Michel saw what The Lord of the Dark had done. He tracked down the very wolf that had done the terrible deed.

'Unto the wolf he said, "You have done a sorry deed. There is but one way in which you can repent and atone for your sin." The wolf cowered as light and sparks flew from Saint Michel. His angel wings were so bright and white that it hurt its night eyes just to look at him. A single feather held a radiance that could blind a creature of the night.

'"From this moment forth you will carry the saddlebags of the Donkey from the hermits to the townsfolk and back."

'But there was a problem. Saint Michel knew that the townsfolk and the merchant would be scared of a wolf and would not stock it with food and support it on its journey. So Saint Michel changed it. He softened its features, changed its colouring and shortened its teeth. In an instant, it became a huge, fluffy, white dog, with the size and power of a wolf, standing almost as high as the donkey, but with soft features and big brown eyes. The wolf was grateful that its life had been spared and this gratitude shone in it eyes.

'The next day it appeared in the village. Initially, the people were wary. But the children could not help themselves. They ran up to the wolf-dog and ran their fingers through its soft white fur. The wolf, so used to evoking fear, gave in to the love lavished upon it and fully accepted its new self. This new feeling was wonderful.

'As demanded, it approached the most successful merchant's door. The merchant walked up to it and hesitated. The children were all over it. He recognised the saddlebags. He knew them well. He had first seen his father load them when he was but a toddler. The leather was thick and well oiled. The stitching was rough, but made to last.

'What witchery is this, he wondered? He looked into its eyes. He saw no evil. But how could he be sure. Should he entrust it with his goods? In the end, as a careful merchant, he only gave as much as he felt he was prepared to lose.

'But the wolf-dog held true. It took the goods of the merchant and the townsfolk to the holy men and did so month after month, year after year.'

'But why didn't the Lord of the Dark come and do anything? After all, he was the one who sent the wolf?' Pieter asked.

'You have a mind that likes completion,' said The Big Man. 'The Mont has much to offer minds like yours. Yes, there is a reason that the Lord of the Dark allowed Saint Michel to change the wolf into a big dog and to take over the role of the Donkey. We might think that the Lord of the Dark did not notice how events turned out, but no. It knew that Saint Michel had stepped in.'

'So why did the Lord of the Dark not do anything?' Pieter asked.

'The Lord of the Dark was recovering. He was in no state to take on the Lord of the Light.'

'Recovering from what?' asked Pieter.

'To answer that question. I need to refer to an old book.' The Big Man drained his big mug. 'It is called the *Book of Revelation*.'

'You can read?' said Pieter, impressed. 'Where I come from the only one who could read was the monk in the next town and that was two days ride away.'

'Young Squire, the Mont has had Monks for a thousand years past. You will be welcome at their school if you are prepared to apply yourself. Now, to go back to your question of why Satan, as he is also known, did not intervene. Let me find the book.'

The Big Man wandered over to the bookshelf. He ran his finger along the heavy books until his finger stopped over one with leather bindings and gold, embossed print on the spine. Absently, he murmured to himself, 'Thirteen, one.' It seemed to fall open where he wanted it to. He only had to turn one page before he started to read.

> *"Then a battle started in heaven*
> *Michael and his angels fought the dragon*
> *The dragon fought and so did his angels*
> *but they did not win and they no longer had a place in heaven.*
> *Then he fell, the great dragon, the ancient serpent,*
> *he who is called Devil and Satan...*
> *And he landed on the sand by the sea."*

'You see Pieter, The Lord of the Dark was a little battle-weary and a little careful. He had just had his insides kicked out of him by none other than ...

'Saint Michel' chimed in Josephine, right on cue.

'And guess where the *"sand by the sea"* was?'

Pieter knew this one. While he had only been at The Mont for a few days, he knew what happened at the great tides. At the peak of their range, they rose twelve yards. Along with the quicksands, this was The Mont's greatest defence against warrior and brigand. The tide went out so far that one could no longer see the water. It became nothing but sand 'by the sea'.

It was only when the tide was out that enemies could attack. But when the sea came in, only the swiftest horse could outrun it. No soldier on foot could beat the water once it was upon them. It would often take even those who had been warned by surprise. A phalanx of armed men could drown in minutes. Oxen and the canons they drew had no hope.

'So it was here that Satan fell?' said Pieter.

'Yes it was here that Satan entered the physical world. In the beginning he thought it was of less opportunity, but he quickly realised the fields were more fertile here than from whence he came. There were many weak souls of deprived lives ready to embrace his offerings. He had much to do. The last being he wanted to tangle with was the one who had just beaten him and thrown him out of heaven and into the mortal world. That time would come, but the Lord of the Dark was not yet ready. So he left the wolf, now dog, to do Saint Michel's bidding and proceeded on his other evil tasks.

'And there endeth the legend,' said The Big Man.

'May I ask a question?' ventured Francis.

'Certainly my young Squire.'

'You spoke of The Light and then you spoke of the Lord of the Light. You also spoke of the Lord of the Dark. If the Lord of the Dark is the equal of the Lord of the Light, then where does God fit in?

'My my. Your mind is not of young men of your vintage. I have told these legends to many young people and adults over many years and you are the first to ask such questions. For you have picked up the scents of deep issues, only some of which I, with all my reading and communing with the men of wisdom can answer. Let me tell you this.

'Christians refer to "God". While we respect their God, we here at The Mont see that as too narrow. God in the likeness of man is a figment of the imagination of men. We see God as "The Light". Something that is in all places - even in each of us. The Apostle Thomas saw it this way, but this was not good for building a church-based following. It allowed people to go their own way to come into the light. The Church went with John because he said the only way to know the love of God was through Jesus, and thereby through the Church.

'The Light is the glue of existence. But we need to learn to tap into it, to let it flow. The Light is the very essence of love and creation. Power without The Light is not real power. The most skilled knight, without The Light will not prevail in the end. If he is prevailing, it is not yet the end.

'The Light is there for all of us to touch and be empowered by. The Knights of the Mont have a sacred saying. It is said only rarely – only before they go on an epic Quest, into battle or before a great challenge. They do not give the blessing lightly and only a True Knight can give it to another.

'You are here Francis, to train as a Knight, or as we call them a "Chevalier". Did you know that it was the French who invented the knight? What you English have forgotten in creating your version are the codes of conduct that make a warrior a true Chevalier.'

Francis had not known this. While he knew that King Arthur and the Knights of the Round Table were a creation from the imagination of a great storyteller and had never existed, he had assumed that the English had created the knight. He admitted as much to The Big Man who nodded and then turned to the younger boy.

'When you turn fourteen Pieter, you will no longer be a Page. You will become a Squire, like Francis, and begin your training proper. While each of you may qualify as a knight, whether or not you will be a Chevalier of the Order is another question. As you know, the Knights of the Mont are the greatest knights in the world. Nowhere in all the kingdoms have knights done what the original Chevaliers of the Order of Saint Michel did here at the Mont. Their secret is The Light.'

Francis knew the story that had made the Chevaliers of the Mont legends across all Christendom. Indeed, there was not a squire who would become a knight who did not know the story of those knights whose valour and determination earned them such an esteemed place in history.

'What made the knights from here so famous?' Pieter asked.

'That is a story for another time my young friend.'

Disappointed, Pieter went on, 'So, what is it that they say to each other?'

The Big Man lowered his voice to a whisper. 'I can only tell you if you promise never to say it to another in the form of a blessing. They say that to do so, when you are not a true Chevalier and presuming to be something you are not, brings the very opposite effect. It brings the speaker and the person to whom it is said the very worst fortune. I can only tell you *of the words* but I cannot say them to you as a blessing. For me to tell you, each of you must swear on the life of your mother.'

Each of the three did so.

The Big Man looked to each of them and then lowered his voice, 'They simply say, "May the Light flow through you."'

For a moment they were all quiet. The Big Man spoke again.

He spoke very softly and very slowly as if remembering a special time. It was as if none of them were there and The Big Man was talking to himself. With some reverence, he said, 'This is what made the difference in the first great war. What I can tell you is that The Lord of the Light is Saint Michel. He is not The Light, but he is of The Light. The Light chose him to represent itself in battle when Lucifer declared himself the Lord of the Dark. The two sides were evenly matched in power – except for one difference.

'Satan led his warriors by fear and greed – fear of his wrath should they fail and greed for the spoils. These motivations were no match for those nurtured by The Light. No angel, or man, will fight to the death when motivated by fear or greed. If you are in fear, you will fear death more than anyone's wrath and greed cannot be satisfied if you are dead. They will fight well-enough, but great battles are not won by fighting well-enough.

'People only fight to the death when it is for a cause that is bigger than their own life. The safety and freedom of those you care about is such a cause. It takes a great leader for angels and men to believe that risking and giving their lives will not be a waste.

'It was leadership that won the day. Saint Michel, the Archangel, was a great leader. Great leaders are able to make clear the motivation for battle in a way that speaks to the hearts of warriors. When other things are equal, battles are won or lost on the heart. Many leaders stand back and send their men into battle. Saint Michel stood *before* his warriors, not behind them, and led them into battle. While they are otherwise immortal, an angel can be killed by another angel.'

The Big Man's Eyes glazed a little, as if he was losing focus on the audience in front of him.

'Before the great battle, he said to his angel warriors, "We do not fight for ourselves, we fight for all beings on all planes that deserve to know The Light and to know The Truth. Without The Truth, they cannot know Love. Without Love, there is no point to existence. Do nothing that I would not do. Risk no more of your lifeblood than I do, but know this: I will go first into the theatre of battle and will fight until I can no longer lift my arm. If any of you see me waver then cease to fight and return to those you love, but if you see me fight until I can do no more for The Light, then I ask that you do so yourself."

The Big Man sagged, as if exhausted. Josephine, who knew this to be unusual and had never before heard the words of Saint Michel in the storytelling asked, 'How did you know what Saint Michel said?'

Francis also sensed the shift.

The Big Man replied quietly, 'I do not know. I have never said those words before. But my heart is heavy as if the weight of other lives rested on my conviction.' The Big Man was surprised. The words that he uttered were not of his knowing. He sensed that his small audience had drawn something from him that he did not know resided within him. He found his attention drawn to Francis, the older boy. He was a slight young man, almost sickly in appearance. He had an air about him. His eyes missed nothing. Those eyes were now focussed steadily on The Big Man.

Tired, The Big Man drew the evening to a close. 'That is enough for one night. It is way past your bedtime. Off you go now.'

VI THE TRUE CHEVALIERS

Fortitude is the marshal of thought, the armour of the will, and the fort of reason.

At breakfast the next morning, Francis sat opposite The Big Man and his wife, Catherine. His wife surprised Francis. In every way he was big, she was small and slight. Francis stood almost six foot tall and he still looked up to The Big Man. Catherine's head did not clear Francis's shoulder, so she was dwarfed by her massive husband. It is as if, between them, they must equal the size and weight of an average couple, pondered Francis.

'So young Francis, I am told that I am to teach you matters other than those of warfare. I am to bring some balance to your training in the sword and the dagger under the tutelage of The Duke.'

'I have much to learn, and I look forward to what you can teach me, as well as my lessons with The Duke,' Francis replied.

'Ahh, but do you know who he really is?' The Big Man asked.

In the short time that Francis had spent on The Mont he had come to realise that things were often not what they seemed. There was more history of special meaning here than he could have imagined. With interest he asked, 'I know he is the best of the Chevaliers of the Mont'.

'Aye he is that. To understand fully you need to know, not a legend as I told the younger ones last night, but a part of our known history. What do you know of the Hundred Years' War? The Greatest war of mortal existence?'

Francis took a moment to gather his thoughts and then said, 'Ever since the Duke of Normandy from France took the English throne in 1066 the line between the two royal houses on either side of the channel was confused. It was the war that finally defined Britain and

France as countries. Until I studied the war, I was not aware that French was our official language in Britain for three centuries up until the late 1300s.' Francis said.

The Big Man was pleased by Francis' knowledge of the French influence in Britain. He was also impressed by the young Englishman's command of the French language. 'So they did not entirely waste your time at Cambridge,' he said in good humour. 'Indeed, it is a pity that you Brits have lost the language of love and chivalry.'

Francis did not argue. He was starting to realise that The Big Man knew much more than the average gendarme about such matters. Indeed, all the people of The Mont appeared to be unusually well educated. While Cambridge University was founded in 1209, he had heard that education at The Mont went back much further in time than that.

The Big Man went on. 'The Hundred Years' War was also the war that almost saw the loss of the knight as a fighting force. The English long bows could penetrate our armour and take down our magnificent and valuable horses. In the end that was good for us. It made us stronger. We designed lighter, stronger armour – for our horses as well. However, that was not the real learning. We learnt to fight with a weapon more powerful than our swords and crossbows. We fought with our minds. The Chevaliers of the Mont were artists of the battles of the mind.

'In 1469 King Louis XI, in recognition of their supreme battle record, created the military order of the Chevaliers de Saint Michel. In English that translates to, The Knights of Saint Michael. You know the mighty cannons that lie at the entrance to The Mont?'

Francis nodded.

'It is a grim reminder of the great battle of 1433. You know that the Knights of the Mont took on the entire invading army of Britons?'

Francis nodded – there was not a squire or a knight, young or old that did not know at least something of this famous battle.

'But, do you know how few there were? How many stood against the might of the invading army numbering in their thousands?'

'Less than a thousand,' Francis guessed.

'No, no. The Mont was defended by a garrison of only 119 Knights and their bearers.' The Big Man paused to let the fullness of this statement sink in.

Francis tried to imagine 119 Knights doing battle with wave after wave of marauders coming at them from an entire army.

'They faced the greatest strength of the English invaders. The invaders were deeply frustrated with The Mont. Do you know why?' The Big Man did not give Francis time to answer.

'The Mont was the only fortified town the English were unable to take. All of France had been conquered by the Britons. The Mont was the only remaining bastion of our history – of who we are. The Britons thought it would be easy. How hard could it be to take a small island with a huge army?

'The Mont was ordained by Saint Michel from the start. It was always meant to be a fortress that could protect the knowledge, history and secrets it holds. Otherwise everyone from pillaging barbarians to great armies could burn and destroy centuries of powerful secrets. Under the guidance of Saint Michel, the tides and the quicksand were powerful allies to the Knights. But ultimately, with the blessing of the Archangel, it was up to the Knights and their skill in warfare.

'Assisted by our great tides and our quicksand, the Chevaliers repelled attack after attack. The Duke Louis d'Estouteville of the Mont led them. The Duke realised that winning a great battle is not about how many you kill, it is about *who* you kill. He knew that battles are won through instilling a fear of defeat rather than by actual defeat. He also knew that the average soldier was full of fear. Their fear was held at bay by their leaders. This was a powerful understanding.'

'How did he use this understanding?' Francis asked.

'Take out their leaders and the fear flows. The tide turns. The battle is won. Wars are not battles of the flesh nor are they about the skill of a fighter, wars are battles of the mind. The theatre of battle is not the bloody field. It is in the heads of the men, commanders and soldiers alike. This knowing will become clear to all students of The Mont.

'The Duke had his men target the knights and the commanders. All were trained to identify, in the midst of battle, any soldier on the other side who was clearly a strong fighter, looked up to by the men around him. They would then target this man. At times, much to the enemy's surprise, the knights would leave the safety of The Mont to take out a knight or commander they had targeted. Once their task was done they would make haste back into The Mont.'

'Did not their return make The Mont vulnerable as they opened the drawbridge to let the knights inside?' Francis asked.

'A good point. Normally this would be so. But The Mont is unique. The Duke and his men knew the quicksand sinks like the backs of their hands. After their quick sally forth, they would spin their horses on their hind legs and race back to The Mont avoiding the sinks in their way. As the enemy followed, burning with murder in their eyes for the loss of their leader, they would charge into sinks that could swallow twenty men without as much as a belch.

'In time the knights and officers, realising they were special targets, lost their nerve and the war was over. Why risk so much over an island not much larger than a King's palace? Saint Michel knew this from the moment he ordained The Mont.'

Francis remembered the words of the crusty guide who brought him out to The Mont across the sea of sand. 'With three rivers emptying into the bay – the Sée, The Sélune and the Couesnon – the channels are always shifting. At times, the rivers seek new entrances and enter the bay as underground springs. Thus creating the quicksand. These sinks can swallow a horse and carriage in a minute or so.'

Francis had noticed the reverence with which the guide spoke of the quicksand. These men, who knew the sand better than any others, respected its capacity to deceive. They were expert at reading the shifts in the sands and springs. Seemingly normal sand could suddenly give way to a soup of sand and water that was too thin to support a man's weight but too thick to swim through.

The Big Man continued, 'Through the actions of the 119 the order of Chevalier de Saint Michel is now the most esteemed throughout Christendom. Your teacher, the Duke is the direct descendent of the Duke who led the 119 Knights. You are lucky, he has only just returned after a long absence. Apparently he has been on a quest for the King.'

'Actually there is no record of his bloodline.' Catherine pointed out.

'Yes, that is true,' The Big Man said to his wife. 'but you only have to look at the painting in the Abbey of Duke d'Estouteville to see they are related. Indeed, they look like twins.'

'Yes, he is a great Knight,' Catherine agreed politely, 'but the Mont has much more to offer you than skills that will entice you to your death. Is that not right dear?'

'That may be so.' While he did not appear to entirely agree with his wife, Francis was intrigued to see that he did not argue with her. Through this and other interactions, he could see the respect that he gave his wife. It was not usual to see a man allow his wife to take control in this way. It was even more unusual to see such a tiny woman do it with such quiet influence over such a big man.

By and large, women were chattels, like one's horse or house, to be treated, or even traded, at will by their father or husband. The only time he had seen a woman treated publicly with respect was his own Queen Elizabeth. He often witnessed this first-hand. For reasons he had not understood until recently, he often found himself in the Queen's company. He had been quite surprised when the Queen had taken the time to visit him when he was at Cambridge.

But Queens were different – or were they? Francis had pondered on this. On what basis could women be inferior to men and then be superior to them? Was not a Queen still a woman? It would not be unusual for a husband to slap his wife if she disagreed with him. The Rule of Thumb, as written in the Bible, decreed that it was fine to beat your wife, as long as you did not use a stick thicker than your thumb. Francis could not imagine such a thing. His father respected his mother. While it was not so obvious in public, it was very clear when they were in private. He would no more consider raising a hand to her than he would the Queen. But he knew many men who thought it was of no matter to strike their wife.

These Montois, as the residents of the Mont were known, appear to hold to higher values, Francis reflected. He wondered whether this was unusual or the norm?

Catherine went on, 'Accompany me on my rounds of the prison and you will learn the real power of a great knight. You will begin to learn the power of the mind. As you have heard, conflict is not won simply through skill with a lance, sword or dagger. The most powerful weapon you have is the one between your ears. It informs the next most powerful weapon, which is the one between your jaws.'

Francis could not imagine how prisoners could teach him to be a great knight, but there was something in her words that held his attention.

VII DIABLO

*In order for the light to shine so brightly,
the darkness must be present.*

Diablo, the war horse, was magnificent. Carrying his head and tail high, he seemed to know that he was superior to other horses. Shining black and heavily muscled, he stood as high at his shoulder as a tall man. His black leather saddle and bridle were inlaid with pure gold.

Diablo's light armour was silver plate polished to a high sheen that reflected the late afternoon sun like a mirror. While this stallion saw battle frequently, it did not need armour for protection – this was provided by its rider.

Like his horse, its rider was all in black. His finely tailored clothes were covered by a black cloak embedded with precious stones. Straight shoulder length black hair fell either side of a prominent brow that sat above a long, but not too large, nose and a square jaw. He held himself, as would any Lord of his domain, with confidence and bearing. A sword with an elaborate inlaid ebony hilt, hung at his side. Despite his obvious wealth, he travelled without an entourage of armed men. He travelled without fear. When fear was required it was well supplied by those who crossed his path.

Just one manservant accompanied him. He too was dressed in black, but without the ornate inlaid fabrics of his master's livery. He wore with pride a long, vertical scar extending from the side of his left eye, down his cheek to his jawline. He was also on a black horse, not quite as large or as powerful as his master's, but a fine horse nevertheless. It was armoured with bronze plate. Its rider carried a grey handled sword that reflected the menace in his eyes of the same colour.

As the two riders trotted along the road, rising easily in their saddles with the step of their black steeds, the world around fell silent. The birds and all the insects simply stopped singing and buzzing as they approached. It was not until some time after they passed that the wildlife risked making noise again. Diablo's rider filled the void with a soft, tuneless whistle.

The thieves, six of them, coming the other way from the South, could not believe their luck. As they came upon the two men with such beautiful horses and obvious wealth, their eyes lit up.

Jean-Paul, the leader of the band, felt his spirits lift. Pickings had been slim lately. Two men were no match to the hardened marauders of his little band. Fighting, raping, pillaging and plundering was their profession. As they approached, he addressed the man with the beautiful inlaid cloak, who was clearly the master. 'That is a nice animal you have there.'

The two men in black said nothing as the six men on horseback surrounded them. All but Jean-Paul drew their swords. They took confidence from the fact that the stranger on the larger horse did not make any attempt to reach for his weapon. Two of the men put their swords to the throat of the armed manservant whose hand was on the sword at his side.

To his manservant he said, with the cultured tones of the educated, 'Gaspard, relax your hand. Leave this to me.'

'Excellent decision m'Lord.' Jean-Paul the famous brigand said with exaggerated politeness. 'If you would now be so kind as to dismount and empty your pockets. We won't detain you for long. And I will have that cloak of yours while you are at it.' Despite the swords on him, the man on the armoured horse did not move. Something about him began to cause Jean-Paul to feel unsettled. The man did not appear afraid ... and then there was the silence. It was eerie. Not a sound. It was as if the very wind had gone elsewhere and taken all life with it.

For the first time in a long time, Jean-Paul felt a growing disquiet. It was fear, good and proper, but he could not back down now. Not with his men watching. He ruled them with his raw power. There was something not right about the man before him. It took a moment for him to work it out ... it was the stranger's eyes – they were deep black pools. At first Jean-Paul did not realise what was wrong ... and then it hit him. There were no whites to those eyes. They were like black, bottomless pits inviting deep despair... they were not human. Jean-Paul averted his gaze, as the earth under him seemed to move.

Jean-Paul's lieutenant, a stocky young man with red hair and a matching beard, was keen to back up his leader. From the side, he could not see what Jean-Paul could see. Wanting his leader's favour and to show his strength to the other men, he put his sword to the stranger's throat and said, 'I think it would be wise to do as he said.'

Slowly, Diablo's rider pulled his glove off his right hand and brought it to the sword at his throat. With a smile, for he was enjoying this immensely, his fingers slowly wrapped around the blade. As he did so, he turned his eyes onto Redbeard. His eyes were no longer black pools, now they glowed a burning fire-red. Against this background, the shape of his black pupils could be seen – they were vertical, like those of a creature of the night.

Redbeard's blood turned to ice in his veins. His fear seemed to give the stranger further strength. With his hand around the razor-sharp knife-edges of the blade, he slowly pulled the sword from Redbeard's hand. The lieutenant could not take his eyes from the hand around the well-sharpened sword blade. The hand should have been cut and bleeding badly. How could any man do that? No sooner had he finished the thought when he realised what his boss already knew ... that was the very point, *no man could do that.* The awareness was brought home as Redbeard's sword shattered between the fingers of the man in the beautiful black.

Redbeard, Jean-Paul and his men looked in awe as the fragments of sword fell from the red-eyed creature's hand, like beach sand running through a child's fingers.

The stranger on the magnificent horse spoke again. His voice was no longer that of a well-spoken noble, in this moment it came out in a chilling otherworldly voice. 'On the contrary, I think it would be wise to run for your lives. Not that it will make any difference,' he added. As he spoke, the youngest of the band of six, no more than a boy, wet himself.

More out of fear than valour, another of the men, who had not seen the rider's eyes, thrust his sword towards the stranger's chest. Faster than the eye could follow the stranger grabbed the thief's blade, saying, 'Here, let me help you with that,' and thrust the blade into his own chest. For a moment, he paused – but it was just for effect. As he started to laugh, he pulled the blade out from his chest. It was as clean as when it went in. Not a man could take their eyes off the bloodless blade. His cackling laugh grew as he watched the expressions on their faces – he was really enjoying this.

The men needed no further prompting. As one, they turned their horses and took off the way they had come.

As Redbeard galloped away he felt a burning pain deep inside his body. The pain grew quickly. It was like his insides were on fire. As he breathed out, smoke seemed to come from his mouth. Blissfully, he lost consciousness as his body convulsed and exploded in flame. Jean-Paul watched as each of his men exploded in fire. With a quiet certainty, he knew he would not escape. As he started to burn, he crossed himself and wished fervently that the burning would not be eternal.

Diablo's rider spared the boy. This was not because of any mercy for the young, but because he was old enough to be believed at the next town and young enough to probably not be a well-known thief. This way he was less likely to be thrown immediately into gaol and would have time to tell his story. The stranger liked having the townsfolk aware of his arrival in advance. It made things so much easier.

By the time Diablo trotted up to the bodies of the men, there was little left of them but their larger bones and smouldering ashes.

'Nothing like a good smoting before tea,' he chuckled to Gaspard.

'Indeed, Sire,' he responded with a glint in his eyes, 'and no richer wellspring of fear than amongst thieves.' Killing was one of the few things that lit up those cold, grey eyes.

The stranger in black laughed in agreement and kicked Diablo into a canter, but Diablo wanted to run free. His rider agreed and gave him his head as they moved into a full gallop. Faster and faster they went, as the riders unloosed on the road. Diablo was very, very fast and pulled away from the manservant's horse.

As the sun set, it was easy to see where Diablo had been – his hooves, glowing red hot, left perfect smoking hoof-prints on the road behind them.

VIII CATHERINE

He that will not apply new remedies must expect new evils;
for time is the greatest innovator.

As they walked up the steps to the prison, Catherine turned to Francis and asked, 'So why did you stop studying the Law?'

'Well it was not entirely my choice to stop, but then it had not been my choice to start.'

'Your parents?'

Francis nodded and did not clarify the question of who his parents actually were. He was still trying to make sense of that. The man he had known as his father, Sir Nicholas Bacon had made the law his life and it had taken him far. While he never told Francis that he expected him to do law, it was spoken of as a forgone conclusion. 'But coming here was my idea,' he added.

'And where did that idea come from?'

'I am not sure. I'd been told of The Mont when I was young and since then I have always wanted to come here. Then I heard of the knight training under The Duke.'

'Was there any other reason to come here?' Catherine enquired.

Could he trust her? One look in her eyes told him he could. 'It sounds foolish …'

'Go on,' she said gently.

'I … I am on a quest.'

'For …?' prodded Catherine.

'I am not sure. I had a teacher at Cambridge who told me to quest for my purpose. I argued with him: "How could I quest for my purpose when I have no idea what my purpose is?" For some reason I have never forgotten what he said next. He said, "A True Quest may not take you where you expect to go, but it cannot help but take you closer to your purpose." Given that questing is what knights do … well here I am.'

Francis did not notice, as they walked, that Catherine smiled as if enjoying her own secret. She said, almost to herself, 'A wise man, your teacher.' She said no more and Francis was happy to drop the subject and walk on in comfortable silence.

As Francis came to realise, Madam Catherine enjoyed special access to the Bastille. This was not just because she was the wife of the head of The Mont's Gendarmerie. She was also the physician of The Mont. A natural born healer, she ministered to all, pauper or rich man, with a grace born of a deep concern for others.

Indeed, it was Catherine that Dr Pierre Clost, the dream-reader from the coach, was coming to visit at The Mont. 'Dr Clost and I, unlike most of our colleagues, have a particular interest in the mind, although he knows much more about it than I,' she had told him.

The warder at the front gate greeted her warmly and waved her through. Evidently her position was such that even the presence of a young guest went unquestioned. As they descended the worn, stone steps to the cells of the Bastille, Catherine returned to their earlier discussion.

'Why do you need to be a knight to go on a quest for purpose? You come from London's aristocracy. Queen Elizabeth herself has taken a special interest in you. I suspect the world is yours for the taking. Is not becoming a mere knight a step down?'

Her brown eyes were too closely set to be considered beautiful. They gave her a mouse-like appearance, albeit a soft, friendly mouse. As Francis looked into those brown eyes, he saw both a genuine interest in him and a strong intelligence. He realised that she would see anything less than the truth for what it was.

'Truth be told, Madam Catherine, I am not sure what I want to be. That was how that teacher and I got to the discussion of purpose. I realise that if I have any good fortune, it is that I am in a position to consider different options.'

'So true. That is indeed a rare privilege. Rarer still for you to see the fullness of the freedom of choice. Most people, even when offered it, do not wish to take it. Life is much simpler if one just goes along the preordained path of least resistance.'

'Is that what one should do, follow the preordained path? And how is it preordained, by others or God?' Francis asked.

'I said simpler, not better. The path that most take, while simpler, is the path to unhappiness. By preordained I am talking about others trying to make it so. Even God cannot preordain your path. Only you can discover the path that is best for you.'

'By using my feelings as a guide?'

This made Catherine chuckle, 'Aah, you have spent some time with Dr Clost. Yes, that is so. I expect that he also taught you that feelings are only a part of it. While they are the guide, we then need to be sure. This is done by taking time to reconsider while evaluating the options with careful thought.'

'Yes, I do remember.'

'And yes, a rare privilege ...'

Francis knew he was privileged. For so many young men their options were limited to farming their father's land or being apprenticed to a father or an uncle with a trade. For a young woman it was even worse. They were destined to become a wife and a mother – unless they became a nun. Their fortune became that of their husband's.

'Indeed, I find it burdensome having so many choices. At Cambridge my eyes were opened to so many things I could do. Now, with this trip to France I have diplomatic opportunities to marry to my legal studies.'

'Do you like the law?'

'I am not sure. Except …' He hesitated as he had not voiced this thought before. 'I enjoy thinking. I like words and ideas. I like the idea of justice. I like the idea of the knight who pursues a just cause, who goes on a great quest and who has the skills to deal with whatever comes his way … ' His voice trailed off.

Catherine stopped and turned to him as they arrived at a stone landing. 'How old are you now Francis?'

'Sixteen.'

'And how old were you when you started at Cambridge?'

'Twelve.'

'My, my. So very young to be thinking at such a level. What is the average age of boys who start at Cambridge?'

'Sixteen,' replied Francis without a hint of hubris.

Catherine could see that he had a questioning mind. She had already noticed that he was not concerned with the issues that occupied most young men of his age. He was interested in ideas themselves. How they worked and interplayed with each other. He asked questions not just to get an answer, but also to understand the principles behind the subject under discussion.

'My father loves hunting and riding. I think he feels I am a bit of a weakling. I have often been ill with one thing or another and I have been more interested in books than hunting.'

Catherine heard the pain of having disappointed in his voice. She knew how desperately every son needed his father's approval. 'Has your father ever said that he sees you as a weakling?'

'No, but when I do not want to go hunting or practice archery with him he seems disappointed in me.'

'Maybe he would just like to see you become more skilled and stronger to round you out. There is a big gap between wanting these things for a son and being disappointed in you as a person.' Catherine ventured gently.

'Maybe. But I do like the idea of being a knight. I want to learn the skills of swordsmanship. Battle strategy also fascinates me. And I think about chivalry, of what it means to be a good person. So many rules seem to be made just to suit adults and to make you serve their needs. From what I know of chivalry, it seeks something more. I have heard that French knights place a higher value on it, and have a greater understanding of chivalry than the English.'

'Yes. That is true. For we French it is as much about how you go about your quest as whether or not you achieve it. It was largely why your army of 16,000 destroyed our army of 80,000 at Crécy. And then, for the first time, completely against the code of chivalry, the English murdered prisoners and the wounded.' Catherine spoke with a touch of bitterness over the senseless acts men did in the name of honour and patriotism.

While becoming a knight was not a career that Catherine could support, she knew better than to tell a 16-year-old, no matter how smart he was, not to do something because of the physical danger involved. They see themselves as immortal as God, she thought. She sensed she had a better chance of discouraging him by getting him to think himself to a different position. 'It was not that almost a third of our nobility died that day. It was that chivalry was mortally injured that day. I fear that the era of the knight and his chivalry is coming to an end.'

'What is it about being a knight of chivalry that we should try to keep alive?'

The question pleased Catherine. This was just the kind of question that Francis asked that made him so different. She had hoped he would start to explore the idea of what a knight stood for, rather than simply wanting to be one.

Chivalry centred on the idea of noble action. Catherine chose her words carefully. 'I have heard a Master say "Nobility is not about being better than other men. It is about being better than the man you were." I think there are many positions of influence that a man can aspire to that would benefit from this truth.'

Francis seemed deep in thought. Catherine knew when any further discussion would weaken an argument. Or in this case, declare that you were having one. She changed the subject. At least, she appeared to be changing the subject.

'Do you know the story of Robert du Mont?'

'No.'

'I must tell you about him. He was quite a man. The Mont's first true Master. But now I need to see my first patient. Just give me a moment with this man. I need to dress a wound on his leg.' She allowed Francis his thoughts. She wanted him to think on what she had said.

The grey, cold stonewalls reflected the level of comfort on offer to their inmates. Catherine started her rounds in the very depths of the Bastille's bowels – the dungeons. It was here the most violent prisoners were held.

Francis remained deep in thought. Catherine's words on nobility had struck a chord. So much of what he saw in the nobility of London was about the pride of being better than other men. And why? On what basis? Through birth right? How could one take pride in something that one had had no hand in?

He had also noticed that those who took the most pride and vanity in their noble birth were also the most tedious and petty. All too often would they remind those around them of their status. They appeared to take no interest in becoming better than the men they had been. Then there were some higher-ranking men, often those who had lead men into battle, who were quietly calm and confident. They appeared to not have the need to assert their superiority over lesser men.

Clearly, the problem was not just because of rank. He recalled more teachings from Dr Whitgift. He was one of the grey-bearded

Cambridge Dons, who had spoken to Francis about the quest for purpose that he had spoken of to Catherine. The Don had also once said, 'Reminding others of one's status, or pulling rank, is to openly declare one's insecurity. This is not information about yourself that you want to be giving to people who threaten you in some way.' At the time, Francis had not thought much about it. Now, in the context of Catherine's words on nobility, he could see the fullness of the issue.

It was then he realised why he was attracted to the knighthood. Great knights were not deemed to be great by birth right. While knights sat at the lowest level of the aristocratic ladder, they were given a special respect. A famed knight was recognised for his achievements in battle. On the field of battle, birth right counted for nothing. If anything, it decreased your lifespan. If your men found you proud and tedious, they would be less inclined to watch your back. It was recognition for individual achievement, rather than the luck of birth right, that attracted Francis to the knighthood.

Francis had dropped behind Catherine as he played with his thoughts. Up ahead he heard Catherine greeting the jailor. There was a jangle of keys and the rasp of the iron door as it grated open.

He was pulled from his thoughts by a yell. Catherine was being dragged out of the cell on the left by a man who towered over her. His arm was across her throat. The jailor had drawn a dagger along with his sword. The prisoner was using Catherine as a shield between himself and the jailor. There was a bandage around his right leg.

'Make a sound or a move and I will snap her neck in two. At the very least, I will crush her windpipe and she will die gasping.'

The prisoner was facing away from Francis as he came up behind the man. He was naked from the waist up and Francis could see the battle scars on his back. While the man was weakened from his time in prison, he was clearly a fighting man who knew what he was doing. Undoubtedly born of desperation, this was not a well thought out plan. While it might get him past the jailor, there were many

85

guards to deal with before he would make it out of the prison. Nevertheless, the threat to Catherine was real.

'Drop your weapons now,' the prisoner demanded. There was a desperate edge to his voice. He stood with his legs well apart to balance himself against Catherine's weight. The prisoner wanted the jailor's blades. With a knife to Catherine's throat, he would have more power than he had now.

Francis realised that the prisoner did not know that he was coming up from behind. Normally Catherine did her rounds on her own. The jailor hesitated. He knew that the moment the prisoner gained the weapons along with his hostage they were all in danger. Desperation and a dagger were not a good combination.

The prisoner roared at the jailor, 'Do it now, or she dies.'

Francis had not been good at wrestling at Cambridge. His slight frame and his relative youth meant that he was no match for most of the other boys. He had not gained height until his fifteenth year. His good speed, which made all the difference in fencing classes, was of little use in wrestling. But Francis, as always, was learning something more than what was being taught. Francis paid particular note when the instructor spoke of what they were not allowed to do for fear of serious injury. Knees were particularly off-limits.

Then the jailor made a near fatal mistake. He saw Francis coming up behind Catherine and her attacker. The jailor's eyes locked on Francis' eyes, reflecting his presence. Francis realised that if he did not act now, the prisoner was bound to notice the jailor's reaction to him and the element of surprise would be lost. Francis took three running steps to get some momentum. He knew this would alert the prisoner. His only hope was the benefit of surprise and speed. He could not hope to overpower the man. He had one move.

At the sound of the footsteps, the attacker started to turn his head to look behind him – but was reluctant to take his eyes of the jailor's dagger. The hesitation gave Francis the time he needed. By then Francis was beside him. With his full weight behind it, he kicked out to his left at the side of the man's right knee. He kicked as hard as he could.

With a popping, tearing noise, the ligaments in the inside of his right knee, attaching femur to tibia, were ripped from their points of attachment taking shards of bone with them. Even the ligaments inside the knee joint ripped through. Knees were only made to bend forward or backwards. There was no plan for any sideways give – so the tendons had to rip from the bone or snap.

The pain was worse than a clean bone break. The man screamed and grabbed at his ripped knee, releasing his grip on Catherine. As the leg gave way under Francis' foot, with his momentum still carrying him, Francis grabbed for Catherine with his left arm and took her with him as he recovered from his burst of speed.

The man would never walk very well on that leg again. At that point, however, walking was the very least of his worries. Fear leapt into him, as did the jailor, with pent-up fury. The prisoner had known that if his escape attempt failed, no mercy would be shown. There was perhaps no one more dear to the Bastille than their beloved Catherine. With her in the clear, the jailor could do his job. There would be no clemency for attempted escape and threatening the life of the head of the Gendarmerie's wife. All, prisoners and the Montois alike, revered her for her care and healing skills.

Dropping his sword, the jailor's muscled left arm closed around the prisoner's neck. He drew the prisoner close to avoid the head butt. At the same time the dagger in his right hand was driven up under the left side of the prisoner's rib cage. The long blade travelled through the thin diaphragm, ripping open the left lung on its journey to the man's heart. At full penetration, he twisted it to ensure maximum damage. As the blood from the ripped lung travelled up his windpipe and out his mouth, the prisoner's heart stopped. He slumped to the floor as the jailor released his dead weight.

'Are you all right?' Francis asked Catherine as they lay on the hard floor together. His heart was pounding and he was starting to shake. 'Did I bruise you?'

'Bruise me!? Silly boy. I should take you on my rounds more often.'

IX THE DUKE

*He that gives good advice, builds with one hand;
he that gives good counsel and example, builds with both.*

It was one of the few, grassed areas on The Mont. The Knight's training area held a commanding view back over the water to the forest lining the coast of France. Not a safe place for donkeys, even those guided by God, Francis thought idly.

The sun had only just risen. All the squires were there. This weekly meeting was the only contact they had with The Duke. No one wanted to miss a moment. In the cold air, their breath smoked when they spoke, but there was little talk. There was an air of expectancy. It was like waiting for a great show to begin. As it had been explained to Francis, the Duke would start with a teaching demonstration of a fighting skill and then he would speak for a short time on a particular subject.

Francis waited with more anticipation than most. This would be his first sight of the man he had come here to be trained by. He had noticed that people appeared to revere The Duke more than a king or queen. There were no jokes about The Duke. No light put-downs. People held him in the highest respect. When Francis had asked why, people simply said 'Wait until you meet him.' This apparently did not happen often. The Duke kept to himself.

Minutes later, The Duke walked quietly and deliberately from the small building to the right of Francis. Two other men-at-arms followed him.

Duke Louis d'Estouteville carried the same name as his ancestor. At six feet six inches with black curly hair falling to his broad shoulders, he had chiselled features and a powerful jaw. While approaching middle age, he had the physique of a much younger man.

It was evident from the way he carried himself that he came from a long line of nobility. Chivalry was in his blood. He had recently returned to The Mont after a long absence. Nobody quite knew where he had been. No one dared to ask.

The Duke now stood in the centre of the fighting circle marked on the ground. The Duke held a sword in each hand. What surprised Francis was the presence of not one, but two knights standing on either side of him preparing to fight. Elegantly, he turned to his right as he brought the blade of the sword in his right hand to touch his own forehead. With reverence, he bowed to the man on his right. He did the same with the sword in his left hand as he bowed to the man on his left.

On cue, the two men began to circle The Duke, making ready their attack. One wore a blue tunic and the other a red one over light chainmail. While squires practiced with wooden swords, here they used sparring metal swords with flattened tips and dulled edges. Nevertheless, the risk of injury, including broken bones, was still real. Serious injury was less likely, but not unheard of. No strikes were allowed above the shoulders or to unprotected arms and legs. The Duke, in his pure white tunic stood in the middle, swords by his side. Unmoving, he appeared almost disinterested.

Francis understood what they were playing out. On a battlefield, once dismounted a knight did not usually face a single opponent. To focus on one opponent was sure death.

Francis had learnt fencing at Cambridge. He knew enough to know how difficult it would be to take on two skilled swordsmen at once. So much of fencing came from getting one's opponent into a position of vulnerability and then attacking with the killer thrust. How could one do that with a second skilled opponent coming at you? Maybe one of these knights was not as skilled. Maybe one would not attack at full pace.

As one, the two knights finally attacked. The Duke's swords came up in an instant and sparks flew as four blades made contact under full muscle. As the parrying and thrusting began, Francis realised that each of the attacking knights were highly skilled. This was no contrived routine. Each wanted to prove that they were a match for The Duke. They were not holding back. Francis saw why. It was not just their personal pride motivating them.

She was stunning. Off to one side in a doorway was perhaps the most beautiful woman that Francis had ever seen. He guessed she was in her early twenties. She was tall and slim with long, gently curled, lustrous black hair that fell to her slight, but well shaped bosom. Her skin, without blemish, was a soft golden hue, darker than the ladies of London. Her perfectly balanced, fine features only added to her regal air. She paid close attention to the fight.

Francis followed her gaze back to the ring. The Duke moved lightly on his feet with the agility of a dancer. He kept moving, bringing the fight first to one man then the other. In full flight, his blades were a blur of steel. Francis had never seen a broadsword move with the speed of a light rapier. The Duke moved the sword in his left hand just as deftly as the one in his right. Most swordsmen had their fighting hand and their 'off-hand' in which they held a weapon of defence. Clearly, The Duke had no off-hand. Wherever his attackers' blades were, The Duke's was there to meet them.

Francis studied The Duke's movements. For the most time his shoulders were relatively still. All the movement was in his wrists and elbows. Shoulder movements required upper body movement, which was much slower. That was part of why his blades could move so fast. How could he watch two opponents at once? Francis moved his attention to The Duke's eyes.

What was he doing? He never looked directly at his attackers. Yet when they parried and then thrust, his blade was there to parry in turn. Occasionally, The Duke would completely stop his sword at the point of a parry, as if to give the other knight a moment to recover. At these moments, Francis could see that The Duke had turned his sword to take the blow on its flat side rather than its cutting edge. This extended the life of the sword and minimised the risk of fracturing the blade. Often, in heated battle, one did not have the time to turn the blade. The Duke seemed to have all the time in the world.

The Duke moved with the fluidity of well-crafted poetry. It was as if he had eyes in the back of his head. Francis watched more closely. At no time did he allow either man to move behind him. The most he allowed was a man directly to either side. But even then, he looked at neither. He moved his head slightly in each direction. He has trained himself to only use his peripheral vision, Francis realised.

As the man in blue moved in behind him to his left, the Duke bent his knees and spun, just as the man in red on his right thrust at his chest. Red's sword found empty air. An instant later, the blade in the Duke's left hand made contact with it. Over-extended by the surprise of vacant space, The Duke's blade swept Red's sword out of his hand and across the ring.

Blue, who had been trying to position himself behind The Duke for a surprise attack, was now standing frozen. It took the audience a moment to realise why as their focus had been on Red losing his sword. Blue looked down to find The Duke's other sword sitting at the base of his throat. His own sword was wide, preparing for a sweeping cut. In moving around for a surprise attack, he had let his guard down. The Duke had done what he was famous for – he made the most of an instant of weakness.

Both men knew they had been outclassed. As masters themselves, they could have been embarrassed. There was little shame in being bested by The Duke. The Duke had no peer.

They were breathing heavily. The Duke appeared to be completely relaxed. He might as well have been out for a morning stroll. Slowly he stood to his full height and raised his swords, in turn, to his forehead as he again bowed to each man. He handed one sword to the man in blue and sheathed the other at his side. He then made his way across to where the squires sat.

Most of the other squires had begun their training at the earliest opportunity – from the moment they turned fourteen. The earliest they could be a knight, if accepted, was their twentieth birthday. Thus, they had six years to learn the skills of combat and war.

Slowly, The Duke stepped into the semi-circle of the squires from all over the country who had the good fortune to be present. Few of them did not appreciate this fortune. For every ten noble families that requested that their sons be trained at The Mont, only one was accepted. Who would be accepted, and why, was never made clear. Sometimes it would be those from the most powerful families, sometimes from the least. Sometimes it was the strongest of boys, at other times it was the weakest. Some said he asked Archangel Michael, the idol of The Mont, for guidance. Either way, they knew that they were the lucky ones.

The Duke stood for a moment in front of his charges saying nothing. He stood, evenly balanced on both feet. One sensed he could move very quickly in any direction. His muscular arms ran down to his long and powerful fingers. His hands were those of a skilled musician, rather than a fighting man, Francis thought.

The younger boys revered him for his unequalled skill with the sword and dagger. The display of skill they had just seen, etched in their minds. The older lads revered him for different reasons. They had started to realise there was a wisdom on offer here. Here was a teacher with knowledge that they rarely come across. Maybe it was also that The Duke was not their father – wisdom is often discounted when delivered by a relative.

Finally, he spoke. His voice was not loud. It held a quiet strength. It was as if he was not going to force you to listen. You had to choose to listen. As one, they leaned forward. They did not want to miss a word. Most of their training was with the knights under The Duke. These times, with the man himself, were treasured.

'When you saw me fighting, did you notice which part of my opponent's body my eyes were on?'

A young lad with more than his fair share of freckles, Antoine, jumped in. 'On their swords. I was taught to never take my eyes off the sword.' He was keen to gain the master's attention.

The Duke's response was good-humoured. 'Well, young squire, I hope your tutor is either fortunate enough to avoid a duel with a master, or soon learns otherwise.' A soft chuckle ran around the seated squires. 'Any other thoughts?'

An older squire, around Francis' age, with blue eyes and fair hair, called Christian, raised his hand. Francis turned to look at him. With his even features, good teeth and broad shoulders, Francis felt a twinge of competitiveness. He was acutely aware of his narrow shoulders and less than perfect teeth. In the way that young men assess such things, he knew that the girls would prefer Christian over him – all other things being equal. Maybe he was an idiot, Francis found himself hoping. His luck was not in. Christian spoke with confidence and an educated tone. 'Their body stance? You looked to see where they will place their sword from their body position?'

'Good. That is getting closer to what I am looking for, but there is more.'

There was silence. Francis spoke up, partly to not allow Christian to dominate the proceedings. 'You seemed to operate in two modes. At times you looked directly at neither opponent and responded from your side vision.'

As Francis paused, The Duke smiled gently. His fine teeth white in the soft morning light. 'Ahh. Our Englishman can speak. Go on.'

'And when you did look directly at them you seemed to focus on their eyes.'

'And what else might I notice while I am looking at their eyes?'

Francis took a moment. If there was one thing he had learned at Cambridge, it was to gather his thoughts before responding. Fools rush in where angels tread carefully. The silence was just starting to get embarrassing. The Duke went to speak, as Francis finally said, 'Then your side vision takes in their stance.'

The Duke studied Francis for a brief moment. 'Yes, and between looking into the windows of his soul and observing his body stance, you will know when he will attack and where he will put his sword before he does.'

The Duke went on. 'Mind you, it takes years of practice for your mind to learn which stance goes with which sword movement. Practice enough and trust your mind to remember. Do not watch a sword fight idly. Look closely at whichever man is facing you. Allow your mind to really see him. If you do not do this, you deny your mind access to all the information it will need to work out which stance leads to which position of the sword. Your mind is all-powerful, much more than you know. Do not choke it off by not allowing it what it needs to develop your power.

'When you are sparring or fighting, keep your eyes wide open. Allow the information in so your mind can learn. I call this nonthinking learning. Can anyone think of something that most of you have become expert at just by virtue of allowing your mind to learn without thinking how to do it?'

It was Antoine, anxious to redeem himself, who said, 'Riding a horse, Sir?'

'That is it. Over the years spent on the back of a horse, this part of your mind has been learning – often while you have been thinking about other things, mostly girls in Christian's case!'

After the laughter settled, The Duke continued, 'Have faith in this process of learning. Most learning occurs at this deeper level of the mind. The greatest mistake people make, because they do not know of the mind's power, is to not give it a chance. You cannot become a skilled horse rider by reading about it, but ride often and your mind cannot help but learn.

'Should one not use the thinking mind when one makes mistakes, Sir?'

It was a good question from Christian, but it was his comfort in questioning The Duke, after the joking around, that aroused feelings of jealousy in Francis.

'Yes we do need to think about our mistakes. But there is a bigger issue here. If you make mistakes, do not beat yourself up for not having done better. Indeed, if you are inclined to beat yourself up for your mistakes, save your energy and do not worry, your opponents will do it for you! Making mistakes is the very essence of learning. No one begins their training in anything as a master and, of course, even masters make mistakes. If they are not making mistakes, then they are not pushing their limits. They are not continuing to learn. *Mistakes mean learning.*

'The fast learners are the ones who know this truth. They have a comfort with making mistakes. The slow learners are the ones who do not. The slow learners are the ones who beat themselves up because they think they should be able to start learning from the position of a master.

'While you need some inborn talent as a starting point to develop high level skill, mastery will come to he, or she, who knows that mistakes mean learning. Any one of you that sees setback and mistakes as failure, rather than as learning experiences, will then, and only then, become a failure.'

Francis was jarred by the sudden reference to the fairer sex. Squires were all men. But then he turned. The black-haired angel still stood in the doorway. Off to one side also stood young Josephine and her cousin Pieter – clearly in awe of The Duke. Indeed, a small gathering of both sexes of all ages, stood behind the circle of squires. *He is not just teaching us about swordsmanship, he is teaching us all about life*, Francis realised.

'Now, what follows from what I have said about the need to look into the eyes and consider the stance of your opponent? What does it mean for you?'

Francis, not wanting to be out done by Christian, spoke up. 'You need to be careful about the information you are giving away in your eyes and in your stance.'

'Precisely.' The Duke replied. 'Never forget what I am about to say to you. During your training, it is five parts mind and five parts body. Your body is where you hold your physical skill. As I have explained, you must give it time to learn, but once you are in the fray of the fight, as with all challenges we take on in life, success is nine parts the mind and only one part the body.

'Now what do I mean by "the mind"?' This time he did not pause for a response from the squires. 'It is not about what skill you have. It is about when and how you deploy it. What do your eyes, face and body say to your opponent? Do you adopt the stance of a warrior, confident in your abilities? Or do you convey fear?'

The freckled Antoine spoke up. A little more tentatively this time he suggested, 'You convey confidence?'

'Yes, but a certain kind of confidence. Many a fight is won, before it begins, through a display of quiet confidence. I say "quiet confidence" not loud bravado – that is more likely to invite your opponent to cut you down to size.

'Conversely, sometimes a lack of confidence can also be the key to winning. If you can appear to lack skill, you can lull your opponent into a false sense of security. He is then more likely to drop his guard and you can strike.'

'So when do you show you are skilled and when do you hide it?' asked the young freckled squire.

'Anybody?' The Duke asked.

On this, they were all silent. The Duke went on. 'As I said, before it begins, be confident and you might avoid the fight. When you have an aggressor who wishes to fight no matter what, hold back. Let them feel they have the upper hand, but make sure you do not let him look into your eyes. Your eyes, as will his, always tell the truth. Fortunately, many people do not know how to look into the windows of the soul and see the fullness of the truth therein.

'As with all conflict, never push against your opponent. Any fool can do this and most do. It wastes precious energy. Use the direction they wish to go in, to your advantage. Use your mind not your muscle.

'If they press forward in the attack then back up – as long as you are not being backed into a corner. By doing this, you are doing three things. First, you are saving energy. Second, you lull them into a false sense of security. Third, as you back up, study their moves. What is their weakness? Finally you strike, quickly and decisively.

'As they then show surprise and often fear and are backing away in retreat, press your advantage. Only then may you allow them to see your eyes and your confidence in their pending defeat. This is often the decisive moment. Be swift but, above all, be merciful. You are never served by an absence of mercy. A true Chevalier is mercy in armour.

'A final point about your relationship to your sword. Do not see your sword as in your hand. See your sword as of your hand. Of you. When your sword sits between your fingers and the palm of your hand it becomes an extension of you. This means that you do not think of where your hand is and how to move your sword – allow your nonthinking mind to take over. The sword is an extension of who you are, just as your hand is an extension of who you are. When you move your arm, do you think about how to move it? Or do you just do it? You use your nonthinking mind to become one with your sword as with your arm. There is no separateness. Oneness is a high truth from which the greatest skill flows.

'In all things in life, moving into oneness will put you where you most need to be to achieve what you wish to achieve. Be at one with those around you. Be at one with nature. The energy of what you become one with, will become your energy.'

With two hands, he began to spin the sword around its balance point at the hilt. Like a fire twirler gathering speed, his blade spun faster and faster until it became a wall of steel. Then he went faster again. The wall of steel turned clear, as the blade did not appear to be where it was. 'To spin the blade like this I first did it slowly. I practiced until my mind knew how to do it.' The Duke explained. 'Once my mind had worked out how to do it, to go faster, I had to approach it differently. I had to stop trying to work out how to get my hands to go faster. I had to hand over to my nonthinking mind. This is the hardest part. I had to not think of what my hands are doing, but of what I wanted the sword to do. I see it spin at speed in my mind and I allow my hands to connect me to the sword to make it spin in reality.'

The Duke then threw the spinning sword high into the air. As it fell, he caught the handle in his right hand with the blade vertical in front of his nose. With his usual speed and precision, he threw the sword lightly up in the air, not so high this time, caught it with a reversed grip and slid the sword straight into its scabbard on his belt.

'To achieve any goal in life we first need to see it in our mind. If we cannot see it in our minds, we have to wonder why? It usually means we do not want it badly enough. If this is the case, it may be time to spend our energies elsewhere.

'On this matter, I will leave you today with the following truth. *Everything worth having is created twice. First in your mind and then in reality.* To attempt to do it the other way around is folly.' With a wry smile The Duke added, 'It is also unnecessarily tedious. You will find that as you start to do it in reality, your nonthinking mind will then start to apply its learning and will refine how you see yourself doing it.'

The Duke paused and looked slowly around the squires. 'Know this, as it is an important way to work out who you are and what you are here to do: If you cannot imagine yourself as a great swordsman, a great archer or a great general, you will never be one. If you wish for something but find your mind on other matters, take note. There is nothing wrong with realising this early on and choosing a different path. There is a lot wrong with realising it once you are in battle.'

The Duke paused and looked at each squire in turn.

'But there is an even greater tragedy in dying to find out you were not doing what you were meant to be doing. At a higher level is the fact that while you pursue something you are not meant to be, you deny your friends, family, and indeed your country, *what you are meant to be*. This is the ultimate waste of your life. Each of you needs to pursue your individual purpose.'

The Duke turned and started to walk away. He paused and turned back.

'You, Englishman. You did a good thing in the Bastille. See me in my quarters a week from tomorrow morning after you break your fast.' He turned his powerful shoulders and walked away, leaving silence behind him. All eyes were on Francis, including those of the beauty in the doorway.

X MARGUERITE

There is no excellent beauty that hath not some strangeness in the proportion.

Later that day, after his first contact with The Duke, Francis was wandering along the main street of The Mont. He had walked back to the front gate to see the cannons taken with the defeat of his countrymen in 1433. However, his mind was not with warfare. The dark cloud that had troubled him as he was leaving Paris was back. After a few moments spent with the rusting hulks of the siege that failed, he turned and walked back, uphill.

As his shoes clicked the cobblestones, he found his mind going back to The Duke's words. What was his purpose? He had no idea. He knew from his dream that he had to be the author of his life, but of which life? What was he meant to be? A knight? Catherine's comments also had him thinking. While he liked the idea of it, he found his mind going to other matters.

As he wandered up the Grande-Rue, he found himself thinking more about the process of learning itself. He pondered how The Duke's wisdom could be applied to life more widely. Truth be told, he thought about sword-fighting very little.

The Duke was not the only one who intrigued him. Catherine, the physician, had a pleasing intensity of thinking, balanced with a caring nature. The love between her and her storytelling husband was obvious. Even the children Josephine and Pieter, were different. They had enquiring minds. Thinking seemed to be nurtured here amongst everyone. Where he was from, it was reserved for the upper classes and was considered almost heretical in those without privilege.

Even at Cambridge, they were taught to think in a particular way. The eloquence of an argument seemed to be more important than searching out and understanding the underlying truths behind what was being debated. Hair-splitting and intellectual debate was more important than building new knowledge.

Dr John Whitgift, his tutor at Cambridge, was the closest to the people he now found at The Mont. His long beard had earned him the nickname 'Greybeard'. He did not speak often, but when he did, Francis found it was usually worth listening. Greybeard seemed much more interested in clever ideas and real truths, rather than just clever words.

What was it Greybeard had said about learning? Francis could not remember the exact words, but they went something like: *'Experience is the most powerful way to learn. Unfortunately, it is also the slowest way to learn.* Whenever you find someone who appears to be good at some aspect of life, a master of sorts, move on from your envy quickly and ask them to share what they know before they move on. All true masters are happy to oblige. A fear of appearing inferior stops most people from seeking what the masters have to share, so they are not overly burdened. Then, when people finally ask, they often do not listen to the answer. This is never more so than when what is being proffered requires effort to bring it about. *Life is simply too short to learn what is required through direct experience.*'

Francis remembered asking a question with some impudence about this. 'What if you do not meet many people with anything to teach?' he had asked. 'Then clearly you need to become more interesting Mr Bacon, to attract their attention.' With that, his classmates had had a great laugh. But Greybeard was just warming up, 'If that fails then there are always books. Great thinkers have a tendency to write. I doubt that even you could repel a book Mr Bacon!'

Through his embarrassment and the echoes of laughter, Francis had heard the message and had never forgotten it. This had been during one of his first classes with Greybeard. The good-humoured delivery had held no meanness. Over time, he came to respect

Greybeard's thinking and knowledge more than that of any other teacher at Cambridge. Greybeard seemed to have a soft spot for him too. Before leaving for France he had returned to Cambridge and sought Greybeard out. As always, his door was open so Francis walked into his musty office. His desk was piled high with books making it unusable. The Don sat reading in his armchair. He motioned Francis to sit opposite him.

'Aah, young Mr Bacon. Off to Paris on her Majesty's business with the English ambassador.'

No "Hello, how are you?" Greybeard never wasted time with small talk.

'You are to attend Court with King Henry III I am told. It is good to see that you have made yourself more interesting!'

Francis was only a little surprised that Greybeard remembered their interaction of almost three years ago. The man had a memory like a steel trap. 'Yes Dr Whitgift. I have come to say goodbye. You were away when I left to go to Gray's Inn to study law. I wanted to thank you for the wisdom that you shared over my time here. You have encouraged me to search for higher knowledge and for that I am grateful.' The fullness of it was that Greybeard had given Francis faith in himself, in both his ability and his right to think at the level of any great thinker.

As if reading his thoughts Greybeard said, 'You have much to contribute to this world Mr Bacon. Indeed, you have a responsibility to do so, to become the best man you can be. To whom much is given, much is expected.' The weight of these words was not lost on Francis. It was an uncomfortable experience. The Duke had spoken of similar ideas, making it hard for Francis to now ignore them.

'Do you have any final words of advice for me Dr Whitgift?' Francis had not forgotten the point of their confrontation all those months ago.

'Be aware of crossroads in your life Mr Bacon. Most people are not aware of when they are making critical decisions that change the direction of their life. Worse than making a poor decision, they make no decision. Often they do not realise the opportunity and the choice that sits before them. You cannot author your life if you do not know you are making a choice. Authoring is hard enough when you know you face a choice. It is impossible when you do not know.'

'How will I know when I face a choice?'

'Here is a clue. There are always signposts and those signposts are people. These people will *make you feel a certain way*. It is not a pleasant feeling. Authoring is uncomfortable. It might be the person, or they may just carry critical information quite unwittingly. Develop the skill to feel when you are at a crossroads. Crossroads have a certain feeling to them. Learn to know that feeling. Then when you notice the feeling, slow down. Think deeply on what is happening. If you can, speak with others. They do not need to be great thinkers, just good listeners. *The process of telling another requires us to organise our thoughts to a much higher level than when we think alone.*

'The greatest regret we can have in life is to turn, or not turn, and not even know we have made a choice.'

Did Francis detect a hint of sadness in his Don's voice? Francis realised that the Don was allowing Francis to learn from his own experience. If Francis could learn this lesson, maybe he could avoid the pain he heard in his mentor's voice. How long had it taken Greybeard to learn this lesson he was sharing? Five years? Ten Years? Francis did not want to learn from the most powerful, but slowest teacher – experience – if he could avoid it.

'Then when you make a choice, whatever it may be, be clear on why you made this decision. Maybe write it down. So that later, you can recall clearly why you did what you did. This is the way to avoid regrets. We do not regret making wrong decisions if we know we thought it through fully at the time. We will rightfully kick ourselves for a long time, when we realise we did not.

'Thank you again Sir.'

As Francis stood to leave, Dr Whitgift said, 'By the way, you know when I confronted you in that class three years ago? I would not have done so unless I had seen that you were strong enough to take it.'

'Thank you Sir.'

'One last thing. If you have a chance on your sojourn in France, see if you can get to Mont Saint Michel. They have one of the few remaining, and perhaps the best, knight-training programs there. If they will take you, they have extraordinary teachers there. '

'I have always wanted to go to Mont Saint Michel ever since my mother told me about it when I was a young boy. Maybe I will.'

'Have a good trip Mr Bacon. May you know when you come to your crossroads.'

As Francis reflected on his last meeting with Greybeard, he realised that, here at The Mont, he had found some crossroads. Undoubtedly, Greybeard had known he would, when he had suggested Francis come here. There were 'signpost people' here. He was starting to understand what his teacher had meant by those strange words: they have 'a certain feeling to them.'

It was not a pleasant feeling. Francis realised that his natural inclination was to ignore it and distract himself. He also realised that no one can teach you to recognise a feeling. Greybeard had done the next best thing, he had explained what to look for and where to find it.

His life at The Mont in the few weeks he had been here was simple and almost idyllic. Every morning, except Sunday, was spent in training from daybreak until noon. While the fighting drills were gruelling, he had already noticed the changes in his body. His lanky body was starting fill out. He felt stronger. He did not tire as easily as when he had first arrived.

He also noticed he was feeling more confident in himself. His greatest embarrassment at Cambridge had been that he had been a slow developer. A couple of the other students had been merciless in pointing out that he was still a boy. Most around him had started to shave and had grown the hair of manhood. Finally, not long after his fifteenth birthday, it all happened.

He gained four inches and his voice had deepened. It was not until his training under The Duke that he had started to feel the fullness of that height he had gained. He sensed that his new-found sense of stature had more to do with his thinking than his practice sessions.

The afternoons were given over to the squires' reading and free time. They were given access to The Mont's great library to study matters of warfare. It was at these times he was able to spend time with the intriguing Catherine on her rounds. She was a tender, wise soul. She had 'signpost' written all over her, Francis thought. And then there was the weekly demonstration and talk from The Duke himself. The Duke was a signpost in capital letters!

He walked through the marketplace targeted at the thousands of pilgrims The Mont attracted each year. He came to a shopfront only a short walk up from the front gate, on the left hand side. It sold arms. He wandered in. The elaborate daggers shifted his attention from his thoughts. Carefully, he slid his hand into a particularly complex design with two blades. There was a curved blade that came from the back of the handle and all the way around his hand and back to the front of the handle as a guard. This guard-blade balanced the deadly, foot long blade sprouting from its elaborate hilt.

As he felt for its balance, he was startled by a voice at his shoulder.

'My, what a big dagger you have there.'

Francis turned. It was the woman he had seen watching The Duke. She was close enough for him to smell her lightly perfumed scent. She had been another subject of his thoughts from the moment he had first laid eyes on her. A few steps behind, stood a Lady-in-waiting. He was not surprised to find she was of noble birth and had attendants. While he had noticed the Lady-in-waiting as he had entered the shop, the woman she served had been standing in an alcove. He had not seen her, until now.

For a moment he could not speak. Her beauty was even more breathtaking up close. While her eyes might be considered by some to be a little too close, her nose a little too pug, it was lost on Francis. Even more than her appearance, it was the raw energy radiating from her, that took him aback. Something was wrong. Then he realised, he had stopped breathing. Breathe, he said to himself, just as he had at Cambridge, before presenting to the class.

Never before had he felt this way in the presence of a woman. Her smell, her proximity. He found himself entranced by a few strands of her hair, black as a raven, that had escaped and curled around her left eye ... She was a tall woman, not as tall as himself. He could have reached out and touched her. He dared not, not through impropriety, but for fear that her entrancing energy would increase with physical contact, overwhelm him and leave him incoherent.

Did she sense it too? There was a very long pause, intensely, deliciously uncomfortable. It was as if they were communing on a different plane. Finally, his mind came back to him. He started to breathe again. Francis resorted to the spoken language, the one place he felt at home.

'All the better to protect you m'Lady.'

'Oh,' she said demurely, feigning innocence, 'But, what would you need to protect me from? Maybe a rampaging prisoner?' Was that respect in her voice?

Clearly, his actions with the prisoner were common knowledge. 'With your beauty, I imagine there would be many unwanted suitors for your affections.'

'And would you protect me from a position of quiet confidence or would you lull my assailant into a false sense of security?'

She had brushed over his obvious compliment. Her beauty was clearly not any news to her, Francis realised. And she had clearly paid close attention to The Duke's words, but then, they all had.

'Given your confidence m'Lady, I think it would be best if I balanced you out by appearing somewhat timid.'

That brought a flicker of a smile to her lips. For some time now, Francis had noticed how the fairer sex seemed more taken by strength with words than by strength in muscle. Men flexing their muscles, in one way or another seemed to repulse the more thoughtful women – unless it was to defend the weak.

'Is that what you are doing – pretending to be timid, or are you really timid?' Marguerite asked tauntingly.

At that, she looked straight into his eyes. Hers were big, brown and sparkling with a teasing element. She held his gaze just for a moment longer than a woman, particularly one of noble birth, should. He felt both weak and infused with energy at the same time. Was he wrong, or did she feel it too?

'What do you think?' He returned her gaze with more brazenness than he felt.

'I think you may be bolder than you appear.'

'Are you dallying with me m'Lady?' It was a bold line indeed, but he would have few chances to know her mind. She was a woman above his station both in age – he hoped she was no more than five years his senior – and in nobility. He would not get many opportunities to impress himself upon her and he wanted to know.

Turning to her Lady-in-waiting she laughed and said, 'Come Mary let us leave him to his toys.'

As she spun on her heel and marched off, he called after her, 'What is your name?' He did not expect her to answer. What had The Duke said when the other side was in retreat: 'Press your advantage.'

'You find out,' she called over her shoulder.

That made Francis smile.

XI A BETTER QUESTION

A prudent question is one-half of wisdom.

Francis made sure he was early. He sat in The Duke's antechamber on a short wooden bench. Across from him a parchment with flourishing script adorned and softened the hard stone wall. Its elaborate frame and markings declared the translation to be of eastern origin.

> *DISCOVER NOWHERE*
> *Yesterday is a history*
> *To be learnt from not ruminated on*
> *Tomorrow is a mystery*
> *To be hoped for not worried upon*
> *Today is a gift*
> *It is where wonderful memories are made*
> *That is why it is called*
> *'The Present'*
> *Only those who discover 'now here' can rejoice in it*

Francis was fascinated by how language worked – how simply placing a space after the 'w' completely transformed the meaning of the very same letters in 'nowhere'. Adding a little nothing, nothing more than white space, changed it completely.

More than this, respelling it with just a space completely reversed its interpretation – from a nothing place to the most important place. He realised that feeling that you were nowhere, or going nowhere, was always an opportunity to practice being in the all-important now. Then it dawned on him that, given you could only make wonderful memories by being present, you really were on the path to nowhere if you were not in the now here.

As he turned the wonder of language over in his mind, the inner door opened. The time had come to meet The Duke. A manservant he had not seen before took him into the parlour. While he greeted Francis with a friendly manner, all he said was, 'This way.' The Duke appeared at the doorway to the sitting room, greeted Francis and invited him in with a wave. The servant took his leave.

The Duke's quarters were simply furnished. His status, however, was evident from the position of his spacious rooms up high in the Abbey. In days past, his lodgings were used by visiting nobility. They enjoyed a spectacular view through a large window to the ocean and along the coastline of Normandy. Francis was particularly taken by a large looking glass set in a heavy stone frame of cream marble. It was beautifully carved and polished with an inscription in an ancient language along the bottom. Francis knew it was not Latin. Could it be an older language?

Noticing his interest, The Duke remarked, 'An old family heirloom that one. Please take a seat Mr Bacon.' Francis sensed it would not be appropriate for him to ask further about it and sat in the chair he was offered.

Francis was pleasantly surprised that The Duke had taken the time to find out his name. While he was no longer 'the Englishman', he was a little anxious. He had been told that The Duke rarely gave private interviews. Nevertheless as he connected with his surroundings, he felt a serenity and calmness emanating from the great Chevalier. He felt his anxiety soothed just by being in his presence.

The Duke moved surely and precisely, but unhurriedly, as if he had all the time in the world. He sat and crossed his long legs. 'First, allow me to thank you on behalf of The Montois for your actions in the prison. Your swift thinking avoided a major problem. Catherine, our physician and inspiration, is dear to us all.'

'It seemed to be the right thing to do, Sir.'

'It was a crippling blow. Where did you learn it?'

'Wrestling at Cambridge. We were taught not to do what I did because it would seriously damage the knee joint.'

'The key to breaking rules is first knowing why they were created in the first place and then being clear as to when and why they should be broken. It would seem you understand these lessons.' The Duke paused.

Francis waited patiently. The silence was not at all uncomfortable.

'Tell me Mr Bacon, what is the difference between information and knowledge?'

Francis paused to think about it. The Duke was about to speak, assuming that Francis had no idea. Sensing this, Francis spoke up.

'I think that information relates to the facts. Knowledge requires critical thinking about the facts and marrying them to other information from one's experience before it becomes knowledge.'

'Very good, knowledge is an English word from two centuries ago. It harkens from the word *knowlechen* which means 'to acknowledge'. Facts are facts whether you are present or not to acknowledge them. They cannot become knowledge until you interact with them. The process of acknowledging is a process of selecting only those facts and teachings that are relevant to the problem at hand.

'However, often selecting the right facts is not enough to solve our more complex problems. For this we require the next level up – wisdom. True wisdom – the furthering of knowledge – comes from building on the known facts and teachings in a new way.

'The human race has gained supremacy over all species through one ability. Which is ...' The Duke paused to see if Francis could fill the gap.

'... the ability to acknowledge and process information?' Francis ventured.

'Correct. It is what humans do. And how do they acquire this knowledge?'

'Through asking questions?'

'Correct. And what is the greater challenge, coming up with the question or the answer?'

Thinking of all the questions that confused and confounded him at Cambridge, he said, 'That is easy – the Answers.'

The Duke did not say 'Correct' this time. Instead, he sat quietly and raised one eyebrow. Francis caught on. Quickly he said, 'As I was saying, it is the question that is the greater challenge.'

With that The Duke laughed. It was a rich, warm sound coming from deep down. 'With your first answer you reflect how most people see it. They think the answers are the challenge. We live in a world where people spend too much time looking for answers and too little time coming up with good questions. The greatest limitation on an answer is its question. A bad question will stop the person from gaining the knowledge that could be theirs. So often great understandings sit just in front of people, but are missed because they ask the wrong questions.

'I will put to you Mr Bacon that the answers will eventually be forthcoming once you can ask the right questions. The human mind is built to answer questions. Hold a question in front of it long enough and it will always find the answer, whether it involves reading more books or finding the right expert. Coming up with the answer is not the hard part. It is far more difficult to come up with a better question.

'For your good deed with Catherine, I will answer one question for you. In two weeks' time I would like you to return and ask your question. I suggest you take your time and make it a good one. I promise to give you the fullest answer I can.'

'Thank you Sir. I will make the most of your offer.'

'Very good. I will see you in two weeks.' The Duke stood.

Their meeting was over.

XII THE FIRST MASTER

Money is like manure, of very little use except it be spread.

'Robert of Torigni or Robert du Mont, as we know him, was the first of our Masters. While a monk of the Benedictine order, and master of higher spirituality, he was also a master of the material world.'

Francis was accompanying Catherine on her rounds in the prison. He had just enjoyed a luncheon of fish cooked in a delicious selection of Catherine's own herbs along with freshly baked bread washed down with a mug of light ale. As they walked to the Bastille, Catherine spoke of the history of The Mont.

'He was the most famous and successful of The Mont's Abbots and administrators. During his rule, The Mont prospered as never before and never since. He was our first Master.'

'What made him a Master? I hear this word used here on The Mont but I am not sure what it means.'

'A fair question young knight.'

Francis noticed, the change in his title. Normally one was not referred to as a knight, young or otherwise, until one had been formally recognised. Valour in conflict was the other way of earning the title on the battlefield. Since the attack on her, she had not been the first to use this title.

'We refer to a Master as someone who has gained mastery of not one but at least two domains. The four core domains are Achievement, Material Wealth, Relationships and the Metaphysical. There are other domains but these are the basic four. Most of the others fall under the domain of achievement. For example, Socrates and Aristotle mastered the achievement domain of intellectual thought and logic.'

'So to be incredibly wealthy would not make you a master?'

'No. Not on its own. Material wealth can often be the result of just a skill with money and good fortune. Others inherit material wealth through nothing but the luck of birth. Either way, these people are often not of particular interest, nor necessarily honourable people. We are looking at higher levels of mastery. Indeed, often material wealth follows from mastery of another domain. Show me a person with material wealth and mastery of a second domain and I will show you a person whose counsel is of great interest.'

I could live with just the 'skill with money and good fortune', Francis thought. Instead he asked, 'What do you mean by "relationships"?'

'Mastery of relationships is the most difficult of all the domains. It is much easier to amass material wealth than it is to be a good leader. It is also much easier to amass material wealth than to operate with honour in relationships with your partner and family. Few people attain mastery of this domain. For every great leader there are a hundred rich merchants. For every great marriage, there are ten bad ones. Most people, even most good people, struggle in relationships.

'The first relationship you need to get right is the one with yourself. This is the most important of all your relationships! Learning to love yourself has nothing to do with vanity – that is another matter altogether. The physician who fails to care for his own health and becomes tired and stressed such that he becomes sick or dies young, denies hundreds of people his healing skills. It is unhealthy to care for others at the expense of oneself.'

'How can it be unhealthy to care for others? Maybe that is the case for a physician but what about in normal life? It does not make sense.' Francis argued. He felt more comfortable voicing his disagreements with Catherine, now he had come to know her.

'It is unhealthy to care for others *to the exclusion of nurturing oneself.* That is the point I am trying to make. The mother who cares for her children, and does not nurture herself, teaches her children that it is not good to nurture oneself, only others. It propagates the tragic message that you are only good if you are giving and that you are not worthy of giving to yourself. This message leaves people feeling so guilty about nurturing themselves. This is especially the case for girls, who are already given the message they are here to serve. *To fail to nurture your own growth is to deny others of the value you might bring to this world.* We all need to nurture ourselves with rest, relaxation, healthy food and stimulation of the mind.'

Their shoes clicked on the cobblestones in the silence that followed. Francis could not deny the logic to these words. Hearing the words from such a kind soul as Catherine made them even more confronting. Clearly, she cared deeply for others. He turned her words over in his mind: 'It is unhealthy to care for others to the exclusion of nurturing oneself ... you deny others of what value you might bring to this world.'

The Duke had used similar words when he spoke of how important it was to work out who you are and what you do. To fail to do so is to deny the world what you can offer. What Catherine was talking about, Francis realised, was creating the nurturing soil in which the flower of purpose could grow.

'So how does the domain of material wealth compare to that of relationships? Which is greater? Francis asked.

'What would be your opinion, Francis?'

While there was a part of him that was drawn to the wealth, he sensed this was not the answer. 'Relationships?'

'Absolutely, relationships yield the greatest rewards by far. While people pay lip service to this idea, few really embrace it. When forced to make a choice, it is usual for people to put the pursuit of material wealth before relationships. It is the odd person, a true person of honour, who puts relationships ahead of money. What most people do not realise is that material wealth often follows from good relationships built on trust and honesty. Do you know how I came to realise the power of relationships young knight?'

'From a great master?' Francis ventured.

'Not quite. This insight came from working with many people who knew they were going to die. Either they had a serious illness or they were sentenced to death.'

Catherine paused. She seemed to be with those souls, facing their mortality. After a moment, her focus returned. 'Not once did I see a man or a woman want material things for their dying days – unless they represented someone, a keepsake. They wanted to spend time with friends and family. It was very sad when they had led lives that had pushed their friends and family away. They realised this too late.'

'Material wealth cannot be all bad though.'

'No, no, wealth is not bad at all. The trick is to know how to use it. The best use of material wealth is to buy time. Time with those you care about and time doing what is meaningful to you. Remember this Francis, it is relatively easy to make more money, it is rather difficult to make more hours in a day.'

'What of the metaphysical domain? What is that exactly?'

'That is the exploration and understanding of the spiritual world. I will leave its elaboration to others. I want to go back to The Mont's first Master. Robert de Thorigny. He was elected Abbot in 1154, over four hundred years ago.'

'Which domains did he master?' Francis asked.

'Actually ... all of them. As well as material wealth and leadership, he mastered the domain of achievement. He was published as an author and renowned as an architect and builder. As a monk, he was steeped in the metaphysical. Few in the world have been his equal in terms of his mastery across domains."

'As one always finds with true Masters, he did not pursue material wealth simply for his own gain. Nor did he just want to amass money for ego and security – he had a purpose for it. With these funds, he beautified The Mont. As well as the hostelry he built for pilgrims, he finished our magnificent Romanesque monastery. Most importantly, he fortified The Mont to ensure that it would prevail against the ravages of marauders, nature and time.'

'How did he do it? How did he make so much money?'

Catherine stopped walking and turned to him. She looked him in the eye. 'He did it the way everyone who makes lots of money does.' She paused to ensure she had Francis' full attention. She had it.

'Three steps:

'First, he believed, at a deeper level that he had the right to attract money. Most people want money or wealth in whatever form, but very few *hold the belief* that they are entitled to have great wealth. At a deeper level, people who want more money believe that with money, comes problems. This may be true.'

'Or perhaps they fear that money is the root of all evil?' Francis offered.

'That can be a problem. They forget, however, that it is the *love of money* that the Disciple Thomas said was the root of all evil, not the money itself. People have as much wealth as they feel, deep down that they are entitled to have. They may make a lot of money, but if they feel they are not entitled to it then they will often come up with ways to lose it. On the other hand, there are those who feel entitled to wealth who can earn much less but end up with much more. They do this through investing, buying and selling wisely.

'Money itself, of course, is neither good nor bad. Like a bow and arrow, whether it is used for enforcing law and order or for killing, is up to those that wield it.

'Second, he saw the opportunity that others had not. He worked out what it was of true value that he had to offer and found the people who wanted it.

'Third, he persisted and followed it through to completion. Any fool can have intention, it is only completion that matters. While these are simple truths, few appreciate their power.'

The third step confused Francis. 'Why would people not follow an idea through to completion if it was going to give them lots of money?'

'In simple terms it is either because they fear failing or they fear succeeding or, often, they fear both. What I call "Failure Fear and Success Stress."'

As they walked on, Francis reflected on his fear of failing. He recalled his discussion with Dr Clost in the carriage about the fear of following one's dreams. At times with his studies, he had found himself not working as hard as he could have. On other occasions, he would allow himself too little time before a test. That way, if he then failed the exam he could explain it as a lack of effort rather than as a lack of intelligence. 'So why would people fear success?'

'Again there are many reasons, but they fall into two main areas. People fear the unfamiliar world they will enter if they succeed. Second, and it is much more of a problem, they have grown up not feeling entitled to be successful. Often they were given the message that they would not amount to very much. They were told that they would never rise above their station. These messages can hold one back more than any cast iron ball and chain. These messages we have been left with must be confronted first if success is to be won.'

Francis let these ideas sink in as he wondered what messages he carried. After a while, he asked a simpler question. 'So what was the opportunity that Abbot Robert saw?'

'It was the fact that The Mont was the greatest place of spiritual pilgrimage outside of Jerusalem, and it had one great advantage over Jerusalem. Travel through the Levant to Jerusalem was dangerous. The Knights Templar were becoming very busy working to ensure the safety of the pilgrims from the infidels. The Mont had no such problem. The Mont was particularly popular amongst the nobility of Europe right up to Kings and Queens.'

'How did he bring about completion on that opportunity?'

'The hostelry he built was for people of higher station. He invested in the nobility. He made them feel respected and valued. When they are here in the midst of a pilgrimage, Kings, Queens and the nobility alike make offers and bequests to the monks. The most valuable were the offers of lands and farms that provide produce or rental income.

'He did something that previous Abbots had been reluctant to do. He followed through. He would procure the title deeds of the promised lands while the promise was still fresh. Often he would ask them to sign a promissory note while still at The Mont. He also argued for the deeds for lands that previous Kings had offered The Mont.

'Robert du Mont was a master diplomat, this came from his mastery of relationships. He personally brokered peace between the King of France and the Duke of Normandy, Henry II of England. This peace lasted until the beginning of the thirteenth Century. For such a man, procuring a title to a property was a walk in the field.'

Francis had never known a woman to know such things. At the risk of appearing rude, he had to ask. 'How do you know so much about this Madam Catherine, if I may ask?'

'Here at The Mont, we have detailed historical records on what I have told you. They are there for the reading by anyone, male or female, who wants to read them. Few men seem interested in reading them. Myself and a group of my female friends usually outnumber the men in the library four to one. The monks here teach all children, girls and boys, to read.

'I have never forgotten what one of our Masters once told me *"That men do not learn very much from the lessons of history is the most important of all the lessons of history."* We women, will not fall into that trap,' she said with a teasing sparkle in her eye. 'Abbot Robert has written of his strategy in detail. Anyone can read it. In fact, he wrote that he expected that few men would take the time to learn from him.'

'So did Abbot Robert pursue particular people when they came to The Mont?' Francis asked.

'No. This too he wrote about. He called it the Strategy of Determination and Detachment. He was determined to raise the funds for The Mont, but was detached in his dealings with each potential donor. In particular, he was detached from what they might donate or when they might donate it. Indeed, he was detached from whether a particular noble would donate at all.

'He noticed early on that the greatest gifts often came from the least likely people. He made everyone feel welcome. He never pursued a gift until after the offer was made. Then he gently, but firmly, held them to their promise. He was determined to achieve his outcome to enrich The Mont. He said it was this detachment from exactly how it would come about, that he came to see as his greatest power and allowed him to amass real wealth.'

'But what is wealth really? How do you define it?' Francis asked.

'True wealth is having enough wherewithal to be able to fully pursue your purpose, your passion, while spending time with those you love.'

As Francis thought that over, Catherine went on.

'The Abbot's other legacy, rightly or wrongly, is this very prison we are on our way to. Any great administrator needs to be able to enforce their law. Robert du Mont needed the capability to imprison. He built two dungeons in the western basement. King Louis XI, a fervent pilgrim to The Mont, saw what a secure prison The Mont made. What made it such a powerful stronghold that repelled invaders, made it the perfect prison to hold would-be escapees.'

Francis' attention waned. There was a much more pressing issue he wanted to raise. As Catherine seemed to have finished talking of the famous abbot, he took a breath and asked his question. 'I was wondering about the woman, who came to our training the other day?

She was standing in the doorway. Do you know who she is?' He tried to sound detached, disinterested, but it did not work.

Catherine stopped walking to turn and look him in the eyes. This time she smiled. Her eyes twinkled. Francis felt uncomfortable. 'Aah. Lady Marguerite de Valois – the third in her family by that name. She arrived recently, on a pilgrimage of sorts. Some interesting people are gathering here at The Mont in this time.'

There was a touch of mystery to the way she spoke of this 'gathering' but, in that moment, he did not pursue it. He was more interested to hear what Catherine had to say about Marguerite.

'She is the daughter of the late Henry the Second and the Queen Mother, sister to our King Henry the Third, and wife of King Henry of Navarre, who may well be our king one day. Her eldest sister was the wife of the King of Spain until she died in childbirth nine years ago. At that point Marguerite was also offered by her powerful mother, Catherine de Medici, to the King of Spain, but he said no. I think he felt that a younger sister could never replace his beloved Elizabeth. Nevertheless, Marguerite is a most influential woman in the greatest royal family on the continent.'

Francis tried not to let his disappointment show. She was married, to a King! Francis was surprised at how much this upset him. Catherine, knowingly or not, came to his emotional rescue.

'Henry of Navarre openly sports a mistress. Marguerite does not seem to mind. I think it frees her up. Indeed, it is said that she keeps the score fairly even.'

So, the door was not entirely closed, Francis thought. 'Can you tell me anything about her interests?' Francis tried to sound disinterested, nonchalant.

Catherine pretended to not notice his feigned disinterest. 'Despite her reputation, her greatest love is clever thinking. She does not tolerate fools well and, it is said, she has more learned men – and women – at court than any monarch in history. She encourages debate on philosophical issues and is a talented writer of letters.'

To sound less interested in Marguerite, he asked, 'Where is Navarre exactly?'

'It lies between France and Spain along the mountains known as the Pyrenees.'

They entered the prison in silence as Catherine left him to his musings.

It was in the very dungeons of Robert du Mont that Francis and Catherine met her first patient for the day. Francis waited outside the cell. Catherine attended him at its entrance. The jailor stood close at hand. He need not have worried. At first, Francis was also on edge, given what had happened on their first rounds together. He relaxed. The man was too weak to sit up, let alone attempt escape.

Catherine lowered her voice to the eternal tone of the carer of the dying. She asked after him. He stirred from his near coma. A smile fluttered across lips that were almost as thin as butterfly wings. His eyes opened wide for just a moment and beheld Catherine as if she were an angel. He was too weak to speak. She mopped his brow and held a bowl of cool water to his lips. He drank weakly. After a minute or so, he lapsed back into unconsciousness or slumber, Francis could not tell which.

Their next patient had a simpler ailment. 'He has a disease of the nerves,' Catherine explained. 'He has lost feeling in his legs. He had a sore that the rats expanded into a large ulcer while he slept. Catherine removed her bandage from the day before and bathed it with salt water. Carefully she removed the dead skin from the edges of the ulcer until pinpricks of fresh blood appeared. 'The red blood will heal the flesh,' she explained. 'But only if we remove the skin that does not bleed. As long as we stop the rats with the bandage he should be fine.'

Catherine gathered up her instruments and placed them in the small leather bag she carried. Thanking the jailor, they walked out as she spoke to Francis. 'Our next patient is a Master with much to offer you. This prison, like The Mont, is not what it seems. People are imprisoned here for one of two reasons. They are here either because they did wrong or because they were great in some way. The wrong-doers end up in the dungeons, where we are now. The great are upstairs.'

Francis was confused. 'Why would you have a prison for the great?'

'Some people threaten the King with a blade. Other people threaten him with something much sharper and more dangerous – their minds. Guess which concerns the King more: the threat of sharp blades or the threat of sharp minds?'

'The sharp minds,' Francis offered.

'Absolutely. It is much easier to defend yourself from sharp blades. Sharp minds can come at you from afar and undermine you from many sides at once. Sharp minds can create influence that sweeps through the populace like the plague. What would you rather defend yourself against: the plague or an assassin with a dagger?'

Francis nodded his recognition of the point. 'The plague showed no mercy to beggar or nobility alike. From what I have read, the only people who protected themselves steeled away from the world.'

'Precisely, and that is how the King deals with great minds. He steels them away from the world and imprisons them.'

'Why does he not execute them?'

'Ahh, young knight. That is a good question. We here at The Mont are blessed by its answer. You see, history has taught the Kings and Queens of the world that you execute people for murder, treason and witchcraft. You never execute someone for being a great thinker. To do so is to draw attention to their thoughts and writings – for great thinkers nearly always write. They write on the edge of treason – not enough to be clearly charged, but enough to get people thinking.

'The moment you execute someone for thinking, is the moment you validate their argument. You declare to the world that they have a way of thinking that you cannot denounce through a logical, more intelligent rebuff. Therefore, if you execute them, you appear to be cruel and mean as well as stupid and insecure!

'The King, or if not the King, the powers-that-be, are smart and powerful. To threaten the King you must also be smart and powerful in some way.'

Francis started to see where this was going. The excitement started to grow within him. This was what he yearned for. 'Are you saying that these great thinkers are here, here at The Mont?'

Catherine had seen this in him, this love of thinking, of challenging new ideas. It was a deep hunger for questioning and not accepting things at face value as most people did. She saw it in him easily … because when she was his age, she had been the same. 'This is the most secure Bastille in the land. The smartest and the most powerful thinkers are sent here. We are lucky indeed. In return, we look after them for who they are. In return for making them comfortable, they share with us willingly what they know.'

With that glint in her eye, that Francis was coming to respect she said, 'When Archangel Michael ordained the creation of The Mont as a repository for sacred knowledge, he had a lot more in mind than just a grand library.'

XIII   THE TEMPLAR

Prosperity is not without many fears and distastes;
adversity not without many comforts and hopes.

Francis was intrigued as he followed Catherine up the stairs. A prison that was the very opposite of what it seemed. Rather than a place of evildoers, it was a place of great knowledge, a repository of wisdom. And what was the gathering that Catherine had mentioned? How was Marguerite involved?

As they walked up the stairs, higher and higher, Francis noticed a change. Here the air was not so heavy. It seemed to have a different energy. Here there were no tiny, open, cold, barred cells but locked rooms that offered privacy to the prisoners.

'So, who am I going to meet? What kind of Master?'

'Jean d'Anjou. He has been accused of being a Knight Templar. No one threatens the King more than a senior member of the Order of the Knights Templar. Do you know why Friday the thirteenth is seen as unlucky?'

'No,' responded Francis.

'On October 13, 1307 Philippe IV of France, along with the Pope, declared the Knights Templar to be heretics, sentencing them to death. It marked the beginning of Templars across France being hunted down, tortured and killed by the King. The 13th was a Friday.'

'It was certainly not a good day for them,' Francis remarked dryly.

At Cambridge, Francis had been enthralled by the story of the fabulously wealthy order of the ironically named 'Poor Knights of Christ and the Temple of Solomon'. It was The Don, Greybeard who pointed out the fullness of the name. It was under King Solomon that the Hebrews enjoyed their greatest wealth. Individual Knights were technically poor as personal ownership was forbidden. All the wealth, and there was lots of it, was owned by the order.

Francis recalled how it had become the largest and wealthiest international organisation in history. He had no difficulty recalling other facts, as they had fascinated him. At its peak in the thirteenth century, it had a staff of one hundred and sixty thousand, which included twenty thousand fully-armed Knights to protect its operations. They owned nine thousand castles and manor houses in Europe alone. Their income, back then, was estimated in one year alone at an unimaginable six million pounds sterling. And then, as a charitable organisation, it paid no tax.

Despite this fortune, it was said that their wealth did not lie in their gold or vast real estate tracts. These things followed from their real wealth, their secret. It was said that they were founded, at the start of the twelfth century, just to protect this secret. It was in Jerusalem, that the Keepers of the Holy Sepulchre gave the first Templars something ancient, from the time of the Essenes, for safekeeping.

The Essene monks had existed for over a century before Jesus came along. Both John the Baptist and Jesus himself were said to have been either Essenes or influenced directly by the Essenes when they lived amongst them. Exactly what the Keepers gave the Templars was unclear. Some say it was ancient knowledge, while others say it was more tangible than this – the Holy Grail.

Whatever their history, it was their material wealth and power that brought the Knights Templar undone. Most of the Monarchs across Christendom were in debt to the Knights Templar. In England, the King had handed the Royal Treasury to the Templars to secure his loans from them. Across the channel, Philippe IV was even more in debt to the Templars. Inept financial management and war had kept him chronically poor. The presence of the wealthiest organisation the world had ever known, or could possibly imagine, at his doorstep, taunted him. The fact that it paid no tax was doubly galling.

To both clear his huge debt and to seize their wealth by simply denouncing the order proved too tempting for Philippe. Gaining the support of Pope Clement, who already had ties to Philippe, was not at all difficult. The Templars' wealth was to be divided between France and the Roman Catholic Church. So the purge of the Templars began in 1307 and was at its most vicious in France. Finally, the Grand Master, Jacques de Molay, was slowly roasted over a fire in 1314.

Catherine interrupted his thoughts. 'Jean d'Anjou, the man you are about to meet, is a wonderful man, but don't take my word for it.'

'But I thought the Templars were wiped out when they were hunted down two and a half centuries ago,' Francis said.

'People forget that the Knights Templar had a deep presence through the whole of Christendom. Some say they even had branches amongst the infidels. Executing the Grand Master was like cutting off a man's right hand – tedious, but not fatal. Scotland was at war with the English, so they took no notice of the papal edict to prosecute the Templars.

In Spain, Portugal and Germany the Templars were too powerful or too popular. Their persecutors only went through the motions of an inquiry. Nearly all the Templars were allowed, or encouraged, to join other orders. In Portugal, they did not even bother with this. They just changed their name to the Knights of Christ and were left alone. Philippe in France, however, remained savage in his persecution. He wanted their treasure.

'I heard that their treasure was never discovered.'

A good treasure story was never lost on a teenage boy, thought Catherine. 'That's right. Their treasury was never discovered. Nor were any of their important documents.'

'Does anyone have any ideas on where it went? Does your Master know?'

'I do not know, I have not asked him. I will tell you one thing that is on record here at The Mont. There were reports that while de

Molay was presenting himself willingly for inquisition, the Templars were on the move. Eighteen galleys were loaded with an unknown cargo at their naval base at La Rochelle ... and then completely disappeared.'

'A naval base? So their shipping was not just for commercial trade.'

'Originally the Templars escorted pilgrims to Jerusalem and provided safe passage by land. With this success they expanded their business into moving goods and money as well as people. There was a huge demand for their services and there was no competition. Shipping followed.

'So they mastered the sea as well as the land?'

'No King owned as many ships as did the Templars. Their maritime operations were probably larger than that of all the other sea-going countries combined. They were master navigators. Their trade and commerce empire was so complex and advanced that none of their persecutors would have known what they were up against. It is said that the Templars knew about The New World way back then. When Columbus found it at the end of the last century, he was just re-discovering what the Templars knew about all along.'

'Why is Monsieur d'Anjou a threat to the King?'

'He has been writing about the need for thinking people to wake up and see what is happening around them. To become interested in more than just their immediate day to day life. It would not matter if no one was reading what he writes, but his books are selling in great numbers. This is what is concerning the King. His books have made him a wealthy man.'

'What is he telling people to do that would bother the King?'

'That's precisely the problem. Jean d'Anjou is smart. He's not telling them to do anything. That would be sedition. The King could prosecute him for treason. No, he tells them how things really are. He knows that if thinking people wake up, understand how they are manipulated and then they are brought together, things will change. Generally for the better. Kings do not like change. They have enough difficulty managing the relative simplicity of things staying the same!'

They approached a cell and Catherine removed a key from the purse at her waist. This was unusual. Normally only a jailor carried the keys to a cell, but then, this was not your usual prison. Francis wondered what kinds of souls were housed in these stone walls of the upper echelon.

They entered the cell – if it could be called that. This was very different. While only half the size of The Duke's sitting room, it was airy. While the window was barred, it looked out over the ocean. It was starkly but comfortably furnished. There was a rug on the floor. A large writing desk, strewn with books. Two comfortable chairs faced each other. There was a small room for toileting off to one side. A bed was beside its doorway.

The room had a particular feel to it. For a moment, Francis could not place it. Then, he recognised the feeling. It was the same energy as in Greybeard's den at Cambridge. There were piles of books everywhere. This was the room of a thinker and a teacher.

Despite Catherine's accounts of his writing, Francis was expecting a knight who could don armour if needed. Maybe someone like The Duke, but then he realised that Templars, while known as fierce warriors on the battlefield, were, equally, bankers, advisors and sailors. This man looked more like a banker. The knight who stood to warmly greet Catherine was short, rotund, almost round, and completely bald.

'Ahh, mon ami!' he said with a big smile.

After the man kissed Catherine on both cheeks, as is the way of the French, she made the introductions. 'Jean d'Anjou, allow me to introduce Francis Bacon, from London.'

'Ah Mr Bacon, I have heard of you. You acquitted yourself well in the service of our physician recently. We are all indebted to you as this amazing woman is our most precious source of love and light.'

'Now you are being silly Jean.' Catherine said this in a way that conveyed an easy relationship between them. 'Mr Bacon was indeed brave. How are those chest pains?'

'Since you started looking after me at this blessed place, they have been much better. I've had no pains for weeks now. That diet you have me on is working wonders. As of today my belt is six holes tighter.'

He must have been really fat when he first arrived, thought Francis a little uncharitably.

'I hope you are not feeling at all deprived with the removal of cake, bread and lard from your diet?'

'How did you know that being fat caused pains in the chest?' The Templar asked Catherine.

'I found it in one of the oldest books in our repository. Someone before me worked out the association. I am not sure as to how it works myself.'

'Well my dear doctor, as long as you keep up the occasional serve of oysters from the rocks of this wonderful isle, I am more than happy to give up those frivolities. Besides, your books here are more than a man could hope for. They more than satisfy any appetite I might have.'

'Well, in that case I am going to get on with my rounds. I will return for Francis when I am finished.'

'Take your time my dear. We have much to discuss.'

'Very well then.' Catherine left the room, locking the door after her.

'Take a seat my young squire.' Jean motioned towards the chair opposite him as he plonked himself back into his own chair. It was positioned to look out the window to the ocean. Obviously, this room had not been designed as a prison cell.

'So how is my old friend John Whitgift? Still holed up in that den of his, piling books around the room?'

This question completely threw Francis. 'How do you …' His mouth kept moving but no sound came out. All thoughts of asking about what became of the eighteen galleons driven from his mind.

'An inspired guess. Some time ago, John wrote me about other matters and mentioned a young boy in his class. He sensed that you have a role of import to play Mr Bacon, both here and elsewhere.'

Francis found his tongue. 'But he just mentioned coming here once, in passing … I almost did not come. Things just fell into place. I had a window of time before I needed to be in Paris …. a coach was going this way with a vacant seat …'

'Nobody comes to The Mont by accident Mr Bacon. The Mont summons you. You might think it was by accident, but it never is. John just had to set things in motion.'

There he paused, waiting. He wanted to see which way Francis would take the conversation. All masters knew that to speak of matters not driven by an interest from their student is a waste of breath. Worst of all, to address an issue before a student is ready, creates the tragic risk of turning the student off a subject they would later have been interested in. The challenge is to accelerate the student's interest to matters of a higher order. When the student asks of such matters, the Master, then, and only then, speaks of them. So, The Templar sat quietly.

It took a moment for Francis to realise that the floor was his. He was still making sense of what he had just heard. To avoid what was becoming an awkward silence he returned to his question that Catherine had suggested he take up with Jean d'Anjou directly.

'Why does the King of France fear the Knights Templar?'

'Aah, as I suspect you know, there is the fear that goes with any organisation that is both powerful and poorly understood. Secrets and wealth are a threatening combination. This all goes back to a very specific event. You know of the torture and then roasting to the death of the Grand Master Jacques de Molay?'

Francis nodded.

'Well it is said that from the flames the Grand Master issued an imprecation, a curse, if you will. He called for his persecutors, Pope Clement and King Philippe, to join him and account for themselves, before the court of God, within a year.'

Francis found his mind imagining the scene. A proud leader tied to a spit like a hog, being roasted. The people gathered around, vying for a view. The stench of human flesh as de Molay burned as slowly as possible. It was a horrible death, slower than being burnt at the stake. It was designed to create as much suffering for as long as possible before the victim passed out. With de Molay's words coming from the smoke as his hair frizzled, it must have been a gruesome and disturbing spectacle.

'This is precisely what happened. The Pope was dead within a month, supposedly from a bout of dysentery. Within the year, Philippe was dead. His cause of death was never explained. Some say the curse was extended to Philippe's entire bloodline.'

'Was it some form of witchcraft de Molay used?' Francis asked.

'Poisoned more likely. Templars were master alchemists. It is said that they had been given ancient knowledge about alchemy. This may be true, but they learnt much from the battlefields. Alchemy is about so much more than turning simple metals into gold. Alchemy is all about chemistry. The greatest benefit of chemistry is the creation of medicines that can advance our health and longevity. Creating medicines and elixirs was a real necessity for knights. Warriors have a bad habit of frequently needing the attentions of physicians!'

Francis noticed how d'Anjou spoke of the Templars as if he was not one himself. He realised that this must be an old habit. To talk as one, would be to immediately incriminate himself.

'Being monks as well as warriors, they were versed in the process of learning. The essence of learning is to record what happens over time to allow the patterns to emerge. The patterns talk to those who wish to learn. By recording which treatments were tried for which wounds, it became clear over time what worked and what didn't. While the rest of the world was still in the dark, Templars were developing an understanding of medicine at high speed.'

'Why do physicians need poisons?' Francis asked.

'They don't. The work of alchemy to develop useful medicines and elixirs is one of trial and error. The errors are the poisons. The successful trials are the medicines.'

'So the Templars assassinated a King and a Pope?'

'No, the organisation would not stoop so low, not even to avenge the murder of its leader. It may be, however, that some of the angry and misguided amongst its ranks took de Molay's words to be an order of sorts.'

'They had ready access to the Pope?'

'Especially the Pope. You need to remember, Mr Bacon, that the Knights Templar had two centuries to develop their organisation. Your average King would be very pleased to have two decades to establish their rule. Then their successor may or may not continue their work. Often a successor would start all over, with a completely new agenda. The Templars were positioning themselves in places of power before the father of a King was even born.'

Francis paused. He tried to get his mind around understanding an organisation that had so long to develop and refine itself. So long to infiltrate courts around the world. The information it would have access to! How could any King know the depth of the Templars? No wonder they were so threatening. It was obvious to Francis that Mr d'Anjou seemed to know a lot about the Templars.

'Mr d'Anjou, you seem to know so much about the Knights Templar, are you still a part of the organisation? Does it still exist?'

'Much of what I have told you has been written ... if you know where to look. I can say this. The Templars are no longer the force they were. We now exist in a different form. That is all I can tell you.' With that apparent admission, he changed the subject. 'So what has our favourite Master been teaching you?'

'The Duke has spoken of many things. For example, he has taught me that if you see setbacks and mistakes as failure, rather than as learning experiences, that is when one becomes a failure. More recently: how asking a better question is more important than getting the answers right to poorer questions.'

'Ahh yes, powerful truths, but he is not the Master I was referring too. He is indeed a great Master, but he is not my "favourite Master."'

'Who ...?' Francis was perplexed and then it dawned on him. 'Catherine is a Master?'

'Very much so. She has mastered wealth, achievement and relationships.'

Francis realised that Catherine's understanding of Masters and their domains was known to others. 'Her mastery of relationships I see and she appears to be a good physician, but wealth ...?'

Jean chuckled. 'She is one of the wealthiest women in France.'

'But how ...?'

'She is very modest about it and would probably rather I did not tell you, but it is too good a story! I told you how the Templars became great physicians through the records they kept. There was a Templar order here at The Mont. Knowing it was built to be a great repository, it was here that the most important records were kept. When the Pope dissolved them, the Templars simply joined the Benedictine monks at the abbey. Catherine has spent months pouring over their writings. At first, she was interested in what they said about alchemy. Then she found her own way to make her gold.'

'She worked out how to make gold!' Francis eyes were wide.

'In a manner of speaking. At the time, she was experimenting with different ways to fight the disease that makes wounds go fetid. The Templars described how cleaning wounds made them heal faster. It was a matter of opening the wound and getting out everything that should not be there from dirt to bits of clothing. For this they would use a special knife heated over a flame to make it clean. The hot knife was also used to melt the points of bleeding to stop the blood loss.

'Boiled water that had cooled was used to wash the wound. Bandages were made from rags that had also been boiled in water to make them clean. The person working on the wound must also wash their hands with soap and clean water. She would say "You must keep everything pure, it is all about purity." Catherine taught everyone here at The Mont these principles.

'So how did that make her rich?' Francis asked.

'Ahh, I am coming to that. Catherine's family owned a vineyard. She was an only child. After the death of her mother, she and her father managed it until she came here on a pilgrimage. That was twenty years ago now. She met the head of our Gendarmerie, stayed and had two boys. There was a physician monk here. He was the one who trained her and showed her the Templar records. One day, in a stroke of brilliance, she realised that the Templar principles of purity in doctoring could be applied to winemaking.

'She went back to her vineyard in Bordeaux and spent half a year with her father applying the principles of wound cleanliness to their wine-making. I have never asked her exactly what she did as this secret has made her wine the best in the land. Maybe we should ask her to give us some idea. Our King will have nothing other than her wine at Court. This, of course, has meant that all the nobles and other monarchs who visit the King get to taste it and then they order it in large quantities. Catherine's wine is considered the ultimate nectar of the Gods. It sells for five times the price of any other wine. To keep the King on side, and to stop him from taking her winery for himself, she sells it to his Court at the same price as normal wine. She is no fool, our Catherine.'

'How did the King find out about Catherine's wine?' Francis asked.

'In many ways it was The Mont that gave Catherine the introduction. The King was on a pilgrimage here when the Abbot, who had taken a liking to her wine, shared some with the King. It all went from there.'

'If she is so wealthy, why does she live here? Her house is simple, although it is large and does have a wonderful view.'

'Catherine is a woman of simple pleasure. The trappings of wealth hold nothing for her. She is here because special things happen at The Mont. She is The Mont's physician. Wise and noble people come from all over to see her. While she would rather be here, she does spend several months every year at the vineyard managing her business.'

'And what became of her two boys? They don't seem to be here.'

'They have become master winemakers and run the family vineyard for their mother. Speaking of whom, here she is.' A key rattled in the lock and Catherine came through the door.

'Ahh Catherine. Your young knight has kept an old man talking for too long.'

'More likely, the old man has talked quite happily with the attention of a young mind prepared to listen to his ramblings.'

'May be so, may be so,' the rotund man chuckled. 'In fact I was telling him a little about the wine business.'

A slight scowl ran across her features. 'I'm sure you could have found more interesting things to talk about.'

'Au contraire, with all respect, your story is a story of great inspiration. Most merchants in France know of it, it is hardly a secret.' Before Catherine could object further, Jean went on. 'I suspect there is a great lesson in it that I have wondered about. I know it is a secret but can you tell us anything of how treating a wound helped you to make the best wine in the country?' He knew that another Master could not resist an opportunity to teach.

Catherine sat down on the dining chair. 'Well it's actually no secret at all. It's just that people don't believe it to be so simple. We did two things differently. First, we started to clean everything that we used in the winemaking process. I had the workers wash their hands. I wanted to pursue purity. We wanted to find out what the real flavours were. My father had always said that the grapes had wonderful flavours, but they were lost amongst the impurities that came from the process of making the wine. It is why so much wine tastes the same.

'We initially focused on one type of grape, Cabernet Franc, which seemed to grow best in our region. Some years ago, we grafted it to the Sauvignon Blanc vine – we call the new grape Cabernet Sauvignon. It has wonderful flavours including blackcurrants, some black-cherry, even a little mint.

'We wanted subtle flavours in the wine that did not overwhelm the foods they were eaten with. Unfortunately, as the wine be became finer, the contaminating flavours also became more obvious. We worked at getting rid of them by being careful about each step of the winemaking process. We wanted nothing in our wine but the flavours from the grapes and their skins.

'As we did this, we found much less wine turned to vinegar. This was how I knew we were on the right track. It was a sign. We tried different things. The second thing we did differently came from what I had learnt from studying the records of the Templar physicians. That was to try different things and keep a record of exactly what we did differently each time.

'Over time, it became clear what made the best wine. To this day, my sons keep detailed records of everything we do. When a vintage is good, we can look back and see what we did differently. Sometimes it was just the weather, but it was also what we did. For example, the time of year we harvested made a big difference, as did how long we left the wine in oak barrels.

'We found that even pruning became important. If we did not prune properly, the vine would put too much energy into growing leaves rather than making grapes. The leaves would then shade the grapes from the sun and this gave the grapes an unwanted "green flavour." Finally, there was the blending. We realised that a small amount of Merlot wine softened and rounded out the Cabernet Sauvignon. How much we add each year is a matter of art.'

'Are not your records a secret? Do you not worry about people copying you?' Francis asked.

'Our records do not apply to other winemaking areas or other types of grape. People come to visit to find out our "big secret." We tell them openly what I have told you. We show them our records. Often they do not believe us. They want a simple secret, a magic ingredient. They don't like hearing that they have to keep records and look for the patterns. It is not even hard work!'

Catherine stood up to leave. 'Anyway Francis, we must along.'

Before they left there was one more thing that Francis wanted to ask. The Templar's comments about 'special things happen here at The Mont' had reminded him. Turning to Catherine he asked, 'What is the special gathering that you mentioned?'

He noticed an odd look pass between the physician and the Templar. The latter spoke first. 'You might as well tell him Catherine. It is a poorly kept secret.'

Francis looked from one to the other. Clearly, something was afoot.

Catherine sat down again. She brushed some imaginary lint from her tunic. She began, 'There is a legend that Archangel Michael pays The Mont a visit every so often. It is said that he was last here around four hundred years ago. It is said that he first visited The Mont around four hundred years before then. This was when he met with the Bishop of the time and ordered him to build an oratory here. There are records of a great teacher being here at that time, but there is no way of knowing if it was really the Archangel. At each visit, he meets with twelve selected people. It is said that he comes at times when the world needs direction.'

'Why only twelve people? Why does he not speak to the masses?' Francis asked.

The Templar answered him. 'He is not a messiah for the masses. You need to remember what history tells you about him. He is the Supreme Commander of warriors, not a leader of the people. That is a job for the prophets like Jesus and Mohammed. Saint Michael's messages are for seekers of truth. Those who will write or teach other seekers.'

'Anyway, there will be a meeting here and if the Archangel makes an appearance, which I do not believe he will, I will be sure to tell you about it. Now we must go.'

Not to be deterred, Francis asked, 'How are the twelve selected?'

Unlike Catherine, the Templar seemed happy to talk with Francis about the meeting. 'Ahh. That is the interesting part. There is a Grail adorned with beautiful gemstones ...'

Catherine, interrupted him. 'Are you sure you should tell Francis about this?' There was an urgency in her voice. Almost a pleading. 'You put him in danger by telling him of this!'

The Templar turned and looked Catherine in the eyes. Softly but firmly he said, 'It is my right to tell him of such matters. I would not do so if I did not think he was meant to be told. Now I have met him, I am sure he is. I am fully aware of where I am taking him with this knowing.'

Francis looked from one to the other. What was going on? What did he mean 'my right'? Why did Catherine react so strongly to the mention of a grail? Could they be talking of *The Grail*?

The Templar went on, 'We have been expecting Francis to arrive at The Mont. He is one of the twelve.'

'What!' Catherine gasped. Now it was her turn to be surprised. It was the same feeling Francis had felt when he had realised that the Templar was expecting him. 'But he is just a boy! We cannot risk it.'

'There have been younger.'

Catherine was not happy. Nevertheless, she went quiet. It was as if there was some hierarchy at play, as she appeared to accept what the Templar said.

Francis waited, not sure what to say. He did wonder what the risk was – it sounded exciting.

'As I was saying, the Grail recently gave up a date. The date is drawing near. As soon as its Keeper noted the date, it disappeared. Over each of the next twelve days a name appeared. I do not know all of the names on the list. Only some have been passed onto me at this time. People are arriving at The Mont from all over the world.

'What will happen in this meeting? Francis asked.'

'No one knows,' the Templar replied.

'How can a grail give up a date and names?'

'There is a metal plate embedded in the stone that shines like a looking glass. It is as if it reflects words that are before it when there are none.'

'Is your name on the list?'

'Yes it is. I will be there with you. We all come by different means. Unwittingly, the King sent me,' he said with a chuckle.

This reassured Francis. He liked the Templar. He could feel his quiet authority. Despite his appearance, he had a certain power. Francis remembered the same feeling with Greybeard, his Don at

Cambridge. Could Greybeard be a Templar too? Francis was learning enough to realise he was not to ask that particular question, but it did not stop him wondering.

'And Catherine will be joining us too. Hers was the second name to appear.'

Catherine had regathered her composure. She spoke as she stood, 'Come Francis. I really need to be going.'

'Be sure to bring him back soon. We have much to discuss. What do you think Mr Bacon?'

'I would very much like that Sir.'

Catherine, her usual serenity having left her, hustled Francis out the door.

XIV A BED FOR THE NIGHT

Chiefly the mould of a man's fortune is in his own hands.

The old butcher was also the mayor of the town. After hearing the story of what had happened on the north road, the tavern keeper had brought the boy to the butcher shop. It was a fanciful story from a boy that no one could vouch for, but the boy looked like he had seen a ghost. A man in black who could set people on fire, no one could imagine such a thing! Nevertheless, soon everyone in town had heard the story. It was closing time. The Mayor, weary with age and wild stories, returned to a house that was less of a home following the death of his wife a few months earlier.

As the beautiful black horses clip-clopped their way through the streets the insects, birds and animals went quiet. Doors and shutters slammed shut. Women grabbed their children and hurried them indoors. Diablo snorted and pranced as he flexed his bulging muscles and flicked his glossy mane and tail. His rider sat easily upon the energetic stallion.

With the man and his horse in town, just as the boy had described them, even those who thought the boy's story fanciful, suddenly became believers. Perhaps what convinced them most was the eeriness that accompanied their passage. The tavern keeper sent a runner to the mayor's house. He had an easy run as the streets cleared.

Diablo's rider smiled at the fear. An entire town of fear – now there was some energy! He began to become one with the energy. Outside the tavern, the Mayor came to meet him. He was flanked at each shoulder by the two biggest men in the town, the blacksmith and a farmer who was built like one of his bulls with a face that was somewhat less attractive than the uglier animals on his farm.

The rider saw it for what it was, an attempt to intimidate him. He smiled and toyed with the idea of having his henchman kill the man who looked like a beast, right up front. Put him out of his misery. Nobody deserves to look like that and have to live with it as well, he mused.

Killing someone upfront was always a great way to get obedience. But then, he thought, they may be sufficiently inspired by the story of what happened to the thieves. Cooperation is less tiring after a long day on the road. Besides, after witnessing a smoting, most people became completely useless. He needed a good meal, a soft bed and Diablo and the other horse cared for. When in human form, he had to feed and rest the body like any other man.

In his most cultured, educated tone, he settled with saying to the man on the mayor's right: 'My God you are unfortunate looking. When God was handing out good looks, you must have been off taking a long piss.'

From somewhere in the nearby tavern he heard a snicker. Obviously, someone agrees with me, he thought. This spurred him on. 'I guess it could be worse ... it could be me, but then, for reasons you may have begun to realise, there really was never going to be any chance of that.'

The farmer started to seethe in anger and press forward. The Mayor put a hand out to steady him. He realised the stranger was wanting a reaction. It was almost as if the rider fed on fear and anger. It was a test of obedience. He looked into the eyes of the man on the powerful stallion. He realised they were not standing in front of a human. In an even tone the Mayor, realising that they had been foolish to try to intimidate this monster, proceeded carefully. "Good sir, we apologise if we have offended you. We do not wish any trouble. There is nothing here for you in our humble town ..."

Cutting him off, the stranger spoke again. 'Don't talk, just listen. For a start, you will address me as Lord. Second, only I decide whether I wish to stay or not. Third, I need a good meal, and my horse needs water, feed and a good brush down. Fourth, do not try my patience for I have none. Keep me happy and you will all live past tonight. Cross me in any way and I will start with you.'

The old Mayor was not intimidated. He had been a soldier in his younger days. It was as if the personal threat empowered him. He showed no fear as his shoulders went back, his grey head came up and he pulled himself to his full height of six feet. His gaze held firm. 'M'Lord, you will find excellent lodgings in the next town.'

Almost imperceptibly, Diablo's rider nodded to his manservant. There was a flash of shiny, razor sharp steel as Gaspard drew his sword and swung in one simple movement and re-sheathed the weapon. He was clearly a master swordsman. Every movement was precise and quick.

For a moment the onlookers were unsure as to what was happening. Nothing had changed. Then the old man's legs crumpled and as he dropped, his head, cut cleanly from his neck, rolled off his shoulders. The old man's blood pumped from the arteries in his neck, soaking into the dirt road. His eyes, still open, showed no surprise.

Diablo's rider turned and looked towards the tavern, whose owner stood in the dark of the doorway. 'You, tavern keeper, come here. Have your man see to our horses.'

Reluctantly the keeper came forward. He had learnt the lesson just taught. 'As you ask Lord.' Turning to the tavern, he called past the closed door. 'Guy, attend to their horses.'

Diablo's rider sensed the fear in the tavern keeper and smiled. He had a sixth sense for detecting it.

'I have one question,' the rider said.

'Yes M'Lord?'

'I understand that this road will take me down the coast to Mont Saint Michel. Is that correct?'

'It will, my Lord.'

'Good. Ensure Diablo has clean straw, fresh oats and a thorough rub down. We have a party to crash.'

XV THE CODE OF CHIVALRY

If the enjoyment of happiness is a great good, the power of imparting it to others is greater.

Francis was struggling. Not only did he not have a worthy question for The Duke, his lessons in swordsmanship were not going well. It was nothing like the training back in Cambridge. There sword fighting was about scoring points. Here it was about fighting to kill. The broadswords were much heavier. Francis with his slight build, tired easily. Where he had been at the same level as the other newcomers for the first few weeks, it was obvious that they were continuing to improve at a faster rate.

Christian, the good-looking, unfortunately-not-an-idiot squire was often paired with Francis. Initially, they had been more evenly matched. He was now beating Francis quite easily. He was stronger and faster. Anyone but him, Francis thought. Why should one person have good looks, smarts and skill? Why were these things not shared between three boys rather than being all given to one? Or if one was going to have them: why not me? Francis had mourned.

To top it all off, Marguerite haunted him. Her raven black hair, those beautiful brown eyes, her unblemished skin. Was she too old for him, too worldly, too married? Maybe, but his mind kept on going back to her, again and again and again …

Then there was the confusing meeting with the Templar. What was the Grail? Was he really going to meet an Angel? How could that be? Francis was not particularly religious. He was not sure that he believed in Angels. He was not even sure that Jesus was the son of God, for that matter. It all seemed like a fairy tale, but then the Templar seemed to be a reasonable man. Why would he believe in such things?

Today was the highlight of Francis' week. It was the training session with The Duke. If there was anything that could distract his mind from his problems it was The Duke. Francis was not alone in the way he saw their teacher. No squire was ever late for these sessions in case they missed something. The Duke would normally start with a display of a particular combat skill. Then he would speak to the assembled squires.

The morning was fresh and clear. Francis was seated beside Thomas. Thomas was a tall, gangly youth with red hair and fair skin. He had been at The Mont for two years. He was friendly and easy-going. Nothing seemed to trouble him. Francis' tendency to worry, to think too much, was well balanced by his new friend. Thomas, in his good-humoured way, was frequently saying to Francis 'You think too much. Stop worrying. It is nothing.'

The Duke's door opened. He came out with one man-at-arms in attendance. It was Sir Maximilian, one of the squires' head tutors, a battle-hardened Chevalier, and the most senior of The Duke's men. In The Duke's left hand were six knives. He held them like a fan. Francis recognised them as throwing knives. Made of a single piece of steel, they had a symmetrical, double-sided blade. Unlike a normal knife, the twin blades of a throwing knife were not very sharp. It was the tip that was sharpened like that of an arrow. At the opposite end of their training ring, a large flat board had been set on a low easel.

They walked down to the easel. Maximilian stood in front of it. The Duke turned and counted his paces, fifteen of them, away from the easel. The eyes of every squire were wide open as they realised what was about to take place.

As The Duke slowly turned, the man spread out his arms and spread his legs. He showed no fear. It was so quiet, you could have heard a pin drop.

Without any showmanship, The Duke threw his first knife. With a thud and a twang it appeared just under the man's left elbow.

Immediately another followed and appeared on the board below the man's right elbow.

'Wow,' Thomas said under his breath.

A third and a fourth flew and appeared opposite the first two, just above the man's arms. There was a slight pause. Where next? With a thud, the fifth knife appeared between the man's legs only an inch or two below his family jewels. As one, the squires let out a collective groan. The final knife flew. It landed so close to the top of the man's head that it parted his hair.

Slowly, the squires started to breathe again.

The Duke addressed the man. 'Thank you Sir Maximilian. As always your bravery is in no doubt.'

'It is my honour my Liege. Mind you, my bravery in this is simply a matter of my knowledge of your skill with a knife. There is no other for whom I would stand against the board.'

The Duke turned to the squires. He had achieved his goal. He had their undivided attention.

'Not everyone can be a great swordsman. You might find you are better suited to the throwing knife, for another it could be the bow and arrow.'

Is he talking to me? Francis wondered. He desperately wanted to be good at something.

The Duke went on, 'You all have different aptitudes and talents. One of the bigger mistakes you can make in life is to work hard at becoming good at something you are not really suited to. While there are times when this may be necessary for a short while, make sure you remember that you are playing off your main game. What you are doing is temporary by necessity. Forget this at your peril.

'After our talk this morning, meet with Maximilian and he will teach you how to throw a knife. It is up to you to practice. Remember, no matter how much natural talent you have, you will never be a master without practice.

'There is one problem with knife throwing. Does anyone know what that might be?'

The squires were all silent. They were still processing the display of skill they had just witnessed.

The Duke answered his own question with a grin. 'As a general rule when in a fight, it is not a good idea to be throwing away your weapons.'

The laughter was a release for all of them.

'On the other hand, there is no better weapon in the five to fifteen paces range. Knives are for when you need to act quickly and you do not have a bow in your hands. A knife can be drawn and thrown in a single movement. There is no better target than the neck. The neck is one of the few parts of our body we cannot protect well with armour. Few men will survive a double-blade throwing knife to the neck. Aim for the leg if you want to bring an attacker down without mortal injury.'

Changing the subject, The Duke asked, 'What is the key feature of a good knife?'

It was one of the senior squires, Bertrand with buck teeth, who spoke. 'Sir, that would be balance.'

'Correct. Like a sword, we are looking for a point of balance that is close to where the grip joins the blade. When you choose a knife, first and foremost choose a balanced knife. In the same way a Lord, when it comes to choosing a knight for a quest will, first and foremost, choose a balanced knight. While the grip must balance the blade of a knife, what is it that balances the blade of the knight?'

'Chivalry, Sir' said Christian.

'Correct. As you know, the first knights, the great chevaliers, were French. While the English and other countries have adopted the term, few fully understand what it means to be a knight. None of you here will make that mistake. Being a True Knight is about something much more important. It sits behind our skill in combat. It sits behind our deep knowledge of the art of warfare. To be a knight and to not understand chivalry is not to be a True Knight.

'If you become a Chevalier de Saint Michel, you will live by five tenets of our Code of Chivalry.'

The Duke counted off on his fingers.

'First, you serve so much more than yourself. You will serve with your very life your Liege, King and Country.

'Second, you will serve the vulnerable and the oppressed wherever you find them. In particular, respect the honour of women. Protect them and their children everywhere, both in their homes and out of them. Women are our mothers, wives and daughters. They are the custodians of love and care in our lives. Remember, protecting them does not make you superior to them. Many men forget this. It is simply by virtue of your larger muscles that you have this responsibility. Nothing more, nothing less.

'Third, you will be men of honour and integrity. You will, at all times, speak the truth when asked. Even when the truth will cause you pain. We need this pain to remind us to act with more forethought in future. In the service of honour and integrity, you will do what you can to rectify any element of meanness, deceit or unfairness in those you come across. You will not stand for it in your entourage. Being human, you may even find yourself provoked to behave in these less than honourable ways. A True Knight is big enough to recognise his error early on and do what he can to rectify his behaviour.

'Fourth, you will persevere to its conclusion, any enterprise you take on. If you decide not to complete a quest you will do so only because new information makes it unworthy of your efforts. You will not abandon a quest through challenge or fear.

'And Fifth, you will not unleash your mortal force unless you have exhausted all non-violent means of resolution. You are being trained and equipped with an awesome power. It is not given for it to be used lightly. When you strike, you will strike decisively. With equal vigour, when you have won, you will be merciful to the vanquished.

'We reduce these five tenets down to *Serve our Country, Serve the oppressed, Serve the truth and Persevere with Restraint*. This is our Code. If you do not feel you can live by it then do not return to your training tomorrow.'

There was silence as The Duke looked at each squire in turn.

'Today I want to talk about our Fifth Tenet as it applies off the battlefield. Young men, knights or otherwise, have a bad habit of getting into fights. Remember this, the moment you fight, you lose something. Even when we win, we lose something. Just as winning the battle will have meant that some of your men died. Even if you win a fistfight, you will be worse off. At the very least, it will be with bruised knuckles.

'In a swordfight, you can win the fight then die from your wounds. Often your opponent can wound you with a lucky move. I saw one chevalier who accepted a drunken challenge in an unfamiliar tavern. During the fight, he stepped back into the fire. While his burns did not kill him, he was unable to ride into battle again.

'A long-lived, powerful chevalier, is a clever chevalier who knows when to fight and how to avoid a fight.'

'Most men spoiling for a fight are insecure. Quietly confident men never pick fights. On the other hand, bullies are the most insecure of all. Bullies have no idea that as they bully another, they are declaring to the world "I totally lack confidence and need to make you feel threatened to make me look like I am strong." If you witness a bully at work, the second tenet of our code, to protect the oppressed, requires you to intervene. What is our most powerful weapon?'

Francis remembered his conversation with Catherine on this very subject. Was it the right answer though. As he hesitated, it was Bertrand who ventured, 'Our sword Sir?'

'But what controls our sword, Bertrand?'

'Our arm?'

'And what controls our arm, Bertrand,' The Duke asked patiently.

'Our mind,' Bertrand added triumphantly. It took you long enough to get there, Francis thought uncharitably. The truth was that he was more annoyed at himself for not speaking up.

'Precisely, but it is not because it controls our sword arm that our mind is our most powerful weapon. It is because this is but one thing it can choose to do. So how do we best use that weapon between our ears? The most powerful way to avoid a conflict is to use your mind to see it coming and develop a dialogue with your opponent. Find a subject to interact with him over that puts him off guard. When we do this between countries it is called … what Mr Bacon?'

Francis was put on the spot. Presumably, The Duke had asked him for a particular reason. He took a moment to think. He realised that it was public knowledge that he had left England in the company of the English Ambassador to France. He was to return to his service when he left The Mont. 'It is called politics, Sir. Trying to find a political solution to a conflict to avoid war.'

'Exactly. The principle is the same whether we are talking of countries or men.'

Francis almost glowed with The Duke's response.

'Best of all find something to laugh about together. For here is a powerful but simple truth. Humans find it more difficult to attack someone they have just had positive dialogue with. Once you connect, you are shifted in their mind. You shift from the gallery of foes to the gallery of friends. It is much harder to attack someone you are in dialogue with. Silence nurtures conflict. I will say that again: *silence nurtures conflict*.

'Friend or foe, maintain a dialogue. I say to you, *keep your friends close and your enemies closer*. There is one other benefit of keeping your enemies closer. What might it be?'

Thomas spoke up. 'By spending time with your enemies you are also learning more about how they think. You are learning about their mind, their greatest weapon.'

'We will make a knight of you yet young Thomas. He is right. Then, if your enemies do turn on you, you will be ready for them. You will be able to guess with greater accuracy their next move. This gives you more power than an army twice the size of your enemy's. Mind you, often you do not get to socialise with your enemy in the usual sense. Study them when you can, watch their moves, and their patterns will allow you to know them.'

'You can win a fight and still be worse off, but then, of course, if you enter a fight you may not even win. How many knights in the world have no one who can better them?'

The squires were silent. Would not it be "one," Francis thought. Could the answer to the question be that simple? Have I missed something in the question, Francis wondered. There could only be one who was the best and could have no better.

'One.' It was Christian who had spoken up, while Francis hesitated with his thoughts. Francis mentally kicked himself. For some reason, Christian managed to make him feel like an idiot. Worse, he did not even appear to realise there was a competition between them!

'Of course,' said the Duke. '*Remember there can only be one knight in the world who has no better.* There is a good chance you are not him ... not yet. Any fool can fight and any man who does so without a cause greater than himself is just that. Our Code of Chivalry gives us our greater cause.

'One cannot serve one's Country and protect the vulnerable and oppressed if you are dead over some petty fight for your honour. Dying young does have the advantage of leaving a better-looking body, but it is a sad waste of this training and your growing wisdom.' The Duke paused to allow his words to sink in. 'There is no valour in dying without a just cause. A just cause is not, and I repeat, not your personal honour. That is vanity. Only a fool allows an everyday argument to progress to a swordfight. A just cause must involve someone other than yourself. A just cause is not, a wounded ego. A just cause is bigger than you. As a simple guide, the more people who will be freed from oppression and savagery, the more just your cause.

'But even then you need to choose which hill is worth dying on. In a battle there are hills of no consequence and hills of great strategic value. A True Knight is one who recognises that hill. He does not let the hill choose him. If you are on a quest for a higher cause, you do not risk that cause by risking your life on a side issue at the beginning of your quest. Before you risk your life, ask the question, is this hill worthy of my death?'

'It takes at least six years to train you as knights. The cost of doing so is significant. You are the officers of the battle. For every one of you, we could train and arm a hundred foot soldiers. If you become a knight, your life is no longer yours to trifle with. The kingdom trains you and during war you will owe your very life to your Liege, the King.'

It was Christian who spoke up. 'Sir, what if you are on a quest, serving your King, under the First Tenet, and then you come across women and children who are being brutalised. The Second Tenet would require us to act which might jeopardise our quest?'

'An excellent question. In fact, such a scenario brings in all five tenets. The Fourth Tenet requires you to be able to persevere with your quest and the Fifth Tenet requires you to fully explore non-violent means in righting the wrong. There is no straightforward answer to your question as each situation is different. A wise knight will act in a way that meets all five Tenets as best as is possible in each circumstance.

'The five Tenets of our Code are guidelines, not rules. Guidelines require wisdom to inform action. Rules do not. A True Knight is a man of wisdom. A lower man needs rules.'

'I want to finish our discussion today by talking about the need to be abnormal, to be different. It is not normal to be successful. If you stay like most others, you cannot be a success at whatever you aspire to. Of 100,000 trained swordsmen in Christendom how many would we consider to be a *Great Swordsman*?'

'Maybe a hundred,' offered Bertrand.

'Even if there were ten thousand great swordsmen in Christendom, that would still only be one in ten. If you are one, different from the nine around you, you are clearly not like the majority. You do not think like the majority. You are highly abnormal. Never forget that to be successful *you must not think like most people*. You need to become comfortable with being different. So ... how do we do this? I have spoken to you before about needing to learn from your mistakes. Let me take the process of making mistakes a little further.

'First, you need to accept that you will make mistakes. As I have told you, mistakes are learning opportunities.

'Second, you must take personal responsibility for those mistakes. If you do not take responsibility for your mistakes, you cannot learn. If you blame someone else, or the world, *you* have nothing to learn. *The benefit of blaming yourself is you can learn something.* If you cannot learn, you cannot grow.

Third, you do not beat yourself up for having made a mistake. You ask the question: *What does this teach me*? This is the Noble Question. This is the basis of nobility. Does anyone have a definition of nobility?'

Francis spoke up. 'Sir, I have been told that nobility is not about being better than another man, it is about being better than the man you were.'

'That is it. Desiring to be better than who we were and who we are today, is not what most people do. So do not be afraid to do what most people do not do. Go your own way, take the road less travelled.

Also, there is another part to becoming abnormally different, of becoming successful at what you wish to do.' The Duke paused.

'The key is to have faith in your Higher Self. When there is no wise person to turn to for guidance, look to your Higher Self in times of challenge or trouble. It will not fail you. Ask it for guidance. With its guidance, if things do not work out as you had hoped, if you have acted from your Higher Self the learnings will be important ones. These learnings will contribute to your wisdom.

'Most people make the mistake of acting from blind emotion. They make the mistake of not taking the time to consult their Higher Self before they act. The only time you do not have this luxury is when you are under attack and your hand is forced. At these times, your training must take over. But these times in life are rare. More often than not, you can buy time to consult your Higher Self.

'Excuse me Sir. How do I talk to my Higher Self?'

'A very fair question, young Thomas. The best way to awaken your Higher Self is in your sleep. Before you go to bed at night, ask your question of it. When you awaken in the morning, you will often find the answer or the guidance you are looking for. Sometimes it might take a few nights. Sleep is not just rest. When you sleep you commune with your Higher Self and it, in turn, communes with The Light.'

'Some will tell you to act with your heart not your head. Your heart can get you into as much trouble as your head and no more so than when it comes to the fairer sex. For how many maidens have I seen good men wound and mortally injure one and other?'

With a smile in his voice, Christian called out, 'That would be twenty-eight, Sir.'

'That was a rhetorical question Christian,' said The Duke with a soft laugh, 'but in actuality it is many more.'

Damn Christian, Francis thought. Now he is joking around with The Duke while I am tongue-tied.

'I say to you that your Higher Self, your wisdom and knowledge of truth and what is good, is there in each of you. You just need to stop and speak to it. Your Higher Self speaks, in turn, to The Light. Your Higher Self, under the guidance of The Light, brings the best of your heart and your head together.

'Rarely in life do we need to make a decision in an instant. Others may want you to because it suits them. Resist this pressure. Give yourself time to bring your Higher Self to bear. Say to those who want a decision from you that you will give them a response the next morning. There is no rule that says we need to give people answers immediately.

'Come to know your feeling of goodness. Look back over your life. How did you feel when you did what turned out to be the right thing? Often this is not the easiest thing. It may come with feelings of trepidation, but it will have that feeling of goodness to it. Come to know this feeling, like you know your own face in the mirror.

'Here at The Mont, you are being trained to be highly abnormal. To be the greatest of the great. To be the Truest of the True. Do not let yourself down through the making of hasty decisions – build a relationship with your Higher Self. Be abnormal. Embrace your difference.

XVI THE GRAND RUE

Write down the thoughts of the moment. Those that come unsought for are commonly the most valuable.

Francis walked distractedly up the steep, narrow Grand Rue of The Mont. Summer was drawing to a close, but the days were still warm enough for lighter clothing. He loved this walk. He had come to realise that when he needed to think, walking nearly always helped. He needed to come up with a worthy question for The Duke. There were three parts to his walk that kept it interesting for him. Each part was quite different.

First, there was the bustle of the Grand Rue, with its mix of shopkeepers and pilgrims. The pilgrims were from all over the world. As he walked, he heard Italian, Spanish and Middle Eastern accents intermingled with the French and occasional English words. The constant noise, from hearty greetings to arguing and bargaining, gave rich life to these varied languages.

He stopped and just looked at all these souls. Different outfits, different skin colours. So different, but all wanting similar things, safety, reliable food, a partner? Pilgrims to The Mont looking for what? Salvation? The meaning to their lives? Happiness? What was it that people wanted most he wondered? What, indeed, was happiness? As he watched a young, skinny waif of a lad, he could not have been more than ten years of age, swaggered towards him down the steep street. The rags he wore suggested a homeless existence.

The boy whistled tunelessly as he walked past the grocer's fruit display. Without losing step, an apple relocated itself from the stand into the bag hanging from the boys shoulder. Francis recognised an artist at work. The grocer, it would appear, was no less practiced at his end of the game. Maybe he recognised the boy's whistle. With a yell, he immediately appeared behind the boy and grabbed for the bag. Maybe the grocer should have let the apple go, or maybe not warned the lad with his yell. The boy weaved out of his grip and with one smooth motion pulled a tray of apples down between them and took flight down the street. Dozens of shiny apples bounced down The Grand Rue behind him, adding even more life to the colour of the street and its people.

It was masterfully executed. The grocer shouted abuse, but between the bouncing apples and the people grabbing for them, there was no way he could give chase. The grocer desperately tried to retrieve as much of his produce as possible. Francis could not help but chuckle as he saw that the lad had stopped further down the street and was now collecting more apples that rolled down to him. He would eat well that day Francis mused, as he helped the defeated grocer collect some of the surviving fruit. At first the grocer went to say something but as he saw Francis putting the apples in the tray, he relaxed, appreciating the gesture.

The second part of his walk began at the top of the Grand Rue where it veered to the left and the steps began as the path became steeper. A sharper turn to the left and there were the steps going up to the magnificent Abbey that sat atop The Mont. The view at that height, from the entrance to the Abbey to the north, was spectacular.

The third part of his walk took him back down the steps to the Abbey but instead of turning right, back onto the Grande Rue, he went straight for a little while longer, onto the path that led to the Tour du Nord. From there the path turned to the east to the Tour Boucle. From the tower at this point, when the tide was in, as it was this afternoon, he was directly over the water. He spent some time just gazing over the water, connecting to it. He found that the water had a deep, calming effect on him.

From his tunic pocket, he pulled some folded paper that he had been scratching notes on with his graphite stick. A wonderful English discovery, the graphite of Cumbria, Francis thought absently. As he often did, when he sat here looking over the water, he mused over some of the notes he had made after his sessions with The Duke, The Templar and Catherine. Often he would add his own thoughts, sometimes in prose, sometimes in poetic form. He made some notes about the lad and his bouncing apples. Could the boy's skill be turned to good causes he wondered?

The last part of his walk brought him back, parallel to the Grand Rue along the eastern shore of The Mont.

He realised he loved The Mont. It was not at all like London or Cambridge. It grounded him. It seemed to have a deep, calming influence on him. Francis had a more spiritual feeling of connection here than he had ever had at church on Sundays. He was not sure about God, at least as he was described in church. He did sense that there were forces at work that guided his life in a way that was more than chance.

He paused at Tour du Nord looking to the North over the water. Somewhere up there, was home, York House, on The Strand in London. Francis was the youngest of the five boys in the house. Anthony was the brother above him. Francis missed Anthony more than the others. They had gone to Cambridge together and were very close. His mother, Anne, was his father's second wife. They had then had Anthony. Then came Francis. With some pain, Francis realised that he now had to think of them as 'foster parents' and 'foster brother'. He pushed it from his mind.

Anne had given Francis a love of reading and language at a young age. Her father, Sir Anthony Cooke, who had been tutor to Edward VI, in turn, had inspired her. She owed her love of literature, and the classics, to her father. A gifted linguist and a theologian, she corresponded in Greek with her friend Bishop Jewell. When she translated his Apologia from the Latin, it was so accurate that neither he nor the Archbishop could suggest a single alteration.

She made Francis' young world rich with some of the greatest thinkers the world had known. As all the great works were in Latin, Francis began his familiarity with the language from a tender age.

Driven by her love both for him and for knowledge, she had immersed him in the classics as a young child. Spurred on by his voracious appetite for learning, she had given him more time than her other children. Unwittingly, she had given Francis a head start over his peers that he would never surrender.

Francis could see his foster-mother's face and, without difficulty her soft, warm smile. It often seemed to be tinged with sadness. Now, maybe, he knew why. Had she loved him as a son or as a ward? Was there a difference?

Francis had tried not to think of the revelations that had removed the very foundations of his world. Truth be told, as much as he tried to banish them, thoughts of what this meant for him were never far from his mind.

My foster-mother – to think of her as such still felt alien – would love the people here and the ideas they play with.

He walked on past the taverns that looked back to the coast. Just after the Tour de la Liberté, he turned right and walked back to the Grand Rue. From there he turned left and walked down to the main entrance. He kept going, heading south now across to the Porte de l'Avanchée. Here he left the path and climbed across some rocks and made his way towards the very southern end of the island.

He was now alone. He came to a small clearing with half a dozen trees at one end. The largest one was his target. From his pockets, he drew some throwing knives. He had purchased them from the shop where he had first spoken to Marguerite. While they were not as elaborate as the dagger he had admired, they were perfectly balanced.

Checking that no one was around, he started throwing. He had started throwing underarm with the knife not rotating, just as Sir Maximilian had taught him. This gave him a good feel for the weight and flight of the knife.

Over the last couple of days, he had just started throwing overhand. This was trickier as it required calculating the degree of wrist flick, to cause the correct amount of rotation over the distance, for the blade to bury itself squarely in the wood. Maximilian had seemed pleased when he had asked for extra lessons to get the overhand throw technique right. Now he just needed practice. Flick … thud, flick … thud. Then he would walk over and pick them up. Just him, the trees and the birds. He found it all soothing.

As he threw the knives, he remembered the lesson from The Duke when he had spun the sword at high speed. Just as The Duke had described, he realised that he could not work out, or think out, how to throw the knives so they would spin just the right number of times in the air for the blade to be in the right place as it hit the tree.

As he practiced, however, he got it right more often. A part of his nonthinking mind was learning, while his thinking mind knew not what was happening. This fascinated Francis. So, he kept throwing the knives, knowing that he was learning with each throw. He wanted to be proficient in at least one skill from his time here.

Ever since his meeting with the Templar, Francis had felt a shift within himself. One way or another, he had ended up here at The Mont. Not entirely by chance, it would appear. Here everything came into question. The one thing he did not question, however, was that he was meant to be here, just at this time. In a way he could not explain, he felt that this was his home, at least for now. It felt right for him.

Nevertheless, he was still grappling with what the Templar had said. *The* Grail? His name had appeared on it? It all seemed too fantastic. But Catherine did not seem to think it was silly. To the contrary, she had seemed disturbed by the truth of it.

'So this is what you sneak off to do every afternoon.'

Francis, lost in his thoughts, visibly jumped.

'Sorry to surprise you.' Marguerite said with some amusement. She was clearly not sorry at all. She stood smiling, in all her glory and an exquisite, white, flowing dress, just behind him.

'How long have you been there?'

'Oh, a while. You seemed to be lost in thought. What could the boy who has everything be thinking about?' As she spoke, she twisted a lock of her hair with her right forefinger.

'What are you talking about?' His wit had deserted him. She had a strange habit of doing that to him. Francis wanted to sound dismissive, especially at the 'boy' label. Nevertheless, he could not deny that her interest in him, indeed her very presence, affected him deeply. That disturbing, but exciting energy was back. It was quite odd the effect she had on him. An effect he had never known before.

'People are talking about you. You have been at the Queen's court since you were a child. You gained entrance to the great Cambridge University at the age of twelve. The Queen visited you there. Why? Unusual for one so young don't you think? Out of the blue you get offered a job with the English ambassador to come to my country. Then you are here only a few days, you save the head gendarme's wife and you have the attention of The Duke. Next I hear that the Grail has put forward your name too. An impressive run.'

'How do you know all this?' Francis was taken aback, this time by her words as much as the strange feelings that passed between them.

'Let us say I have my sources. Being the wife of a King helps a little too!'

'Should the wife of a King be alone with a man – especially one with knives in his hand.' Francis tried to regather his wits.

'Actually, I don't think it would be your knives that my King or Court might worry about,' she laughed.

That made Francis turn a little red in the face.

'My ladies-in-waiting think I am meditating in my parlour. I take an hour each day. I have a mystic at Court from the East and he has been teaching us the Buddhist way of focussing the mind. As I settled to meditate each afternoon, I would see you clambering across the rocks to come here. I would wonder, who is he going to meet? And then I finally worked it out.'

'Worked what out?' Francis was confused.

'You were going to meet me again. I just needed to turn up ... and here I am.'

Her presumptive air was off-putting. It was if she knew more about him than he did himself. Francis needed to change the subject. 'The Grail put forward your name too did it not?' It was a fair guess, Catherine had almost said as much.

'Apparently.'

'What does it mean? What is this Grail?'

'Surely you have heard of the Holy Grail?'

Of course, he had. '*The* Holy Grail. I thought it was a myth, a fairy tale.'

'The Knights Templar would like the rest of the world to think so. It would make their life easier.'

'You say it so matter of factly, as if it was no big deal.'

'It is both a matter of fact and a big deal.'

'How do you know it even exists?'

'My husband is a Templar. He has seen it and knows its power. It also names each of the Grand Masters. It has done so since the beginning. It names them clearly. It is as old as Babylon.'

'So what is it with your husband, the King? I am told he has a mistress.' Francis hoped to throw her off step.

'It keeps him off my back,' she said, without missing a beat. We are good friends. More like brother and sister. We have known each other since we were children. We both knew that we would be married. It was strategic for our families. We laugh and have fun, but there is no passion. I let him do with others what he pleases and he does the same for me. It works very well.'

'What is your passion?' Francis asked.

For the first time she had no quick comeback. 'A most interesting question,' she observed as she took a couple of light steps towards him.

Francis waited. For the first time he felt like he was off the back foot in the conversation.

'I have never told anyone this before ... only because no one has asked,' she added. Hesitantly, she said, 'I love ideas. I love the magic of words crafted like a great painter paints a painting. I like people who make me think. This is why at Court I surround myself with men of letters and wit.'

'I never quite finished my degree at Cambridge, so I am only three-quarter lettered. As to wit, my tutor would tell me that I spent half the time somewhere else, so I missed half the jokes – so I suppose that makes me a half-wit.'

What happened next, thrilled Francis to his core. Marguerite threw her head back and laughed. At the same time her right hand went to his left wrist. Just touching him ever so lightly. He felt her energy mingle with his own and surge through him. He did not want that moment to end.

'In fact I have written something you might like ...' his voice trailed off. Immediately he wished he had not told her. What if she didn't think it very good? The thought was almost too much to bear.

'Well then, show me.' It was not a request. In that moment she was a Queen.

He was torn. He did not want to appear to be taunting her, to be playing games. He could have said that he did not have it with him – but that would have been a lie. Francis could not lie. He was incapable of it. Slowly, he pulled it out of his tunic pocket and proffered it to her.

She took it graciously and, gathering up her skirts, sat on the stump a few feet away. Her free hair fell around her face as she leaned forward to read his script.

He was about to apologise for his scrawl, but as if reading his mind she said, 'Your penmanship is beautiful.' He shut his mouth again as she read.

Shall I compare thee to a Summer's day?
Thou art more lovely and more temperate:
Rough winds do shake the darling buds of May,
And Summer's lease hath all too short a date:
Sometimes too hot the Eye of Heaven shines,
And often his gold complexion dimm'd;
And every fair from fair sometimes declines,
By chance or nature's changing course untrimm'd:
But thy Eternal Summer shall not fade
Nor lose possession of that fair thou owest;
Nor shall Death brag thou wander'st in his shade,
When in eternal Lines to Time thou growest:
    So long as men can breathe or eyes can see,
    So long lives this, and this gives life to thee.

For a long time, it seemed like an eternity, she just sat there. Her head was down. He could not see her eyes. He realised he was holding his breath. Finally, she spoke, very softly. Francis had to strain to hear her.

'It is quite exquisite.' She looked up, briefly. Her eyes were wet. She sniffed and turned away as she wiped her eyes. Francis breathed. He did not realise it, but his words had changed things between them forever. 'May I keep it?'

'Sure,' Francis nodded as she folded it up and put it in her bodice.

Quickly she gathered herself. 'So show me. How do you throw a knife?' At which she stood up from the stump and came and stood in close behind him. Gently she turned him to face the tree he had been using as a target. He took a throwing knife in his right hand. Her hand closed around his as she said, 'Show me how to do it ... the throwing action.'

As much as he knew she was changing the subject from herself, he was quite prepared to be bought off by more touching. His senses were overwhelmed, she was so close. He could smell the fragrances she used in her hair. Her hand on his. Was it her breast he could feel against his back as she shaped up behind him?

'Start with an underarm throw,' he said, his voice almost as weak as his knees. 'It goes like this.' It took all his will to move his arm. He just wanted to sink back into her bosom, melt with her and stay there forever.

At that moment, there was a call. A woman's voice. 'M'lady? Lady Marguerite, what are you doing?'

'Oh no,' Marguerite groaned. 'That's Henny. She's the King's spy.'

The spell was broken. It was a Lady-in-waiting, but not the one from the shop, this one looked older and meaner as she clambered over the rocks, still some distance away. 'Your husband's spy?'

'No, my brother's.'

Francis wondered what life must be like to have a father, then a brother and a husband who were all Kings.

Marguerite went on. 'He seems to feel my conduct is not that of a woman of my position. He will not be pleased about this. I must go.'

'No ...' he protested, but his words fell on her heels, which he caught a glimpse of as she pulled up her skirts and ran towards the other woman.

At least with her departure he could breathe again.

XVII THE QUESTION

Who questions much, shall learn much, and retain much.

Francis had only just sat down in front of the great man. The Duke went straight to the point. 'So what is your question Mr Bacon?'

'Sir, I would like to know what makes a great knight?'

The Duke paused.

'I could answer that question, Mr Bacon, but it would be a waste of some proportion. Your training will answer that question. You have a much better question in you. Be clear on this. Gaining knowledge is not about the answers. Were you listening in our last meeting?'

Francis heard the soft but clear reprove in The Duke's voice.

'To recap: work hard to come up with the most powerful question. Ask the right question, ask it long enough and the answer will inevitably be yours. On this occasion, you have me to accelerate the process. It would be wise to make the most of it.'

The Duke paused before continuing.

'The answer is the easy part, it is the question that is the real challenge. Favour both of us and come back when you have a worthy question.'

'I am sorry to have wasted your time, Sir.'

'You did not. This is an important part of the process. If you had made it a much longer question, you might have. If I had wasted my time answering it, that would have been my fault, not yours. I am responsible for my time as you are for yours.'

The Duke was not rude. He was matter of fact.

'I look forward to your question in due course Mr Bacon. It might serve you to not think of me as just a knight. Good day to you.'

With that, their interview was over and Francis felt like a fool. He knew that his mind had not been focussed on the matter of coming up with a good question, his mind had been on that other matter ...

XVIII THE GREATEST WEAPON OF ALL

Knowledge is power.

They were sitting in the Templar's room. Francis had been keen to visit Catherine's friend again. After all, he had never really found out what it was that the man wrote about that had brought him to the attention of the King. Nor had he asked his question about what became of the Templar treasure.

'Madam Catherine, said the four domains are wealth, relationships, achievements and the metaphysical, but what of warrior qualities? What of my training as a knight?'

'Ahh, young master, I need to tell you something that you might not like to hear.'

'Go on,' Francis said.

'Knights are romantic. Knights are glorious. Knights are inspiring. But in the end, Knights are pawns.'

'But a pawn and a Knight could not be more different,' Francis protested. 'A pawn is powerless and a Knight is all-powerful.'

The bald man sat across from him in his well-worn chair. As he spoke, he looked into Francis' eyes. There was an earnest quality to his voice.

'So the powers-that-be would have you believe. It is just this belief that makes a Knight a pawn. Truth be told, it is the Knight's ego, his belief in his power, which is his greatest weakness. His ego is what makes him a pawn. The more elaborate and shiny the armour, the more accolades from the Queen, the more prepared the Knight will be to do the bidding of the powers-that-be. The more prepared he will be to take on an impossible task and risk his very life for the powers-that-be.'

'There is a wise saying, "If a hammer is a man's only tool, then every problem will be treated as a nail." A Knight has mighty hammers – lance, sword and dagger – but they, and his training, are all designed for one thing: to fight. So when there is a problem what will a Knight's solution be? Sometimes he will be right, but what of the other times when fighting is not the solution. It will be hard for him to not bring to the table those skills in which he excels.'

Francis was confused. No one had ever said such things of a Knight before. He heard the logic in the man's words. 'The Duke spoke to us recently about choosing which hill to die on.'

'Yes, the knights of which I speak are the majority – those who have not had the benefit of being trained under someone like our Duke.'

'You say the 'powers-that-be,' do you not mean the King?'

'Nay Francis. The King, if he is not careful, is just another Knight with the shiniest armour and the greatest steed of all. Our King is overwhelmed by his job and not interested in most of it. He has two advisors who really run this kingdom. It is these two who are the "powers-that-be". So when we refer to "The King", we refer to a triumvirate – a powerful three. Power rarely lies where it appears to lie. Never assume that the power lies with the person with the title. Look to their left or their right and understand who wields the influence. '

'Is not the King the most powerful man in the land?'

'Only if he recognises that he is not.'

'I am sorry, but that does not make sense,' Francis offered hesitantly.

Patiently, the Templar replied, 'There are many matters upon which the King must adjudicate, matters of very different natures. Matters of state cover all issues from property arguments, through international affairs to religious conflict and many more. No one man can be an expert on them all. He who thinks he is, is overtaken by his ego. Nothing weakens a man more than his ego. In such a weakened state, he will make poor decisions. In time, his poor decisions will cause him to lose confidence. He will not admit it openly, but he will know it at some level.

'He will then look to others for guidance but will not be prepared to admit this to himself or to the others. He will come under the influence of men who see this weakness and exploit it.'

'How do they exploit the King?' Francis asked. He dare not admit it, even to himself, but at some level, it was possible he could become either a King or an advisor.

'These men may be no more expert on a given matter at hand than the King, but they work to make the King feel more confident. These wily men realise that those who are run by their ego crave confidence, as false as it may be. Supply this false confidence and the King is happy. In this way, the wrong people gain power and become "the powers-that-be".

'A great King will recognise his limitations and take the counsel of the would-be-powers-that-be with care. He will take their advice but then take responsibility for the final decision.'

'So even Kings can become pawns,' Francis reflected.

'Absolutely. Meanwhile, knights are often used as pawns in the game of empire domination. Knights are sent to their possible death so that the King will own more land or protect his land from invaders. A King uses a knight the same way he uses his knife to cut his steak. What do you notice about the three words, king, knight and knife?'

Francis thought for a moment then pulled out his paper and graphite. He wrote the three words. With the word, "King" he reversed the "i" and the "n" to give "knig". He realised he now had the first four letters of the word "knight" and the first three letters of the word "knife". He turned the paper towards the Templar.

'Well done. Most can see the spelling similarity, but few see the relationship to the power behind them! A knight is simply the King's knife.'

'Spelling is the building block of words and language. Mastery of words and language can send people to fight to the death for a cause they might not otherwise believe in. Words, especially when they are well delivered, are used to convince people of things. Words bring us back to spelling. The secret lies in the word itself. What do you have left when you take the "ing" off spelling?'

'That's easy, you get "spell" …' Francis paused as awareness opened like a rose bud for him. 'As in what witches and wizards do!'

'Correct. Spells are cast all the time by people who do not look like witches or wizards, people with much greater power over their fellow man. By delivering the right words at the right time to the right person with just the right emotion, masters of spelling can change the course of history. Spelling is not the act of counting out the letters in a word. Spelling is using letters to create words to bring another under one's spell. This is why the pen is mightier than the sword. I sense that you need to remember this truth.' And the people who wield pens are often not easily recognised by appearing to look like witches or wizards.

'I am guessing the men around the King are good at spelling?'

'They are often expert at spelling. This gives them great power. Let me give you an example of spelling. This spell keeps the King, or Queen in power. One of the great spells if you can weave it. Whenever things are very bad or very good, the King holds tournaments and festivals across the country. Do you know why?'

'Well I guess if things are tough for the people they will welcome the fun and festivities of a tournament?'

'That is part of it. These are all funded by the King. Not because he is gracious and wishes to bestow favour on the people of his reign. No, it serves three purposes. First, it allows the people to be angry at someone other than the King, as they come along and engage in mock battle or cheer their favoured knight in the main arena.

'Second, the festivities encourage drinking and the pursuit of pleasures of the stomach and flesh. A great party every few moons with much laughter and debauchery leaves people thinking life is good. They will overlook shortages of food and work. They will overlook their poverty and disease. It is for this reason the King encourages any partying amongst the people. The imperial breweries ensure that beer and wine is both readily available and cheap. The masses think that their life must be good if they can have fun.'

'But why have festivals when things are very good?'

'When things are good and the mood is high there are always those nobles who think they are now strong enough to threaten the king. This is when the parties and the festivals need to be the most splendid and lavish. He who would wear the crown will find it hard to garnish support in overthrowing a King or Queen when life is already good and prosperous.'

'So, rather than targeting the person who wants the crown, it is about weakening their supporters,' Francis added.

'Exactly. Indeed, it is better to keep them alive once you know who they are. Remove them and you may not identify their replacement. The third and final benefit of the tournament is that the festivals allow the powers-that-be to identify any rising talent or threats amongst those who compete. Talented fighters can then be enticed into the employ of the King. Those who refuse and are potential threats are watched closely by spies of the Court.'

Francis had attended many of these festivals over the years. The people looked forward to them with great excitement. Things are not what they seem, he found himself thinking, yet again.

'Do you know Francis, what the most powerful weapon of all is for the oppressor?'

Francis remembered The Duke's words, 'The oppressor's mind?'

'Almost. It is the minds of those he or she oppresses. If you can get the people to be relatively satisfied with their life when they should not be, you have real power.'

'This is why you are here, is it not?' Francis' said as recognition lit eyes. 'This is what you have been writing about. You are trying to get people to see all this.'

'In simple terms, yes. I try to get people to see that things are not what they seem. To know when the powers-that-be are playing with them. I must be careful. I write stories rather than talk directly, as I have just now, about what is really going on. My books and writings have gained a following, not just here in France, but in several countries. They have been translated into many languages. That is really what has bothered the powers-that-be. I have published many of my works under other names, so few realise just how widely my books are read.

'Fortunately for me, the money they make keeps me very comfortably. The invention of the printing press by that German, Johannes Gutenberg, in 1440 has changed the world. Now ideas can be easily spread. The powers-that-be have much to worry about.'

Francis, took his time to think about his next point. The words of The Duke were fresh in his mind. He wanted to ask better questions. 'To what specifically, do you owe your success as a writer?'

'Aahh. A great question. One that I am rarely asked. You would be surprised at how even budding authors fail to ask me such an important question. Let me see. I think there are four points. First, I do not speak down to my reader. I write to communicate, not to impress with fancy words. A good writer is one who can take a complex idea and put it into simple terms using short words that anyone can understand. I use small words in short sentences.

'Second, I use adjectives rarely. You do not make a point more clearly by embellishing it with superlatives and adjectives.'

'And third?' Francis asked. Writing was an art he dearly wished to master.

Third, I write to also entertain. You hold the reader's attention by entertaining them. By telling a good story. If you cannot hold a reader's attention it makes no matter what message you deliver, they will not be reading it to find out.

Fourth, behind the words, behind the stories, you must answer the questions people are concerned about. Why are we here? What is good? What is the nature of happiness? What gives life meaning? Many of my readers may not think about these issues, but at some level, they are concerned about them. I always have at least one such issue sitting in each book. Many tell me that it was months after a reading that something came back to them. Something that made sense of the life challenge they then found themselves confronted by.'

'Thank you, Sir. You have given me much to think about. May I ask you another question on a different topic?'

'Certainly.'

'What became of the treasure of the Knights Templar?'

'Aah ha, ha' chuckled the Templar. 'So you know the story.'

'I know the eighteen galleons all disappeared. I know the Templars ruled the seas. I know that no one had the power to stop them.'

'Aah. You have been thinking on this have you not? Let me tell you about treasures. Treasures are important. Why? Because treasures give us a quest. There is no point, no adventure to life, if there is no treasure to search for. If we have no quest, we have no reason to live. Never forget, the quest always has greater rewards than the treasure ... the quest always has greater rewards than the treasure,' the Templar repeated as if in his own world.

'So ... the treasure?' Francis prompted.

'All I can tell you, because it is all that I know, is that the treasure has more to do with ancient knowledge than it does with gold and jewels. You see young Mr Bacon, as with a good treasure, true wealth is not about what it can buy. *No, true wealth is about what you know and who you can attract to help you attain your desire.* True wealth, as opposed to material wealth, can be summed up in one word – relationships. It is what you have left when the material wealth goes.'

'So what was in the galleons and where did they go?' Francis asked the question directly.

The Templar could see that Francis had had enough of the less tangible truths for one day. 'What was in them I am not privy to. All I know is that their contents are safe, but where, I do not know. If I were to guess, I would say it went to either Scotland or Spain. Both of these countries were safe havens for the Templars at the time that the galleons put to sea. Scotland perhaps the safer of the two.'

Francis could see he was not going to get much farther with the treasure story. He changed the subject. 'The Duke has said I can ask one question of him. I tried to ask him about being a good knight and he said the question was not good enough. A worthy question has escaped me.'

'I can tell you this. The Duke is much more than a great knight. He has much knowledge and wisdom, old wisdom. So yes, you need to ask your question wisely. I can give you no more than that. It must be your question.'

Francis reflected on the Templar's words for a moment, before asking, 'This meeting, the one I have been invited to, when is it and what will it be about?'

'It is always on the full moon of Easter of the year in which the names appear. This is when the tides here at The Mont move the most.'

'That is fifteen days from now,' Francis reflected.

'As to what the meeting will be about. No one quite knows. In the past, those who have attended have been given special information, special insights that were needed. We have one clue. The word "alchemy" came up before the names started appearing. Maybe we are going to be given some insight into the workings of alchemy.'

'Do you mean the making of gold from lead and nickel?' Francis asked.

'That is a very simple understanding of the word. It has much greater dimension to it,' the Templar explained.

'So what is alchemy?'

'That we will find out more about on the night.'

'Do you know who else is attending?'

'I know that people are coming from afar. There will be those coming from the north and the middle-east. They are of all religions, creeds and nationalities. In fact, the only Christians coming are those of the faith of the apostle Thomas – the St Thomas Church.'

'The Duke mentioned Thomas. What is the St Thomas Church?'

'Aah, for that question you need to speak to Bishop Daniel. Well, he was a Bishop until he was excommunicated and imprisoned here. As usual, the world's loss is The Mont's gain. I am sure Catherine can organise a meeting with him for you.'

'There was one other thing. Madam Catherine said that there were three key secrets to attaining wealth. You have to reach the place where you believe you are entitled to have wealth, you find what you have of real value and then you persist until you achieve completion. I have been thinking about her story of the wine-making and I see a fourth element. Is it not also about applying strategies from one area of life to another?'

'Go on,' said the Templar.

'Well, Madame Catherine took the principles of wound healing and applied it to wine-making. I wonder how many other opportunities there are to apply principles from one thing to another.'

The Templar slapped his own leg with a laugh. 'Now you are thinking Mr Bacon! So many people hear a story like Catherine's and lament that they did not see that opportunity. It is as if there is now one less for them. They miss the point entirely: *as long as there are people, there are opportunities for wealth and achievement.* People's needs change, always, as sure as the sun will come up tomorrow. In good times and bad, people need solutions, better products, more knowledge. As the world grows and evolves, entirely new opportunities present themselves.'

At that point, there was a key in the door as Catherine returned for Francis. 'Aaah Catherine, we have a student of life here. He is going to make a difference this young man. I think he is ready to meet The Bishop. Do you think you could arrange it?'

'For you Jean, anything. Come now Francis, we must be off.'

XIX   THE LETTER

Natural abilities are like natural plants;
they need pruning by study.

Francis sat at the small wooden desk in his room. Quill in his right hand, some of Catherine's notepaper in front of him. He smiled as he thought about his brief encounter with Marguerite earlier that afternoon. He had been taking his regular walk up the Grand Rue, the colour and buzz of the visiting pilgrims all around him. As the road veered to the left, just past the entrance to the Musée Gravin, he had looked up as he heard a laugh he knew and loved. There she was, coming towards him.

Marguerite was responding to something Mary, her Lady-in-waiting, had said. With a smile on the unblemished skin of her perfect face, she was as gorgeous as ever. The sour-faced Henny was a few steps behind.

Without thinking, he heard himself blurting out, 'Can I see you?'

Without pause, Marguerite responded with, 'There, you have seen me. Have a good day Mr Bacon,' and walked right on by.

While it was not the desired outcome, he smiled, as he thought of it. There had been a twinkle in her eye as she had spoken. That twinkle had prompted him to write, first a sonnet then a letter to the Ambassador. He needed to find out more about Marguerite. He could not take his mind off her. He realised that he just happened to know the Englishman who could find out more about French Royalty than anyone else in Christendom! In their short time together he had come to see Sir Amyas as a kindly Uncle. He had even taken an interest in Francis' poetry, even though he admitted that it was not a subject that he read. There was no one else and he needed to speak to someone. He felt like he was going to burst.

My Dear Ambassador, Sir Amyas

Firstly, please allow me to apologise if my visit here to Mont St Michel will take longer than I had anticipated. I am eternally grateful for your patience and generous forbearance in this matter. Truth be told, life here is not as I had foreseen. There is an ancient knowledge that survives here that I have only been able to access in part. I look forward to meeting a man known as The Bishop who is apparently steeped in arcane religious wisdom.

The people, even moreso, the political prisoners, are gifted with a surprising knowledge and a free way of thought that heretofor has been a most uncommon find for me. Apparently, I am to attend a meeting of great import, the basis of which has not been afforded me.

I have met a woman – oh what a glorious, woman! She inspires fear and yearning in me in equal measure. Marguerite de Valois – Queen Margot of Navarre and sister to the King. I fear she has my heart. Her marriage, even though to a King, seems to be in name only and the French seem to be rather unconcerned about proprieties in these matters. As you know, I am naïve to dealings of the heart. Anything you can discover, or any advice you can give me, would satisfy my deep hunger in this matter.

Finally, I have found myself writing again. I know that you do not have an easy ear for my poetry as I can often see your confusion past your kind indulgence – of which I am evermore grateful. I would, however, appreciate your thoughts on this sonnet as it is your greater perspective that I value. I fear my legal studies are overburdening my words with its concepts. I seem to have little choice in what my mind comes up with. The words write themselves in my mind and I just have to move the quill.

The words of this poem are true: when it comes to Queen Marguerite my eyes and my heart are in fierce debate as to which can better capture her ethereal magnificence. I would appreciate your thoughts as I cannot risk or countenance the prospect of leaving her unmoved by my words. This is what I have writ:

Mine Eye and Heart are at a mortal war,
How to divide the conquest of thy sight;
Mine eye, my heart thy picture's sight would bar,
My heart, mine eye the freedom of that right.
My heart doth plead that thou in him dost lie,
(A closet never pierced with crystal eyes)
But the defendant doth that plea deny,
And says in him thy fair appearance lies.
To side this Title is impanneled
A Quest of Thoughts, all tenants to the heart,
And by their verdict is determined
The clear eye's moiety, and the dear heart's part
    As thus; mine Eye's due is thy outward part,
    And my Heart's right, thy inward love of Heart.

Your ever-respectful servant and aide
Francis Bacon

XX THE BISHOP

If a man will begin with certainties, he shall end in doubts; but if he will be content to begin with doubts he shall end in certainties.

Like The Templar's 'cell,' that of the Bishop was at the very top of the prison. As they walked up the steps, their footsteps echoed off the motif-adorned stone walls. Catherine spoke softly. 'You asked me a little while back about the domain of the metaphysical.'

'Yes, and you said you were not the best person to talk to me about it. I am guessing that person is The Bishop. He is a master of the metaphyisical?'

'Yes. Let me warn you though that he knows things that may surprise you. He has the gift of seeing. Some would call him a prophet. In any other time, he would have been a victim of the inquisition. Being born into the Church – his father was an archbishop – saved him.'

'But Monsieur d'Anjou said he was excommunicated?'

'Yes he started to speak the truth. He started to talk about the Bible and its limitations. This is not something the Roman Catholic Church wants spoken about publicly – especially not by one of its senior officers. Pope Gregory himself ordered his excommunication and asked our King Henry to imprison him. So yet another Master joins us here.'

'What was it he was saying about the Bible?'

'This is his room here. You can ask him yourself.'

Catherine turned the key in the lock.

'Catherine, how good it is to see you,' came the greeting as they entered. The man who kissed her cheeks was of medium height, with short brown hair and a hooked, aquiline nose. It made him look a little like an eagle, thought Francis.

'Bishop Daniel may I introduce Francis Bacon.'

'How do you do Sir?' The man had the most penetrating blue eyes that Francis had ever seen. He had a sense they both missed nothing and saw into his very soul. He found himself feeling uncomfortable as The Bishop stared intently at him. The growing pause made it even more uncomfortable. Eventually, The Bishop let out a long sigh. It was what the man said next, that really disconcerted Francis. It even drew an odd look from Catherine.

'Yes it is you. I came to The Mont a year ago to meet two people in particular. You are one of those two.'

'Sorry, Sir ... Ahh ...me?' Francis could not imagine what was going on. Why would a Bishop want to meet him? How did he know he would be here? Even Francis had not known he would be here until recently.

Catherine took a step back, as if to take a better look at Francis.

'Do you know Dr Whitgift too?' Francis asked bewildered.

The look on his face indicated that he clearly did not. 'No? Is there a reason I should know this man?'

'No Sir. It is nothing.'

It was Catherine who spoke up. 'Bishop Daniel, I am intrigued. Why is it that you might be here to meet Francis?'

'Mr Bacon will be a man of influence. He will influence the future in many ways. His words will change the world forever. There is one issue in particular that brings us together. It has to do with the Bible. Please, where are my manners, take a seat.'

There were only three chairs in the room. It had the same layout as The Templar's. Like the Templar's there were books everywhere. Catherine took some off one of the chairs, put them carefully on the floor and took the seat on The Bishop's right. This time she was not leaving. Even she wanted to hear what this was all about and where Francis fitted into the story.

The Bishop cleared the seat in front of his, to the left, and motioned Francis to sit.

'To explain, I need to go back a few steps. Have you heard of the St Thomas Church?' His bright blue eyes were focussed squarely on Francis.

'Only since I have arrived at The Mont and then only a little. I know it is based on Thomas the Disciple of Jesus. I understand that he taught that we are all connected to the Light, to God. I have never heard of a separate church of this name.'

'That is because it is a church within a church – within the Catholic Church. There is a bit more to the story than you may realise. What I am going to tell you, you may find hard to believe. These are the facts, as we believe them to be. I am not asking you to believe, but you need to know that there are different accounts of Jesus, his teaching and his life. History is often written by the victors who need to cover some of the tracks they are not so proud of. In the Church at a senior level, I had access to original documents that most people do not get to see.'

'But I thought the Bible was the inspired words of God, written through men of God?' Francis said.

'That is what the Church would have you believe, but nothing could be further from the truth. In fact, the majority of key players who shaped the Bible and church doctrine were not part of the church hierarchy. They did, however, understand the value of the church when it came to wielding power and this was what they wanted.'

Francis looked confused.

'Let me give you a good example. It was the Emperor Constantine who, in 325AD, called the first Ecumenical Council in Nicaea to solve a major problem for early Christianity.'

'What is an ecumenical council?' Francis asked.

'It is the meeting of the Church's bishops, the men, for they were always men, who decided the direction of the Church and what we should all believe.'

'But you said it was called by Constantine, he was not a bishop.'

'And there you have it in one. Indeed, he was not of the Church. He was a great emperor who knew how to lead. He knew religion was his most powerful tool, but the tool was splintered. The problem was this: was Jesus of God or not? Alternatively, was he just an inspired man, albeit with royal blood? Indeed, with over two hundred different versions of the Gospels in circulation, things were rather confusing all round. Constantine wanted to control the souls as well as the minds of his subjects and Christianity was the way to do it. However, as a great leader, he saw the disorganised doctrine needed to be ... shall we say "upgraded".'

'Was not Jesus the son of God?'

'For 325 years after his birth he was not! At best, he was seen by many in his church as divinely inspired, but not of the same standing as *the God*. By many of his followers he was seen as a prophet and to many others, just a man of royal lineage who was a great teacher. "The Son of God" is simply the way all Jewish Kings were referred to. Arius from Alexandria argued against God status. So, Constantine put it to a vote. Rabbi Jesus by a small margin of only four votes – 161 to 157 – was voted to be deified as a God.'

'So you are saying that Jesus *became a God through a vote*?!' Francis said with dismay.

'It was not going to be the last time that a vote was to decide what would become accepted religious thinking either.' The Bishop said cryptically.

'The other problem was that Thomas was as popular as Jesus. The Gospel of Thomas was one of the most popular Gospels being preached prior to Nicaea. Didymos Thomas's second name was Khrestus. "Christ" is the way we say it now.

'Constantine was smart enough to know that two potential gods would confuse the people. To have two leaders of the fledgling Church was asking for trouble, for a potential rift. There was already a Syrian sect called the "Christians of St. Thomas." So their images and their names were married into one – Jesus Khrestus. While things were going his way, behind the scenes he organised the bishops to declare that Jesus Christ was *homoousia* – of the same essence – as God. What Constantine wanted was consensus, not a final truth. He knew that what weakened the Church, weakened his empire.'

'But what did the Pope have to say about all this?' Francis wondered.

'Aah yes, The Pope. The answer to that is simple. Constantine had bought him. He bestowed him with enormous wealth and gifts including half a dozen churches and cathedrals. Not the least of which being St Peter's Basilica in Rome – the largest cathedral in Christendom! The Pope did not actually attend the Council of Niceae, so Constantine was able to run his political agenda in the Pope's name.

'This was a cold-hearted man who would stop at nothing to get what he wanted. Not long after Nicaea, as part of the celebrations for his twentieth year of reign, he had his wife, Empress Fausta, and their first-born son, Crispus, murdered for reasons that have not been clear.'

'Not a particularly Christian thing to do, no matter what the crime,' Francis remarked.

'Actually, Constantine was not entirely Christian yet. Even back then, it was fashionable to not be baptised until one had reached an age where one was too old or too incapacitated to commit any more sins. Constantine first accepted the sacraments from his Bishop Eusebius only weeks prior to his death. But again, I digress. Back to your question.'

Francis had forgotten his question as he processed just how much of an omnipotent, all-powerful law unto himself Constantine was. Not only was he free to kill whomever he chose, he was prepared to murder his own wife and child! And this was the man whose religious agenda was to fundamentally shape the world for centuries, if not millennia, to come.

'While Constantine had the Pope in his pocket, he saw yet another opportunity. With all of the versions of Gospel in circulation, he needed one version that he was happy with. So, to his ever-loyal Bishop Eusebius he instructed him to compile a uniform collection of writings from the many versions.'

'Do some of the other writings still exist?' Francis asked.

'As always, Constantine was thinking about what could go wrong. To be sure that no comparisons could be made and then debated, he ordered all original versions burned. He did not want consensus from within the Church, he wanted clarity, a single, undisputed doctrine. To be doubly sure, he also decreed that any man found concealing one of the original documents was to be beheaded. Eusebius was highly effective in doing this. To this day, no public records remain of these other writings.'

'No public records ...'

With a glint in his eye, the Bishop responded, 'Correct. But the Church has some ... and a few other copies exist ....'

Francis did not need to ask where they might be found. They very likely took up some space on a galleon ...

'Constantine's final act of biblical brilliance was then to have this new, New Testament bound to the Hebrew Old Testament. In this one act, he brought high-level credibility to the books of his new religion. By association with the accepted and respected Old Testament, he gained respect for his new version.

'With the new doctrine in place, all that was left was for him to recruit the masses. This was the easy part as it just was a matter of good old incentives. He offered favours, honors and for some, gifts of a white toga or twenty pieces of gold, to convert to his new Christian religion. People converted by the thousands. He issued edicts forbidding those of other beliefs to assemble or hold meetings.

'He passed laws that any buildings used for such meetings were to be destroyed. Non-believers were banished and their books burned. To avoid persecution many fled to the remote regions of Pagi where Constantine did not have the resources to police his edicts. The people in these areas, or who held contrary views, were called Pagans.'

'Does the Catholic Church now tolerate the Church of Thomas?' Francis asked.

'Well that brings us to my story. The Vatican has his Gospel. They know it to be as true as any of the Gospels. Indeed, in all probability it is one of the earliest Gospels. Parts of it appear to have been written in the first century, only a few decades after Jesus' death.'

'So, are you saying it was not included because it was not simple and dogmatic?' Francis suggested.

'Absolutely. You see over the years the Bible has had several editors ... and it will have one more,' The Bishop paused, became still and wore a look that made Francis uncomfortable. He seemed to glaze over, as if communing at another level. Finally, he moved and shook his head as if to clear it. 'But let me come back to that. Now where was I? Ahh yes, in the early centuries after the time of Jesus, there were many differing Christian sects.

'Collectively they were called the "Gnostic Sects." The word gnosis comes from the Greek word for "knowledge" and this is what they sought. Some of the Gnostic sects were particularly enlightened. Their followers were the more intellectual, the more sophisticated end of society. They pursued spiritual knowledge and debated it with vigour. Based on the recognition that Jesus gave Mary Magdalene, these sects gave equal status to women, ordaining them as priests. Even more problematically – at least in the eyes of what would become the organised church – Gnostics encouraged debate and discussion about the possible meanings of Jesus' teachings.

'While the enlightened Gnostics pursued knowledge and debated the words of Jesus, the church was getting organised. Its eyes were on a different aspect of the debate – which sect would prevail? Which sect would become the dominant one? There are always men driven to impose their views on others. Men who want to dominate. It could be argued that with more women as priests in the Gnostic churches they were doomed because they were not prepared for a fight for domination.'

'Not all men want to dominate. Why is it that some do?' Francis asked.

'First, you have powerful men, autocratic leaders like Constantine. These men know how to wield power, have a plan and believe they can lead the people to a better way. Then there are those who lack personal power. These men are defined by a deep flaw that they mask with arrogant, dogmatic argument.'

'What kind of flaw?' Francis asked.

'These are men who cannot tolerate the differing beliefs of others. They are *men who are insecure in themselves and their own beliefs.* To reassure themselves they must argue down those who hold different beliefs.

'The self-assured and confident man has no problem with others having their own beliefs. He rests secure in his knowledge that his view serves him well while the views of others may or may not serve them well. The quietly confident man discerns when it is wise to speak up or remain quiet. The more quickly and loudly a person needs to argue their viewpoint, the more they declare their insecurity to all present.'

Francis could see that The Bishop could talk at length on many matters with authority, but he wanted to know why The Bishop had such an interest in him. 'Sir, what does this have to do with me? Am I a flawed man?'

'No, no.' The Bishop almost seemed shocked. 'That is not my point at all. You have an important job to do with the Bible and you need to understand that its history is not as clear cut as many would have us believe. As it has evolved, different men have influenced and edited it. To understand the Bible you need to understand these men and their motivations. Only once you understand the motivations of the players do you understand history.'

'I am not sure I have much to offer here,' Francis said. His words did not reflect the fullness of his reaction. At this point he started to wonder if The Bishop was slightly mad.

'I hear your impatience. Let me introduce you to Irenaeus. He was the first to take sides as it were. He set the direction that the Church followed. The real story of editing the Bible begins with him. Preaching in the late part of the second century, he was the first of the so-called Church Fathers to start deciding what was included and what was removed. He decided the Gospel of John was in and the Gospel of Thomas was out.

'As I said, to understand history you need to understand the motivations of the players. To work this out, start by looking at whom they spent time with. Why would Irenaeus support John? Well, Irenaeus was tutored by the very long-lived Polycarp who had, in turn, actually met John. John had little respect for his co-disciple Thomas. He highlighted repeatedly Thomas' tendency to question Jesus rather than accept everything at face value. Thomas was obviously less in awe of Jesus than the other disciples.'

'I am supposing that being "less in awe" is the last thing the Church wants,' Francis said.

'I think you can see where this is leading. According to the Gospel of John, Thomas, after missing the first meeting with the resurrected Jesus said "Unless I see the mark of the nails in his hands, and put my finger in the mark of the nails, and my hand in his side, I will not believe." On top of his other questions of Jesus, this forever labelled him the Doubting Thomas.'

'So Thomas represents the right to question. This is the last thing a Church wants,' Francis added.

'Exactly, and there you have a fair summary of what was to come. John delivered a simple message in his gospel. He told the stories of Jesus' life that made him God-like, especially the miracles like the wedding at Cana where he turned water into wine. Then he wrapped it up in the simple message that "God loves you, believe, and be saved." Mind you, it is unlikely that the Apostle John actually penned the Gospel – but that is another issue.'

'Thomas on the other hand, represented the right to question, to wonder and to debate. This was the way of the Gnostics. Most importantly, Thomas wanted to see evidence of the divinity in Jesus. That is what makes Thomas' viewpoint so crucial. He did question. He was the original *critical thinker*. To have a critical thinker spread Jesus message is much better for the cause. Who has the greater influence? Is it a critical thinker who will question or one of the Johns of the world who are too ready to believe?'

'But back then, the simpler message of John's was easier to sell to the masses,' Francis guessed.

'Precisely. The more powerful message and more complex teachings by Thomas were harder to sell. But there was one more big difference in the teachings of John versus Thomas. John declared that the only way to the kingdom of God was through Jesus and those who taught his words. That is to say, there was only one Church and, through it, only one way to heaven.

'Thomas on the other hand, said that Jesus described us as all being from the light of the father and that light is within each of us. According to Thomas …' At this point the Bishop reached for another leather bound volume. It was clearly very old. He handled it like it was of the finest, most fragile crystal.

Francis realised, as he looked at the obvious age of the book before him, that he was about to hear words from the original Gospel of Thomas. The Bishop had a copy! Poor Eusebius, he had missed a copy or two.

'Jesus said, "If they ask you, 'What is the sign of your father in you?' say to them, 'It is movement and repose.'" What Thomas is highlighting is that Jesus himself taught him that we can all claim to have God in us.'

'So I can see that John's viewpoint is much more helpful if you want to build a religion. His view requires churches and priests preaching God's word. Thomas' view allows everyone to connect with God without any of those things. With respect Sir, what does this all have to do with me?'

'Let me get this right.' With that, The Bishop sat back and took a couple of deep breaths. He looked at Francis, but did not look at him, he looked through him, just as he had done before. Once again, Francis felt uncomfortable. Finally, The Bishop spoke, 'One day, in the years to come, you will do the last major edit of the Bible. You will be given an incredible responsibility. It will become the final version that the world will look to for centuries to come.' The Bishop paused.

'How do you know ...' Francis was lost for words. Even Catherine sat there attentively processing what they had just heard.

'The King will commission a major re-write of the Bible ...' the Bishop repeated.

Francis found his tongue, interrupting, wanting to prove the man wrong. He did not want this responsibility. 'But we do not have a King in my country, we have a Queen, Queen Elizabeth.'

With a distant smile, The Bishop simply said, 'And you think she will live forever?' He paused for a moment, then pushed on.

'She will be succeeded by a King. He will come to rely on you very heavily. You will become his most senior advisor. When he commissions the re-write, he will turn to you, as his most trusted and talented advisor. He will commission a team of religious men to come up with an English version of the Bible. He will instruct them as to how he wants the King to be positioned just below God. Once they finish the manuscript, he will hand it over to you as he will not have the capability to process its complexity himself. He will want you to ensure they have followed his guidelines but beyond that, he will give you free reign to add final touches as you please.'

'Why me?' Francis asked weakly.

'Why not you?'

Francis had no answer to that point.

The Bishop continued, 'Have faith in yourself. When the time comes, and that is some time away, you will be more than ready. I am here to begin your education on the editorial history of the Bible. Without becoming expert in this history, you will not understand what you are dealing with. I am here to give you the history, the context that you must understand so that you will know the fullness of what you will be working with.'

Then the mood changed. Suddenly the Bishop started to look quite agitated. A bead of sweat broke out on his brow. He seemed to be caught up in some kind of internal battle. His head swivelled to the window, looking to the mainland, his eyes opened in fright. He looked back, directly at Francis, his pupils wide in fear. His voice changed. The mellow tone of The Bishop's educated voice was replaced by a demonic hiss. Francis knew that voice. He knew it from his dream, the one he had discussed with Dr Clost.

'I am coming. Coming for you. Coming for you all.'

The voice coming from The Bishop made the blood in Francis' veins run cold. Catherine's face lost all colour.

The Bishop's face contorted. He seemed to be in the midst of an internal struggle. The Bishop's voice came through, 'Go, both of you, go now. He is gaining energy through your fear. Leave me now! I can deal with him.' With the urgency in his voice, Catherine was driven to respond. She grabbed Francis by the hand. 'Come on, we must do as he says.'

As Catherine locked the door to The Bishop's room behind them, Francis' fear started to abate. He started to breathe again. 'Wh wh wh, what was that?' Francis stammered.

'Not what, but who. It certainly was not The Bishop. I think he connected to the wrong spiritual guide.'

'Will he be alright?' Francis asked.

'Few in Christendom are better matched to that battle. He is a warrior of the Light from way back,' Catherine said.

Francis was reassured by her confidence that The Bishop could manage. Truth be told, it was himself that he was worried about. He did not want that voice to reappear in his dreams.

Catherine put her arm around his shoulders and pulled him tight as they walked away. He would not have pushed her away for anything.

XXI FOCUS

In taking revenge, a man is but even with his enemy;
but in passing it over, he is superior.

It was their next session with The Duke. As usual the squires were seated, unarmed, awaiting The Duke. Francis sat with Thomas on his left and Bertrand on his right. They had been kept waiting for some time, which was unusual. As they waited, Francis thought of his meeting with The Bishop. The way it had ended had unsettled him, that voice .... Catherine had since visited the Bishop to report that he was fine. Apparently, the voice had left him the moment they had left the room.

Suddenly, with a shout, a door burst open from behind them. Armed men poured into the courtyard. They were wearing cloths over their faces with eye holes cut out so they could see. The squires were out-numbered two to one ... and unarmed. In contrast, their attackers were heavily armed. Each carried both a sword and a dagger.

Francis was scared – very, very scared. He was not alone. He saw the whites of the eyes of some of the other squires. Defenceless as they were, it would be a massacre. The men surrounded them. They were all on their feet now, but there was nowhere to run. Francis could see Christian, he had adopted a fighting stance and was looking quickly from side to side. Thomas beside him spoke under his breath, 'Do not move suddenly, do not draw attention to yourself.'

The masked men moved in. Blades drawn. Out of the corner of his eye, Francis could see the young, freckled squire, Antoine. One of the men held a dagger to his throat. Antoine did not whimper or plead. He stood quietly. They all did. The young squire's composure settled Francis a little ... and then he felt cold steel at his own neck.

His attacker held him in a vice-like grip. 'So much as twitch and I will separate your head from your neck.'

A voice boomed, 'I want that one, that one and him. Bring them.' Roughly, the masked men dragged three of the squires forward. Francis turned his eyes to see whom they were targeting. Bertrand, from Francis' left, was the first to be manhandled forward. A thickset man dragged him out and pushed him to kneel in front of the man shouting the orders. It was a position of execution. The man who appeared to be directing things held a huge sword.

Christian was next. Ever defiant, as his assailant pushed him forward he struck out at the man. Francis held his breath. Two more men stepped in and held him firmly and delivered him to the man at the front. He too was forced to kneel beside Bertrand.

The third was the youngest of them, Antoine. Francis felt sick. It was Thomas who called out from beside Francis, gentle, easy-going Thomas. 'NO! He is just a boy.'

'Bring him as well.'

Two men grabbed Thomas and dragged him forward.

The thickset man pushed his sword into the ground and threw his dagger across to his right hand. He walked up behind Antoine and thrust his dagger into his back. Francis could not quite see where, but the blood coming out of Antoine's mouth meant that he had probably punctured his lung and maybe his heart. As Antoine fell to the ground, someone screamed. Francis could not believe that this could really be happening.

'That is enough.'

The masked men stopped and turned in the direction of the authoritative voice.

'That will do.' This man stood at the back. He was unarmed. He took off his mask. It was The Duke.

The masked men followed suit. Weapons were lowered and sheathed. As they removed their masks they started to laugh. Familiar faces started to appear. The man who had been giving orders with the huge sword was The Big Man, the head of The Mont's Gendarmerie.

As Francis looked around, he recognised other faces. One was that of the jailor that had killed the man who attacked Catherine. These men were prison warders. Slowly awareness came. This was an exercise. Francis did not know if he wanted to laugh or cry out in anger.

Antoine! As one, their eyes swivelled back to the young boy. He picked himself up and started laughing. With great delight, he pulled out of his mouth a small, double sausage skin that still held some of the pig's blood and tomato mixture. He had been in on it!

The squires looked at each other. Understanding slowly replacing confusion and fear. Some of the squires started to chuckle. Laughter was a release from the fear. Antoine was trying to spit the blood out of his mouth as he laughed. He just seemed to realise how horrible it tasted. His face made fascinating contortions as he tried to spit and laugh uncontrollably. The prison warders slapped their legs and guffawed. Soon all the squires were laughing, it was infectious. As Francis looked at Antoine's face he laughed so hard, he found it hard to breathe. It was good to be alive!

Even The Duke had a smile on his face. Slowly he walked around to the front and stood next to Antoine and rested a hand on his shoulder. Francis realised that they had chosen Antoine to play along, given he was the youngest, so as not to traumatise him.

'Thank you and your men. You did that very well. Please leave us now.'

Still chuckling to themselves, the prison warders moved off. Sir Maximilian stood off to The Duke's right.

'Antoine, you have a great future on the stage, should you wish it!'

'Actually sire, even though I knew it was coming, I was still scared when it happened, so it was not hard. May I please have some water to wash my mouth, the pig's blood tastes disgusting!' This brought another laugh from the squires.

The Duke nodded to Maximilian who handed Antoine a water bladder from his belt.

The Duke turned back to the boys and stood before them quietly. The smile was gone. The lesson was underway. The squires went quiet. 'That was amusing in the end, but it was no joke. As your training with me is coming to an end, I needed to give you a taste of the world of a Chevalier. This will be our last training session. Your training will continue under Sir Maximilian, as I must take my leave.'

The squires exchanged glances. This was almost as unexpected as the staged attack.

The Duke went on, 'Our last lesson today is on two subjects. The first is about managing fear. This is perhaps the most important subject of all. There is little point to having skills or knowledge if you cannot apply them when you are scared and fearful. Any fool can apply what he knows in fair weather. Your real test is to apply it when you have the taste of fear in your mouth. Let me say that again - there is little point to having skills or knowledge if you cannot apply them when you are scared and fearful.

'Never forget how you felt today. I will not waste my time asking you whether you felt fear or not. Only brave men feel fear. If you did not feel fear you were a fool who did not appreciate the danger. If you do not feel fear then bravery and courage is impossible. Deeds done without fear when faced with danger, are the deeds of fools. Never forget how you felt today. Notice that there is always some space around your fear. It may not be a large space, but it will expand as you attend to it. It is in this space that you can still think, you can still act.'

Francis was not sure if he had had any of that space around his fear.

As if reading his thoughts The Duke went on. 'You may not have felt that you had any of the space of which I speak. Not one of you lost your nerve and became blabbering idiots asking for mercy. In that mode, unless you are a superb actor, you cannot think to save yourself or others. You are well selected, but then that was no accident. The exercise today was about giving you practice at feeling fear so that next time, that space will be a little bigger.'

'Christian, I know you worked hard to control yourself, you are very capable and I know it is in your bloodline to be proud. You should have kept a lower profile until the time was right. Experienced soldiers will execute or disable you quickly if you look like a real threat, which you are. You do not want them to know who you are. Remember our earlier lesson on when to appear confident.

'Yes, Sir.' Christian heard the compliment behind the criticism.

Who is Christian really? Francis wondered. What did The Duke mean about his bloodline?

Interrupting Francis' thoughts, The Duke turned to all the squires. 'When you find yourself in the situation that you did today, hide your strength and choose your time. The moment one makes his move, unless it is very ill-timed, you all move. Make the most of the distraction. That was why I had to stop it when I did. I knew some of you might make a move and I did not want anyone to get hurt.

'Make your move sooner rather than later. Take the time to find the point of weakness and then attack it. The longer you take before you attack, the more time your foe has to settle in and become confident. Early in the action, they are also nervous, fearing failure, fearing the unexpected – this is when they are at their most vulnerable.

'And Thomas. Your concern for Antoine was admirable. Your actions were neither right nor wrong. It is a True Knight's quality to protect. It is also in your nature to care. But remember to choose carefully the hill on which to die.

'Now let me talk about managing fear. What is it really? F-E-A-R.' The Duke spelt it out. 'It is all in the spelling. Does anyone know? And, no, it is not: Fuck Everything And Run.' That got a laugh from the squires.

'Let me tell you what fear is: Future Events Appearing Real. Fear is feeling that something bad is going to happen. Most things humans fear will happen, never actually occur. Most future events stay right there – in the future. For every one thing that does happen, there are nine things that you worry about that never happen. Indeed, often the number is not nine, it is ten. Often, the one thing that does happen is the one that you did not see coming at all – like today's surprise attack.

'Today, as you were attacked, you feared injury or death to yourself and or another. Did that actually happen?'

The Duke looked around the squires as they shook their heads. 'Future Events Appearing Real. If we are not careful, we can be disabled by it. How do we stop that? How do we manage our fear, no matter what the situation, so we can apply our skills and knowledge? The paradox is that we often most need to apply our skill and knowledge when we are least able to – when we feel fear. This is life.

'I am not just talking about fear in a life-threatening situation, it might be fear for your health, fear of losing your family or your partner, or your money. Fear comes in many forms. So, what to do?'

No one answered.

'Fear, F-E-A-R, stands for something else. Focus, Evaluate And Respond. Focus, Evaluate And Respond,' The Duke repeated. 'And Focus is the most important. It is the beginning, the essence of survival. Where you focus your attention when you feel fear, more than anything else, will determine the outcome.

'Your mind will naturally go to the cause of the fear and the terrible outcomes. Never forget what I am about to say to you and that is this:

'You get what you focus on – whether you want it or not.

'This is true of life generally, but it is when fear sets in that it becomes critical. You must become master of your thoughts. You must choose what you think about. You must choose what your mind attends to.

'You all have free choice, but you do not access it until you exercise it over your own thoughts.'

'But Sir, how to stop your mind from thinking thoughts you do not want to think?' Bertrand asked.

'Very good question. It is very difficult to get the human mind to "not think." It does not like to stop. This is why focus is the solution. "Focus" means, if I must think, this is what I choose to think about. Today, when you were under attack, what could you have focussed on that would not have been so helpful?'

Francis knew this one. 'I am about to die.' That got another laugh from the other squires.

'Or you could have focussed on how you were outnumbered, or how well armed they were. Focussing on these things will bring you undone.' The Duke added. 'What could you focus on that would help?'

'I am going to live,' suggested Antoine.

'Yes ... but we can go a step beyond that. What did I say FEAR stood for?'

Christian said, 'You evaluate your options and prepare to respond. The fact that you are going to live is assumed. It is a given.'

'Exactly,' said The Duke.

The Duke continued, 'We operate on the basis that we will have a good outcome. We are then free to focus on evaluating our options and how to respond. You start to evaluate the situation and the people. What are my options? Where are their weaknesses? As you move into this mode you will feel the fear decrease to a level that helps you.'

'Excuse me Sir,' said Thomas, 'How does fear help you?'

'With the right amount of fear you will be at your absolute best. We need fear to give us strength and resolve. F-E-A-R stands for something else "Feeling Excited And Ready". You will see this most easily when the threat is less than you experienced today. When you fight in competition, at tournaments for example, that is the fear of Feeling Excited And Ready.

'Focussing away from the thoughts that bring you down and onto evaluating your options and preparing your response will move your fear from that which disables you. It will take you to the excitement of applying your skill and knowledge when under pressure.'

'I said that today, in our last meeting, I wanted to cover two subjects. Previously I spoke to you about our Code of Chivalry. Bertrand can you please remind us all.

'First, I serve more than myself. I serve my Liege, King and Country.

'Second, I serve the vulnerable and the oppressed wherever I find them. In particular, I honour women and protect them and their children everywhere both in the home and out of it.

'Third, I am a man of honour and integrity. I speak the truth when asked.

'Fourth, I will persevere to its conclusion, any enterprise I take on.

'And Fifth, I will not unleash mortal force unless I have exhausted all non-violent means of resolution. This is our Code.'

'Excellent Bertrand. Today I want to talk about an equally important code – a code *between* Knights. Some call it the Code of Friends. Men or women it makes no matter. It is known as the Code of Courtly Conduct, or more simply, The Code. Its origins go back to the time of Babylon. Babylon was a civilised, educated and, mostly, a peaceful place. They had time to think on matters of conduct.

'Initially it was not for knights as there were of course no knights back then. It was for successful warriors who, in these extended times of peace, found themselves spending more and more time in the King's Court. The Court was a place of deceit and trickery as everyone vied for the king's favour and their own power. Warriors, mostly generals, at Court, needed to look out for each other. Not all did of course, but those who did survived longer than those who did not. More used to the battlefield than the ways and wiles of Court, they needed a code that would serve them well.

'Over the centuries, The Code of Courtly Conduct has been both refined and largely forgotten until it was passed onto the first knights.

'So what is The Code? It has to do with matters of the heart. Do not see them as less serious matters. Failure to follow The Code has brought down kingdoms and destroyed allegiances between great countries. On occasions, it has taken them to war. Do not underestimate the importance of The Code.

'This Code, like the Code of Chivalry, has five parts. First, thou will not have intimate relations with a woman who is in a relationship with another. This remains true even if the woman is the one responsible for the pursuit. A strong knight knows there will be other women, the fact that one wants him is no matter. It is the insecure knight who feels he must make the most of every opportunity. More importantly, if a woman is prepared to cheat on her partner, she will be prepared to cheat on you.'

Francis' mind immediately turned to Marguerite. She was in another relationship, but, then at this point, he had no intention of having intimate relations with her.

As if reading his mind, The Duke went on. 'Of course, once their relationship is formally ended, it is a different matter. Indeed, it is not uncommon for people to make poor judgements when choosing a mate. As with the gaining of all wisdom, if one is prepared to reflect and learn, later choices are better made.

'Second, thou shalt not pursue another woman while still in a relationship yourself. This is because one cannot compare an old relationship with a potential new one, for it is no comparison at all. A new relationship is an illusion – this is the very mechanism of attraction. The new one, fresh, promising and uncomplicated will win, irrespective of the woman involved. The honourable thing to do is to first end one's existing relationship. The process of so doing, will force a more real comparison between the old and the new. The moment you end a relationship is the moment of its potential rebirth. The Phoenix, in all its glory, cannot rise from the ashes if there are none.

'If you live by this, it will mean that you think more carefully about whether you can improve your existing relationship, or if you really want to end it, before the decision is made for you. As soon as you lie with the other woman, your first relationship is over, at least in your heart if not in reality. Human guilt usually means you allow yourself to be found out. Your partner's anger at finding out this way, on top of whatever problems you already had, means your relationship usually cannot be saved.

'Third, thou shalt not take a woman who has been a fellow knight's partner unless you are prepared to lose the loyalty and friendship of that knight. Such is the nature of these relationships that few friendships survive them. Take no heed of the approval of the other knight, for a good Chevalier, if asked, will give such approval, for he knows he cannot have ownership over a woman. Generally, you cannot share both a woman who was with the knight and a friendship with this knight. Remember, your life will often depend on the allegiance of a fellow knight.'

I think that just maybe I can give up a friendship I do not have with Marguerite's husband, even if he is a King, Francis thought happily.

'Fourthly, a knight in love will embrace the virtue of patience. He will be patient and take his time in love to be sure that the match is good. If there is a hurry to wed then the couple are clearly declaring their love to be weak, to be just infatuation. True love will not wane, so with true love there is no hurry. And then he will be patient at times of disagreements.'

For the first time in his life, Francis decided that patience would become his greatest virtue.

'Sir?' It was Bernard, thinking of his own parents, who spoke up. 'If two people argue does that mean they should not be together?'

This made The Duke smile. 'Two intelligent, thinking individuals cannot cohabitate for long, before they will disagree over something. You must have conflict, for it is part of all healthy relationships. How patiently this is dealt with, indeed whether it is dealt with at all, will tell of the presence of true love. Indeed, it is not until you have had your first major argument that you will really meet your partner. It is only in conflict that you will discover how much love and commitment there is between you.'

'Then my parents must be discovering much,' Bernard quipped, making the squires chuckle.

The Duke smiled too, 'It is only in argument that one discovers the true nature of a partner's soul and if their commitment to each other is stronger than the anger. You do not want to bring children into a relationship that does not have this commitment, for children will not strengthen a relationship, they will test it further.

'There is no time that clarifies whether or not true love is present, than when one is in conflict. Conflict is the time when you discover how big and forgiving, or how vicious and petty, the heart of your partner truly is. A knight with patience will be slow to anger and will take the time to consider the problem from his partner's view point.'

Francis had never thought of knights have caring relationships. Of course, they had to have a life off the battlefield. Truth be told, times of peace lasted years.

'Fifth and finally, a knight will not make money through dealings with another knight. Any such dealings should be particularly favourable to the one paying for the item or service. Indeed, this should be true for dealings with all people, for you never know when and in what form a person who is unhappy from their dealings with you will seek payback. On the other hand, being generous in your dealings will bring you unforseen benefits in due course.

'This is our Code. Moreover, these matters of honour and integrity that this Code of Courtly Conduct speaks to, will define your reputation. Trust me when I tell you that your reputation will accompany you wherever you go, even though at times it might arrive a little later than you do. It is your reputation that defines your true nature and true value as a person. You can make mistakes, these will be forgiven, but only as long as they inform your learning. Learn and all is forgiven, fail to learn and the world will make your life difficult indeed.'

'I must leave you now. This will be the last lesson that I will take as my time on this magnificent island is coming to an end. You will be well-trained by Sir Maximilian and his men after I go.'

With that, The Duke moved around the group shaking the hand of and speaking words to each of the young squires. To some, he gave some specific advice on what they needed. To others he gave words of encouragement. The young men were subdued. They knew they had been taught by an unusual man who knew about much more than swordsmanship and warfare. That time was now over.

As he came to Francis, he said, 'I hope you have a worthy question Mr Bacon, for today will be your last chance to ask it. See me in my quarters at noon.'

When the Duke had finished, he stood before the seated squires. After a long pause he spoke his final words to the gathering. 'My young Chevaliers, none of you are here by accident. How you apply what you have learnt will be different for each of you. As you have realised, these teachings are not just for knighthood. After you leave this place, your real lessons will begin. It is easy to be a student in a class such as this, surrounded by like-minded peers. It is much harder to be a True Chevalier in a world that does not always aspire to or recognise honour, or our Codes.

'Marry the Codes to your heart and then be true to your heart. No other can know what choice you should make nor what path you should take. When you come to a crossroads, or an opportunity, always take a decision, your own decision. There is no greater regret than the regret of not being author to your own life, of not finding out what you could have been.

'The main goal of life is to learn and grow and you can only learn from a decision that you made yourself. If someone else makes it for you, all you learn is how good, or bad, they are at making decisions. Drink deeply from the wisdom of the wise, but always, always let your final decision be your own.

'I bid you all adieu. May the Light flow through you.'

The Duke turned his broad shoulders and began to walk away. As one, the Squires stood. It was Christian who called, 'Three cheers for The Duke ...' The square resounded with their cheers. The Duke walked on.

The young squires had no way of knowing that, two days later, The Duke would disappear and never be seen again.

XXII THE CHURCH'S GREAT SECRET

Prosperity doth best discover vice,
but adversity doth best discover virtue.

'The church had a big problem with me. Like Thomas, I believe two things: We have the right to debate and explore the teachings of Jesus. Second, we can know God directly without the need for the Church, its buildings or its clerics. We can connect directly with the Light within all of us. Strangely enough,' The Bishop leaned back and gave a wry smile, 'the church had a problem with me thinking they were unnecessary! And if that was not enough to annoy them, I have said more than once that there was the other small fact that the Bible was edited by people who were less than divine.'

Francis had been keen to see The Bishop again. He had tried to talk about the strange way in which their last meeting had ended but The Bishop did not seem to want to revisit what had happened. So, Francis had asked him about why he and his church had gone their separate ways. 'Is it these beliefs that got you excommunicated?'

'Actually, no. There is one last issue with the Thomas versus John viewpoints that we have not yet discussed. Do you remember from our last meeting the differences in their thinking?'

'John had the simpler message: to be accepted by God, followers had to accept the teachings in the Bible as delivered by the priests of the church. Followers were not to question either them or the teachings. Thomas believed we had the right to question. Most importantly, as you have said, he did not believe we needed a church to connect us to God.'

'Aah yes, you have caught the essence of it, young Francis. So, there is one final point from Thomas you need to understand for when you edit the Bible. Make sure you leave in the references to reincarnation.'

Francis still could not accept that he would be the senior advisor to the next monarch and involved in editing the Bible. Could he believe this man's wild prophecy? Reincarnation? He did not seem to know what he was talking about.

'But Christians do not believe in reincarnation. These were beliefs held by Plato and Pythagoras.' asserted Francis.

The Bishop responded patiently, 'Jesus and his disciples believed in reincarnation, but you are right, "good Christians" do not. Not now. Not since Emperor Justinian convened the Fifth Ecumenical Council in 553AD.'

'Sorry. I do not know of this.' Francis said.

'No and neither do most good, God-fearing Christians. Constantine and Justinian had much in common – it was what made them so powerful. They were probably the two greatest Emperors of the later Roman era – the Byzantine empire. Once again, the beliefs of the Church were to be changed, forever, not from within its own ranks, but from without – by the Emperor. By the middle of the sixth century it was time to take another vote.'

'The first vote being the one that you spoke of at our last meeting – the one that made Jesus a God?'

'Correct. Before Justinian saw a problem with it, reincarnation was as acceptable to Christians as it was to Hindus and Buddhists. Justinian knew that you could not have ultimate control while the Christian population believed in reincarnation, as they did. Justinian ruled with an iron fist. The ultimate penalty was death. How could this be a real threat if you believed in reincarnation? Many people were not unhappy about the prospect of leaving their often-miserable lives, when the next one might be better.'

'So if I believe I will come back to a better life, and this one is pretty horrible, getting involved in an uprising against the emperor, punishable by death, might even look attractive. One could not only escape this life but die a people's hero!'

'You have it exactly! Moreover, his powerful wife Theodora, also had a problem with it, because it meant that people were, at their core, equal. Just as a boy who was finishing his education, could not be said to be a better person than a boy just starting. People were just at differing points of growth over their many lives. Being of low-birth and an ex-prostitute she needed to feel superior to others.

'It was not the primary agenda at the Ecumenical Council of 553, but it was an important one for the Emperor and his wife. It was a big ask to destroy the belief in reincarnation, but that would not stop this mighty couple. To get away with it they had to call the greatest theologian of the early Church a heretic. Origen lived three hundred years before Justinian and was a true Church Father. Having written over six thousand works on Christian faith, he was one of the most prolific writers and greatest thinkers the Church has known then or since.

'In De Principiis, his major work on the theology of Christianity, he wrote ...' The Bishop picked up yet another book. 'Every soul ... comes into this world strengthened by the victories or weakened by the defeats of its previous life.'

'They had to call him a heretic and that was exactly what they did. In denouncing Origen, such a prominent Church Father, Justinian had a problem. He also had something else, he had the Pope under house arrest. In the end, without the Pope present, he took his cue from Constantine and pushed his agenda through. The vote, weighted by his own Bishops went in his favour. From that moment forward it became a heresy, punishable by death, for anyone to talk of any aspect of reincarnation. Here is the decree from the proceedings of the meeting.'

The Bishop walked over to the table and picked up another tome. Francis could see from the title that it was a record of the proceedings of the Fifth Ecumenical Council. The Bishop opened it and read, "*If anyone asserts the fabulous pre-existence of souls, and shall assert the monstrous restoration which follows from it: let him be anathema."*

'A thousand years later almost no one realises that we dismiss the idea of reincarnation not because it is false, which it may or may not be, but simply because Justinian and his wife did not want it to be so.'

'You are saying that good Christians do not realise that their problem with reincarnation is a dogma that Justinian fed them?! It did not even originate from within their Church! Can this be true?' Francis asked.

'Do not take my word for it. In fact, I would rather you did not. Research it yourself. You have time. As you can see, the books are all here. The bigger problem is that even people who are not Christians do not realise that they dismiss the idea of rebirth because Justinian told them to. In taking it out of Christian faith, he took it out of "civilised" western thinking. It was quite an achievement – one of many for this brilliant man. To the millions of Hindu's and Buddhists rebirth is as normal and as accepted as it was by … well, Jesus and his disciples.'

'You almost seem to be impressed by Justinian?'

The Bishop chuckled, 'Indeed I am. Think of it. He changed the way everyone in Christendom thinks about perhaps the most important spiritual awareness of all time. I do not like it but I have to respect it. To date I have not been able to come close to such influence. My attempt to do so is what got me excommunicated!'

'So this was what did it?'

'Yes, I know the truth. It is one of the church's greatest secrets. I had to be silenced. Can you imagine how much would change if people realised they lived many lives. Justinian's fears are only a part of it.'

'You said that Jesus believed in reincarnation. How do you know this?'

'That is even easier to prove. There are several references in the Bible. The clearest is that found in Matthew's Gospel, Chapter 11. This is when Jesus was questioned about the Old Testament prophecy that Elijah would appear before the coming of the messiah. Jesus responds by simply pointing out that John the Baptist was Elijah. There was no confusion over this statement. Christianity stands on the very shoulders of reincarnation and cannot afford not to.'

'Let me see if I follow. If reincarnation did not exist, then Elijah as John the Baptist did not come, and so Jesus could not be the prophesied messiah! That would be a problem for Christianity.' Francis could see why the Church had a problem with The Bishop. His logic, using their own evidence, put them in an embarrassing bind.

The Bishop's eyes twinkled. 'Precisely. Justinian overlooked Matthew, but there is more. The most intriguing reference to reincarnation comes from the Gospel of John, chapter 9. It is the comfort with the subject that is so remarkable. Do you remember the story of Jesus healing the man who was blind from birth?'

'That is the one where Jesus spat in the mud and put the mud into the man's eyes?'

'Yes, that is it. Do you remember the question the disciples asked that begins the story?'

Francis shook his head.

'They asked Jesus: was this man born blind because he had sinned or because his parents had sinned? Now think hard about that question. How could a man sin before he was born?'

Francis' mind turned over. He could see where The Bishop was going. 'They must be talking about reincarnation.'

'Precisely. There is no other explanation, except maybe that the man's soul sinned in heaven before his incarnation, but that brings up even greater complexities. All present in that scene with Jesus simply assume that rebirth occurs. It is no big deal. What we are hearing here is a conversation between people who are all comfortable with reincarnation, including whoever wrote John's gospel.

'Jesus' answer does not even deal with the question of reincarnation because all present know of it. When he answers, he simply says that neither the man nor his parents sinned. He was born blind so that Jesus could heal him and demonstrate God's work. The issue of rebirth is a complete non-issue for Jesus and his disciples.' With a wry smile The Bishop added, 'Bit of a pity for the man though, to be blind until Jesus came along just to show off God's power.'

Finally, The Bishop stopped. Francis was almost afraid to ask more questions. Since meeting this man, his world had been shaken to its very foundations.

Catherine seemed to sense it too. Quietly she said, 'I think that might be enough for one day.' Nobody objected.

As they stood to take their leave The Bishop said, 'Take an interest in these matters. Do not take my word for any of it. Make up your own mind. Most of all do not dismiss reincarnation because Justinian told us to. When the time comes, do your precious work on the Bible knowing that it will be read by more people than any other book for centuries to come. Despite the men who have tried to subvert it, use it for the good of humankind. There will be others who work on the Bible before it will be handed to you for the final edit. Ensure they do not take out the clear references to reincarnation that remain.'

That only left Francis feeling more anxious. He hoped The Bishop had it wrong, but the man's honest eyes, looking directly into his own as they shook hands, left him feeling otherwise.

'Go with the Blessing of Thomas.'

After they took their leave, Francis asked Catherine, 'I can see he has mastered the domain of the metaphysical, but you have said that to be a true master you need to have mastered at least one other domain.'

'In The Bishop's case that would be relationships. He is a great leader with tens of thousands of followers throughout Christendom. People believe him because over time he has proven that he does not play with the truth. Nor does he overstate it. People trust him. That is the main reason why the Church has kept him alive – they do not want to martyr him. The other reason is that his followers are the thinking people, intellectuals and the sophisticated amongst those who seek enlightenment. Many of them are very powerful people.'

This did nothing to reassure Francis. A part of him had been hoping that the thinking people had dismissed The Bishop as a crackpot.

XXIII THE ANSWER

There is no comparison between that which is lost by not succeeding and that which is lost by not trying.

Here he was again, back in The Duke's antechamber. Francis was anxious not to invoke The Duke's disappointment in him. Their last meeting had not gone well. It took him a few moments to notice the object hanging on the wall opposite him. It replaced the parchment he had read when he had first visited The Duke.

At first glance, it appeared to be a looking glass framed in black marble embedded with precious stones. As he looked more closely, he realised that it was not glass but highly polished metal. He could see his reflection with ease. He realised that it was a smaller version of the larger one that he had seen in The Duke's sitting room at his first visit. Beneath the polished metal there was an ancient inscription. Francis did not recognise the old language.

He felt drawn to it. He looked again, more intently. Two words seemed to take shape. Francis looked more closely as his lips mouthed the words: 'My Faith.' As he watched, the words changed. He felt compelled to write them down. Taking out the paper and graphite that he always carried with him, he started to write.

MY FAITH

Serves to inform my responses to the challenges of day-to-day life and how I treat others, knowing that there is a higher guiding force that I am able to access from within myself;

If I can remember why I chose this life and find the courage to live it, life will go as well as lives can go;

With all the valour I can muster, I will give voice to the magnificent potential within me, a power that may frighten me and may be the envy of all but my closest supporters;

In turn, I will love by recognising that same glorious potential in others and nurturing them to step into their own fullness;

I will remember that experience is what you get when you do not get what you want, as wisdom cannot be attained without experience;

Though experience is the best teacher, it is also the slowest path to wisdom and, while learning from those with evident wisdom is the quicker path, I am grateful for their patience in my learning journey;

If I can appreciate these truths and aspire to them, I will be as happy as one can be, knowing that happiness, like the blooms of spring, cannot and must not persist year round;

Like the other seasons, all emotions, including anger and deep sadness, are necessary and elemental parts of the human experience - the rich and wondrous journey that I joyously came here to devour.

The words stopped. Francis felt confused. What manner of trickery was this? He got up and inspected the hanging more closely. The metal was now clear, empty. He moved it slightly. There was nothing behind it. Perturbed and dismayed, Francis sat back down again. He stared hard at the wall piece, but it simply hung there. Empty. It did not even stare back at him or reflect his presence. It appeared to be inert, completely disinterested in his presence – just as metal and stone should be.

He looked down at the words he had written. Among his papers was the letter he had received yesterday. To distract himself from this madness teetering on the edge of his mind, he read the letter again.

My Dear Francis,

Thank you for your communiqué as to your actions and intentions.

While I had expected your return by this time, I can see why you feel compelled to stay on.

I have looked into the matter of which you wrote. Queen Marguerite, from what I have heard is both a learned and remarkable woman. Whilst not in high favour with her Queen Mother, she is so with almost all else. Indeed, her mother's disfavour undoubtedly further endows the respect in which she is held!

Although I do not want you to get your hopes up, it does appear that the marriage of which you speak is so in name only. There is doubt as to whether it was even consummated. And yes, there is talk of it being annulled as her husband rules Navarre without her. I shall look further into your prospects.

On the matter of your poetry, my ears are simply not qualified to do it justice, let alone to offer an opinion. As a matter of confidence, I showed it to a woman with a great appreciation for matters poetic and she proclaimed it sublime.

I will write once I know more.

Yours faithfully,

Sir Amyas Paulet

As Francis refolded the letter, his mind went back to the strange object across from him. He recalled the conversation with The Templar. He had spoken of the Grail and how it had polished metal in which words could appear. Was this the Grail? The Holy Grail?

'Aaah, Mr Bacon, how is that knife throwing coming along? Have you been practicing?' Sir Maximilian roused him from thoughts.

Francis liked Maximilian. He had taken the time to give Francis a couple of individual lessons to help him develop this skill. 'I am practicing Sir. I seem to be improving.'

'Excellent. I was just leaving. The Duke will see you now.' Turning to The Duke behind him he said, 'Thank you for your time M'Lord. I wish you all the best on your travels.'

Francis realised that Sir Maximilian was saying his goodbyes.

The manservant was not to be seen. The Duke ushered him in.

'Aah, Mr Bacon, take a seat.'

Francis did so.

'You have a better question for me?'

As always, The Duke was straight to the point. There would be no small talk here.

'I think so, Sir, but before I do, may I ask…? In the waiting room, the object on the wall … the metal … it showed me words … and then they were gone.'

Smiling as he sat, The Duke motioned Francis to do the same. 'Ah yes, it does that from time to time. Most intriguing is it not?'

'Does it give the same words to everyone?'

'Oh no. Indeed, it rarely gives words to anyone. When it does, they are always different. They are for that person at that time. Indeed, they are simply a reflection from your higher self. Whatever words you were given, keep them and reflect on them from time to time and see how they fit with what you have come to understand.'

'Is it … is it the Holy Grail?'

'Oh Lord no,' he laughed, 'it is much larger. Now, our time is short and there is much to cover, so we need to move on.'

Francis recalled the larger looking glass set in the elaborate cream marble from his first visit. It was nowhere to be seen. He wanted to ask about it, but sensed this was not the time. 'I would like to know why I am here? Why are any of us here on this Earth?'

The Duke sat, studying Francis intently. Francis felt uncomfortable. Had he asked a foolish question again? Finally, the great Chevalier spoke. 'Yes, I believe you do want to know. I will tell you. You, and everyone else, are here to remember and to experience.'

Francis thought of how prominent the word 'experience' had been in the message he had just been given as he had waited.

'This is why you will regret not experiencing everything you could do in life so much more than you will regret having an experience that does not work out as hoped,' The Duke continued.

'But experience what, sir?'

'Everything that speaks to your heart, everything that beckons you. Most of all, you want to experience happiness.'

Francis waited. Was there more? This made no sense. The last thing he saw around him was happiness. Misery, suffering, poverty and illness were everywhere. Even the privileged few of breeding and education rarely seemed happy as they fought for more and warred with their neighbours.

'You are thinking that happiness is the last thing you see in this world. Am I correct?'

'Verily, Sir.'

'Attend to your question, Mr Bacon. Did you ask me what is the state of the world, or why are you placed upon it? The truth is that few people work out why they are here. The vast majority stumble through life with no idea as to the greater plan. Remember that many people die in their early twenties. It just takes a few decades before their body realises it and follows suit. They finally die with misery on their left and regret on their right.'

'But Sir, with all due respect… Happiness? What of the greater good? Of helping others? Of great achievements or progressing humankind?'

'How do you think one gains happiness Mr Bacon?'

'By having the wherewithal in life to be able to afford to relax and enjoy the good things.'

'Really?' The Duke responded, raising one eyebrow.

Francis found it disconcerting when The Duke did this. It usually meant that he was missing something.

'Do you really think that if I gave you the wherewithal to relax and enjoy a perpetual holiday of wine, women and song with your friends, that six months later you would be telling me just how happy you felt in your life?'

Francis felt that sink in. He could hear a truth emerging from the great Chevalier's words, but it was still just beyond his grasp.

'Let me help you, young Squire. There is a good chance that at the end of the six months, you will have a perpetual hangover, a woman who is angry with you, both for the disease you gave her from your previous wench and because you rarely come home early enough. This will be because you are out all night drinking with your friends as you solve the problems of the world through the wisdom of alcohol!

'Imagine a different six months. Go back to a time when you worked to master a skill or a challenge. How did you feel, after your initial stumbling frustrations? When, say, you rode the hunt, staying at the front, without falling from your mount? Maybe after your early humiliations, you won a fencing match, or you mastered the Pythagorean mathematics that had initially brought you undone.

'Now, think of a second kind of experience – when you were working at something that completely absorbed your mind. A task that challenged you, yet rewarded you, at the same time. This was a time when you were applying and developing the very mastery that you fought from the jaws of frustration. There is a simple and easy way to recognise this kind of experience. You lose track of time. It just flies by. There is a state of timelessness. You might be building something, writing something or helping another. You are completely absorbed in what you are doing. Your inner emotional stream bubbles contentedly as it flows to connect with the great awareness of the ocean of life experience.'

Francis nodded as he remembered this feeling. Some of the great books he had read had taken him to this place of timelessness as he had immersed himself in the world created by the writer.

'So now, imagine six months of your life during which you were developing and honing your mastery as you work on something meaningful to you. From time to time, you find yourself in this state of timelessness. Then allow yourself, just from time to time, to enjoy the pleasure of the company of good friends. Maybe you have a woman who loves you and values you. Maybe you laugh together. At the end of these six months how will your happiness compare?'

'So, if I have this right, pleasure can build on happiness, but happiness cannot be built on pleasure?'

'You have it Mr Bacon! Pleasure is not on the path to happiness. *Happiness is a by-product of pursuing a meaningful purpose in life.* Adding more spices to a dish, beyond a certain amount, means less taste, not more. In the same way, more pleasure usually leads to less happiness – there is an optimal amount in both cases.

'So, why do you say we are here to be happy? Why not say that we are here to do meaningful things *and be productive*. Is that not what you are saying?'

'That message can mislead too. That message leads people to think that they should all do great things or that the more productive one is, the better. People start to think they have to become a monk or a nun or work hard from daybreak to nightfall. When people understand that true happiness is a by-product of pursuing a meaningful purpose, they have a guiding light. These paths are many and varied – more than you can imagine. The feelings of true happiness start the moment you begin on your path. This guiding light of the feelings that go with pursuing one's purpose is something you can easily look for.'

'So, by saying the goal is happiness, you prevent people from working too much because then they will notice that if they work too hard, they will not feel happy.'

'Precisely. A father will make his wife and children unhappy and annoyed by not being there for them as he works too much. This will interfere with his happiness and lead him to work out how best to meet their needs too. The happiness derived from meaning is what gives the emotional guidance that people need to stay on track.'

'The happiness from meaning … that makes sense, but how does one work out what will give one this happiness?'

'An apprentice stonemason who will become a builder of majestic cathedrals will first notice his fascination with the design of the buildings around him and how curves come together. He will find himself at his happiest when he is working on jobs that allow him to explore ways of building, that talk to his creativity. Such work will not be a chore for him. He might find himself having fantasies of one day constructing a great building.

'On the other hand, this young builder will have doubts. 'What right do I have to be a great builder?' he will ask himself. Jobs that hold no interest for him, he does less well. His master tells him he will never be a good builder, let alone a great one. His master forgets that great builders have others do those tasks that they are not good at.

'As long as he can notice how he feels when he is working on certain projects and take notice of what he daydreams about, he will find what is meaningful for him. As he does what is meaningful, his purpose will become clearer. Purpose is built on meaning. One's purpose will follow from the pursuit of meaning.

'Our young stonemason must remember that neither his master, or anyone else, can know what makes him truly happy – or the fullness of his purpose. His master may help him to work out where his talents lie. Noticing what you enjoy doing as you go through life, noticing your guiding emotion, your guiding light, holds the key.'

'While I can see how this works for the young stonemason, my problem is I have no idea what my purpose is,' Francis despaired.

'Very few do. And when they think they do, they often find that it was not quite what they end up finding to be meaningful for them.'

'It all seems too hard to work out.'

'Precisely what most people decide,' The Duke responded. 'Who am I and what am I here to do, are two of the most difficult questions a human can ask. Largely, this is because they have no immediate answer. Such questions are a special kind of question. What did I say was the answer to the question you brought me today?'

'We are here to remember and experience, but what do you mean by a 'special kind of question'?' Francis asked somewhat impatiently.

'Do not rush on. Do you remember the spell of spelling?'

'Yes, The Templar told me of it.'

'The nature of these special questions is to be found in the very word itself.'

'In which word?'

'When it comes to a question, in which word do you think?' The Duke smiled with a playful gleam in his eye.

Francis thought hard. He sensed the answer was not far from his grasp, but he could not grab it ... then all at once, it came to him. 'It is a Q-U-E-S-T-ion ... it is a question that can only be answered through going on a quest.' Francis laughed with delight at the 'spell'.

'People, so often, when confronted with your great question, dismiss it. They give up and return to their meaningless lives because they fail to realise that this is a very different question. This question will never be answered at the time of asking. It can only be answered over time – and then, only if the asker keeps the question alive in the back of their mind. Too often they let the question die, and so does their life.'

'So how does one begin the quest to answer this question?'

'You start by asking *better* questions of course!' The Duke said with a smile. 'There are six questions. Three looking back. Three looking forward. At least one of the six will help you get started on your quest. Let us start with the past.

'The first question is: When you were young, what did you dream of, or fantasise about – before the world told you what you should or should not be or do? Some will have been flights of fancy, but other ideas will have come from a deeper place. Try to remember. Allow yourself to go way back and remember. What you came here to do lies deep in your soul. While deep, it lies in wait to be found.

'The next question, as you look over your past is: Of everything I have done to date, which tasks did I find truly satisfying? This question looks at what part of a job, or interest, really spoke to you or gave you satisfaction. Often, while we do not enjoy a job, parts of it can be deeply satisfying for us – this is the emotional guidance I spoke of earlier. You need to look back for it.

'Now as I ask these questions Francis, I want you to be thinking about them. Do not answer me just yet.'

'I understand,' Francis replied. 'What are the next questions?'

'The third question, looking back to your recent past is: What aspects of what you are doing now talks to you and gives you satisfaction? Which parts of your working day do you enjoy? Equally, what parts of it do you not enjoy?'

Francis thought of how he did not enjoy the fight training. Truth be told he was always scared he might get hurt. He enjoyed mastering the skill of knife-throwing, which was much safer – until you were on the target side of it! But what he enjoyed the most at The Mont, was learning new information, indeed just as he was right now.

The Duke continued, 'Let us look to the future. The first question is: If I had the wherewithal to do whatever I wanted, what would I like to do? If there is no answer, you need to stay on the quest to find out. I can promise you, one day your mind will answer it.'

Francis asked himself the question. The Big Man came into his mind. Why? Do I want to be a gendarme, he wondered. Then it came to him. When he thought of The Big Man, he thought of a storyteller. What was it about that which interested him? Was it about getting a message through to others in a way that made them listen and pay attention? The Duke intruded on his thoughts.

'Second question: If I were to imagine doing this or that, in the future, how might it feel? Here you need to spend time imagining your life if you were to go down this path of your passion. Push aside, for the moment, your doubts about whether you could do it or not. Just fantasise about how your life would feel if you were doing more of what really speaks to your heart. Also, notice what aspects of this pursuit you find yourself imagining, as this will tell you more about what speaks to your heart.

'Now, the final question. Are you prepared to put aside time to explore your interests? These interests might be old ones that you need to give more time to, or new ones that you have never tried before. Dabble in anything that interests you. Make time by giving up both leisure and work. The most difficult work to give up is that which you might even be good at, but is not that meaningful for you.

'I should give up things that I am good at? What if they earn me money? What if I need it to then fund pursuing my purpose?'

'This issue is much less of a problem than you think. Indeed, the argument, "I need to work now, so I can fund my purpose later," is usually a way of avoiding the challenge. One should never be far from the other.'

'You mean that pursuing one's purpose should never be put on hold for long, while one works to pay the bills and vice versa?'

'You have it in one. As a guide, never let the sun rise and set without doing something that is meaningful. Never let a moon rise and set without spending time pursuing your purpose.'

You will need to do things you are good at that are not meaningful early on, so that you can put food on the table and pay the tax collector, but you must always remember that it is not the main game.

Once you forget the main game, your life is over as you fall into the depths of meaninglessness. Remember to remember.'

'So the signposts along this path are about how meaningful the pursuit feels, rather than how good you are at it?' Francis asked.

'Precisely. Your emotions will guide you if you look to them. Early on, when the path is unsure, explore your interests and fantasies and then notice your reactions. Explore-notice, explore-notice.'

'So inevitably, you move closer to your purpose?'

'Yes, meaning informs purpose. Finally, beware the trick of saying, "I would like to try that, but I do not have time. I will do it later when I can get to it." This is your fear speaking. If you cannot organise your time to pursue it within a week, certainly a month, your fear is winning. The quest begins with you putting aside the time. Initially it might only be a few hours a week. Heed this: if you are not prepared to put aside this time, you are not yet ready to embark upon your quest. A meaningless life will be yours until you do.'

More softly The Duke said, 'So, tell me Francis, what do you dream of doing ... what is your passion? It is all right, you can say ...'

After a moment Francis spoke. 'I want to write. I want others to hear the words and ideas that sing in my mind. I want all to know the great truths that I have been privy too ... but what if I cannot capture these ideas? What if I cannot get the right words out of my head?' Almost to himself, Francis went on, 'To be honest, I do not think I am good enough, that I am worthy of being a writer. I have met great writers, like The Templar and The Bishop. I am not in their league.'

The Duke left Francis with his doubts for a moment. Gently he said, 'There you have the essence of the fear of the quest. This personal doubt, this fear, is the greatest of all obstacles. Faith is your only hope ... faith in yourself, faith in the importance of The Quest.

'But what if I confront my dream to find I cannot do it. What am I then? What is left for me in this life? Can I call myself a man if I simply prove I am not good enough?' As he said the words, Francis recalled visiting this problem right back in his discussion of the dream with Dr Clost and then with Catherine when she spoke of failure fear. 'Fear, it seems, is the mortal enemy of pursuing one's purpose.'

'So true. The courage of overcoming fear is the key to living a rewarding life.' With a smile, The Duke lifted Francis' sombre mood. 'While no one can give you courage – that you must find from deep inside – I can give you one thing. It is a key truth: As long as you are pursuing your purpose you cannot fail … if you persist. So, be Determined and Detached. Those two critical "D" words are your greatest resources and your greatest weapons on your quest.'

'I recall Catherine telling me of how this was the strategy used by Abott Robert. He was the first true master I was told about.' Francis mused.

'Indeed. So, let me recap for you. Be determined to get there and to see all setbacks as learnings. Be detached from exactly how you will get there. Of these two words, Detachment is the hardest for humans to come to terms with. Humans desire certainty as it gives the illusion of control. This desire brings them more suffering than you might imagine. Rarely will life unfold as you would expect. Detaching, surrendering to your higher self and to the universe to look after the details of how it will unfold, will be perhaps your greatest challenge on The Quest.

'Which brings us to my definition of success and happiness – for they are one and the same thing. Five simple words. You will be successful and happy if you are *pursuing one's purpose in love*.

'It has two stages. The first is answering the question, "What is my unique mix of capabilities and talents?"'

'What if you do not have any great capabilities or talents?'

'Aaah, this is of course the usual response.' The Duke leaned forward and looked Francis in the eyes to make his point. 'People assume the important words here are "capabilities" and "talents" but the most important word is only three letters long – M-I-X. It is your unique mix that we are looking for, not great talent.

'That is how it can be true for everyone, not just the great,' Francis realised. 'And the second stage?' Francis asked.

'Taking the leap of faith, overcoming the fear of failure, and maybe the fear of success, and making it a part of one's life. In short, you get on with pursuing it.'

'So, why do you not say the second stage is "living one's purpose"? Why do you say you are still pursuing it?'

'Because even when you are doing what is your purpose, you are still pursuing a higher form of it. It is a journey. Our stonemason-come-architect will always have a bigger and better cathedral to build. It is a never-ending process. And then, one's purpose, itself, evolves. Our stonemason, in time, may decide that to share what he knows is more meaningful than to build another cathedral.'

'So are you saying that it starts as a dream, then we do it around our daily work and then it becomes our work?'

'Usually, but not always. Some pursuits that give us meaning are better kept as a retreat from work. They complement and refresh us for work. This is particularly the case if we have found daily work that is also meaningful in a different way.'

'Can we have more than one purpose in life?'

'Usually there is one purpose that evolves during our life, but it is expressed in different ways at any point in time. For example, our young stonemason before he is able to be his own master, might have a love of sculpting stone into works of art. This might be something he does outside of his work. ' The Duke explained.

'And then one day people decide to pay him for his sculptures and he can give up his job and make a living from his passion?'

'Provided he does not do it primarily for the money. There is no better way to kill a passion or purpose. Moreover, the great paradox of money is that it is most likely to come when you do not focus on it.

'I have heard the saying that "people do not buy from the hungry shopkeeper," but it sounds like we all have to spend some time doing what is not meaningful when we need money?' Francis suggested.

'Yes, and "hard work" is simply work that we do not find meaningful. When we are doing what we love, what is meaningful, none of it is "hard work" no matter how demanding it may be. Even when pursuing our purpose, there are times when we need to work 'off-purpose' – fields need to be tilled, water carried and debts paid. At these times, meaningful pursuits take third place.'

'What's in second place?' Francis asked.

'Actually, your question is: what is in first place? Because work *is* in second place.'

'Like I said, what is in first place?' Francis responded immediately with a smile.

The Duke also smiled. 'Well that is what the "in love" part is about. Whether it is your children, your wife or the men you lead, there are times when relationships must come ahead of all else. There is no benefit in pursuing your purpose at the cost of your relationships. Mind you, the clever person allocates their time so that there is no conflict. By regularly giving time to those we love, they are much less likely to quarrel over the time for meaningful pursuits.

'Indeed, the person who pursues his purpose finds himself in richer relationships. This is simply because people who are inspired by the passion of their purpose are more attractive and have more to give. People who are without the passion of purpose may be nice people, but in the end they can bore.'

'Does raising children constitute a purpose in life?' Francis asked.

'Some men would like women to think this, but no, that is the right of every child and the responsibility of every parent. Indeed, if they are going to raise their children well, mothers and fathers need to model to them, the importance of pursuing a meaningful purpose.'

'Is not all of what we are speaking a luxury? Can everyone pursue their purpose? What of beggars, and the sick?' Francis argued.

'Yes, many would like to say that the matters that I speak of are a luxury. The truth is that the only way the beggar will leave his rags behind and the unwell become well, is through looking inside and beginning The Quest. There are only three benefits of pursuing one's purpose and they are, health, wealth and happiness. Show me someone who has risen above their station, who enjoys robust health, and who is contented with their lot and I will show you someone who is living with passion.

'When people see this as a luxury, they are surprised to find that their life has no meaning. It is Law, *if you do nothing to pursue meaning in your life, it will be meaningless.* It may seem so obvious, but you would be surprised at the number of people who see pursuing meaning as a luxury and then wonder why they are not happy and their life feels meaningless.'

Francis could not dispute this logic. He had another question. 'I sense that the happiness you speak of is not the happiness that most folk think of?'

'You studied Aristotle at Cambridge?'

'Yes.'

'Did you ever read his Nicomacheon Ethics?'

'Yes.'

'Do you recall what he said about the highest state humans could achieve?'

'Was it that the highest of all good achievable by human action is a sense of satisfaction with one's self?'

'Almost. Do you remember the exact word he used? It was not "satisfaction".'

'Not really,' said Francis shaking his head.

'The word was eudaimonia. Do you know what it means?'

Francis shook his head again.

'It comes from the word 'Daimon'. Each individual comes into life with a unique mix of capacities or capabilities. This mix is known as one's 'Daimon'. The central task of life is to recognise and realise these talents.

'The prefix eu- is Greek for "feeling well." The suffix -ia simply forms the feminine noun. So eu-Daimon-ia is the feeling you get as you express your potential. It is the passion of a meaningful life. It is the feeling one has from dancing in perfect time with one's Daimon.'

'I had heard the phrase of how we all need to do battle with our "inner demon". Should it be doing battle with our "inner Daimon"?' Francis asked.

'Precisely. Demons are those painful secrets and memories we all carry. They can be painful to confront. Unlike dealing with our Daimon, confronting our demons can be done in hours, days at the most, if one is prepared to put them out there and talk about them. The truth of the matter is that people would rather deal with their many demons than their one Daimon. Most people deal with neither.

'It takes years to make sense of your Daimon as we have to go on the inner quest to unlock it and bring it forth into our lives. Learning to dance with one's Daimon is one of the most difficult of dances. However, once the steps have been learnt it is the most rewarding dance of all. It is the very celebration of eudaimonia.'

'Whilst Aristotle obviously knew a thing or two, I did have some problems with his logic around the way to grow knowledge. He did not seem to value the testing of ideas and collaborating with others to do so.' Francis was trying to impress The Duke with something that had been a bit of pet subject for him at Cambridge.

'Did you write well at Cambridge?'

'I was told that I did.'

'Good. Could you do me a favour?'

'Anything Sir.'

'I would like you to write down what we have discussed this day, so that it might be copied and available for others. Would you do that for me and leave it with the Abbey librarian?'

'Yes Sir.'

'Excellent. I have one final duty as your Master to perform.'

Francis sat expectantly.

'Your position in the training program is at an end. It is over.'

Francis thought there must be some mistake. Maybe The Duke was joking, but his expression suggested otherwise.

'Sorry Sir?' he asked. What could he have done to deserve this?

'Mr Bacon, it will not feel like it right now, but trust me, I am doing you a great favour. It is not difficult for a teacher, or an experienced person in any field, to work out whether another is suited to the job at hand. You, Mr Bacon, are not a man of arms. You are not one now nor will you ever be.'

Francis felt emotion rising in his throat. This did not feel at all like a favour. It felt like failure. It felt like his last visit with the Queen. Oh please, he said to himself, you are far too old to cry. Especially, not in front of The Duke. He lowered his head in shame.

'I suspect you will be a knight one day, but not from the path here at The Mont. Please listen to me, Mr Bacon. Look at me.'

Francis raised his head and reluctantly looked into the eyes of The Duke. He felt them reach past his disappointment and shame. Was it kindness in those deep green eyes? As he looked, they seemed to shine like emeralds of the deepest hue.

The Chevalier spoke with a gentleness Francis had not heard before. 'This is no matter of shame. You need to be set free from this path. It is not for you. I would do you a grave disservice if I did not deal with this directly. Determination is a wonderful thing, but it can hold us all back when it is misdirected. That is why I need to send you away. You are too stubborn to give up yourself. You may tell the others you resigned.

'Besides, you have ideas to think, intellectual paths to explore and for that you need a fascinating world of complex and great people to negotiate. Most of all you need to be on a path that allows you to fulfil your Daimon – because one day, you will write … you will write like an angel.

Tears came to Francis' eyes. Not from shame. He felt the encouragement behind the words. The Duke's eyes … at some level in his body knew he was being given a great gift. A tear from his left eye rolled down his cheek. He did not wipe it away. Quite strangely, he did not feel embarrassed in the company of this extraordinary man. He felt … well the only word for it was love – from the very depth of his being. It was a feeling of grace. He did not want it to end.

'Goodbye Mr Bacon.'

Their time was over. Francis stood and turned towards the door.

'By the way, Mr Bacon.'

Francis paused.

'If anyone wants you to resign in future, and you respect them, do yourself a favour. Thank them for the gift, resign, swallow your fear and ask your Daimon to go dancing with you. If you are being asked to go, you are not yet on the right dance floor.'

'Thank you Sir.'

'My pleasure, Mr Bacon. And one last thing.'

'Yes Sir.'

'Remember the way of The Quest, resist the urge to forget. May the Light flow through you.' With that, The Duke stood and turned to look out the window. The meeting was over.

'Thank you, Sir.' As he left, Francis remembered this was the blessing used by the Chevaliers of old. The Big Man had told him about it not long after he had arrived. What had The Big Man said about it? That was it – it could only be offered by a true Chevalier to another Chevalier.

XXIV THE MEETING

The great end of life is not knowledge but action.

The Abbey's bells proclaimed midnight. Three rows of four wooden chairs faced a large fireplace at the front of the room. The burning timber crackled quietly as if respectfully aware of the portent of the meeting. The most tardy and disorganised of the twelve invitees, the Bishop, had been early. He sat next to The Templar. Their heads bowed as they conversed softly. To their left in the front corner was the main entrance to the room – a heavy door of oak with black metal strapping.

Outside the door, on guard, stood The Big Man and another experienced gendarme called Delano. They had served together in two major battles and were prepared to die for both their Liege and each other. Amongst other duties, they were ensuring that no swords were worn into the room. Given who had been invited, this was not surprising. As Francis had entered the room he had noticed the glass fronted weapons cabinet outside. The Big Man was requiring all men of arms to leave their weapons in this cabinet. Of course, he did not ask Francis to disarm.

As he had walked in, two Persians were handing over their scimitars. One had the air and finery of royalty. His turban was heavily jewelled and his tunic and cloak were of the most lustrous purple and gold coloured silk. The other, with the battle-scarred appearance of a seasoned warrior, was a military man of the highest rank. Both sides, Christian and infidel, Francis realised, had a right to the Archangel Michael.

Francis had no idea what to expect. He thought there was every likelihood that nothing would happen and that after a while, they would all leave with muted embarrassment at having attended a meeting called by a bejewelled piece of metal and rock.

He did have at least one worthwhile reason to be there. She was sitting in the front row directly in front of his seat. Oh Marguerite! His young heart ached. He was positioned at the end of the second row closest to the door. Catherine sat to his right. He chose a seat for the two of them in the middle of the three rows to maximise his chance of being close to Marguerite. When she had finally entered the room, she had completely ignored him.

He had recently sent her another sonnet that he had written, but had received no reply. He desperately wanted to know what she had thought of it. Maybe she had not received it?

He could live with the fact that she did not immediately acknowledge him, but his spirits had gone downhill since then. She had arrived early, when few others were in the room and even though it was safe to do so, she had not looked at him once. It would have been so easy for her to steal a glance at him after she spoke with The Duke, before taking her seat. Now she could not even look at him without turning completely around. The roof falling in could not have crushed him more!

Sitting with the weight of her disinterest upon him, he looked up at the door as two more men walked in. It took Francis a moment to register and then his jaw dropped. One of them was Christian. He was dressed like a Prince with a perfectly tailored richly coloured tunic overlayed with the purple sash of royalty. It was as if the total colour in the room was limited, such that Francis' mood darkened further with the rich colours of Christian's attire. He was accompanied by an older man, even more regally dressed. The family resemblance was obvious. Even more annoyingly, the young prince nodded in a friendly fashion to Francis when their eyes crossed. Once again, Francis tried to dislike him, but struggled to do so. Why was he here?

'Who are they?' he asked Catherine, pretending to sound disinterested.

'That is Frederick II, King of Denmark and King of Norway and his son, next in line to the throne, Chr…'

'Yes I know – Christian.' Francis tried to hide his displeasure. So, Christian was a Crown Prince! Francis found a part of him stirring in response to this news. A legitimate Crown Prince. That was a pain he did not want to re-visit.

Apparently, Christian's father was not also invited, or maybe one family representative was sufficient, Francis wondered, as Frederick II spoke briefly with The Duke and then left the room.

Dr Pierre Clost arrived. Francis remembered him from the trip in the coach to The Mont from what seemed a lifetime ago. He had called it The Mont of Legends and Francis had come to see why. While he had seen the physician several times when he had visited Catherine, one had been arriving as the other was leaving. In these brief meetings he had always felt a generosity of spirit and reassuring calmness from the kindly, wise Frenchman. He and Catherine had much in common.

Then, a big and welcome surprise. His old tutor from Cambridge, Dr John Whitgift, walked through the door.

Francis jumped up and greeted him with a vigorous handshake. While the Montois with their open doors had been so hospitable, there was nothing like seeing a familiar face from home. He inundated his old mentor with questions. Why was he here? Where did he fit in? Did he know The Duke? While the older man was friendly, he made it clear that the time for conversation would come. After brief introductions. he sat to Catherine's right. Graciously, Catherine had recalled Francis talking positively of his old mentor and said so to Dr Whitgift.

In the row behind him sat the two Turks. Speaking in their own tongue, Francis could not understand them. He wondered how they had managed to make it to The Mont without incident. He remembered reading that in the 1540s the Turkish navy, led by Barbarossa, had fought alongside the French against the Spanish over Nice. And this was not the only time the Crescent of Islam had flown beside the French King's own banner, much to the concern of the rest of Europe.

The two Turks made eleven. The twelfth was an elegantly, but sedately, dressed woman Francis did not know. She appeared to be in her late twenties. Like so many in the room, she exuded fine breeding. She sat beside Marguerite and from time to time they exchanged words as if they knew each other. She appeared to be of Germanic extraction. As if she was reciting from a book, Catherine had explained the connection.

'That is Anna of Austria, first daughter of Maximilian II, Emperor of the Holy Roman Empire of the German Nation. She is the fourth wife of Philip II, the King of Spain. Marguerite's older sister, Elizabeth was his third wife who died after a miscarriage nine years ago.' As an afterthought she added, 'His second wife, as I am sure you know, was your Queen's half-sister and predecessor, Queen Mary.'

As Francis sat there quietly, he had time to ponder on how he had come to find himself amongst such eminent company. He realised that in this room were representatives of all the major powers in his world. Then there were those with less evident but 'behind the scenes' power such as The Templar and The Duke. Dr Whitgift, Catherine and The Bishop were the thinkers and writers with influence. It was a careful mix. He was particularly intrigued by the multiple interconnections between the royal families. Despite its vastness, it was a rather small world. He could not help but wonder where he fitted in.

They waited patiently.

Nothing happened. The clock chimed the half hour. The Turks started to shift in their chairs and mutter to each other. By one o'clock most of the audience was becoming restless. They shifted in the uncomfortably hard wooden chairs. The Bishop and the Templar were engaged in a quiet conversation. In the back row, The Duke sat still, leaning back in his chair. His eyes closed. His long legs, stretched out and crossed before him at the ankles.

Deciding it had been a waste of both time and the long journey, the Turks stood to leave. At that moment there was the sound of shouting at the door, followed by the sound of sword against sword. The room came alive. The Turks, already on their feet, headed for the door. The others jumped to their feet. Only The Duke stayed where he was, unmoved, as if asleep.

Before the Turks got to it, the door burst open. A tall man in black strode into the room. He bore the air of man who was relaxed and used to being in control. His cloak, stitched with what appeared to be black diamonds, seemed to absorb the firelight. The Big Man stood in the doorway at the point of Gaspard's sword. Behind him, the other gendarme, Delano, was nursing a deep cut to his sword arm. Blood was seeping between his fingers and dripping to the floor as he held the disabling wound.

The man in black spoke with quiet, menacing authority. It was if they were all gathered there to see him. 'Gaspard, leave them outside and join us. Close the door behind you. Everyone, back in your seats.' To The Big Man he commanded, 'If you come in here before I summon you, one of these women will die.'

Francis looked back to The Duke for reassurance. Surprisingly, he was still seated, head down in the back row. Why did he not do something? As he watched, The Duke looked up and gave The Big Man a slight nod. The Big Man backed out of the room and Gaspard slammed the door shut.

A small table stood beside the fire. The man in black wandered over and sat upon it. He surveyed the room. 'So, where is our beloved Michael? Do not tell me he stood you all up? And such a distinguished group too.'

There was silence in the room. All eyes were upon the man in black with the long straight, jet black hair and the strong, square jaw.

'How rude of me. I should introduce myself.' Slowly, he loosened the cord at the neck of his cloak. With a flourish he threw it to Gaspard, who caught it in one hand. Collectively the room gasped. The Turks took several steps backward and sat in their chairs. The Bishop crossed himself fervently.

Slowly the wings under the cloak unfolded. They were a glossy, jet black and they were immense. Each wing was as wide as the Fallen Angel was tall. They had a sinister majesty to them, like a powerful bird of prey. As he turned slightly, Francis could see that at the base of his wings the roots of the first row of feathers were a dull white. He realised that once upon a time these wings had been all white.

Satan threw his head back and laughed loudly. He appeared to be enjoying himself. He fed on the rising fear in the room. His laugh became a cackle and as his head came forward, his eyes were now glowing red. His vertical black pupils sent ice into Francis' veins. As Lucifer had intended, the fear in the room increased and he breathed it in deeply. His chest swelled. It was a demonic voice that said, 'So where is your precious Michael now?'

Francis was scared. His mind was having difficulty processing the turn of events. The creature before them was real. Evil personified. He looked behind him to his right, once again seeking the guidance of his mentor – possibly the only man in the room who could help them. How could even The Duke take on the very devil himself? Francis was stunned to see the great Chevalier still sitting with his eyes closed, as if he were in another world. Slowly, The Duke opened his eyes, uncrossed his muscled legs, stood up and spoke.

In a loud but calm voice he said, 'Good evening brother Lucifer.'

All heads turned. The Duke was walking down the far side of the room towards the front. The room was silent. Francis turned to look at Lucifer, for the first time, perhaps in a very long time, he appeared less sure of himself.

It took Francis' mind a few moments to register what The Duke had said: Brother Lucifer? Something else was strange. There was total silence in the room as The Duke walked to the front of the room to confront the evil standing there. It took Francis a moment to work out what was wrong. Finally, he realised what it was … his teacher's boots made no sound as he moved along the stone floor.

The Duke continued, this time speaking to those gathered. 'Listen carefully to me. Do not be afraid. He feeds off your fear. Without your fear, he is powerless to hurt you. If you show no fear, he cannot raise a finger to you. That is why he needs his evil human henchman – to do his dirty work to those who do not show fear.'

'Ahh Michael, so good to see you again and thank you so much for your sermon.' Satan's words came out with syrupy venom. 'I did not notice you up the back there, you have changed your hair. You are looking very, shall we say … human … and you hid your Angel smell. I am so sorry to barge in like this but I seem to have not received my invitation to this little soiree.'

'O contraire, mine old enemy, yours was the first name on the invitation list. Indeed I have been warming a chair for you while we awaited your arrival.'

This took Lucifer aback. Saint Michael pressed further. 'As you know only twelve, other than myself, can attend. You need to ask your man to leave us.'

The Lord of Evil was not about to be told what to do. Certainly not with all eyes upon their exchange. 'Gaspard, choose one of these fawning, common-kissing foot-lickers and kill them. As he says, we need to keep the numbers at twelve.' To those in front of him he added, 'And while Michael here is giving away heavenly secrets about me, let me give you one about him. Your wonderful Michael will not save you. He is unable to raise a weapon or injure a human being – and that includes my decidedly charming friend here.

'If you look closely at your history books, you will note the strange behaviour of The Duke who fought the British in 1433. While he lead his men, he never drew his sword. He could not. He had to stand by and watch them being attacked and killed.'

The Archangel responded, 'That may be true, but you speak as if death is a bad thing, something to be feared. We both know it is not so.'

'There is one thing I have learnt since I left the heavens and made my home with the humans. Despite the teachings of your confused preachers, humans still fear death. No small thanks to that wonderful Justinian – he was very helpful in outlawing beliefs in reincarnation. Your power-hungry preachers are more concerned about who can get the largest following than they are about teaching the truth to these poor idiots. Those who know the Great Truths are more often found outside the Church than in it. But, we waste time with this idle banter. Gaspard, choose one to die. He cannot stop you.'

Gaspard looked around the room. The fear level in the room rose again. Lucifer smiled. The fear energised him. His gaze settled on one of the gathering. Francis' heart froze.

Marguerite! NO! He screamed in his mind.

The scar-faced man brought his sword up and walked over to where Marguerite stood in the front row. 'I will take this haughty bitch. She is a fine one. Can I have my way with her before I kill her? No I suppose it will have to be afterwards while she is still warm.' He grabbed her by the arm and pulled her roughly to the front of the room.

Without warning Marguerite spat in his face. She has no fear, thought Francis. He did not think he could have admired her more until that moment. While that will stop Satan, her flesh will not survive the manservant's sword he thought. Through feelings of desperation he tried to swallow his own fear so as not to attract Lucifer's attention and empower him further.

Gaspard wiped the spittle from his face. His scar turned purple as his face twisted with rage. He drew his sword back for the blow.

It was Saint Michael who called to him in a commanding voice. 'Gaspard! Do not do this thing. It will only add to all the remorse and regret you already carry as you depart us for the other side.'

All eyes turned to the being they had known as The Duke but his resemblance had changed. Massive wings had sprouted from his back. As much as Lucifer's were an oily black, the mighty Archangel's were mostly a brilliant white with sparkling emerald green feathers along the outer edges. He hovered off the ground. His hair colour had changed to blonde and his skin glowed from within. The long, beautiful Sword of Truth had appeared at his side.

Francis could almost see the energy radiating from the Angel. He could certainly feel it. It was warm and empowering. It was similar to the feelings of care he had experienced when The Duke had told him he was to leave the training program, but this was much more powerful. He felt a gentle urge, like a vibration, but he had no idea what to do with it. At least he felt calmer. The ice in his veins was melting.

Saint Michael was summoning his full presence to discourage the man with the scar from what he was about to do. It almost had the desired effect. In awe, Gaspard started to lower his sword.

'Gaspard, do not listen to him, you are not going to the other side just yet. No one can stop you, their swords are at the door. Now despatch her and give them something to fear.'

Gaspard, while a proven warrior, was still fearful of his other-world master. His heart, heavy with his crimes, did not allow him to be free of his fear. To disobey the very Devil himself would mean a painful death of slow burning from the inside out. He drew his blade back to strike the death blow.

Saint Michael could do no more.

Marguerite stood with her arms by her side and calmly waited, not taking her eyes off her executioner. Her calmness won her the respect of all in the room. The muscles in Gaspard's face tightened as he pulled his sword back for the death thrust – as a knife sprouted from Gaspard's neck! It cut both his windpipe and a major artery. He died as he fell to the floor clutching at his torn throat, drowning in his own blood.

For a moment, those gathered could not work out what had happened. Marguerite was the first to react and realise who had saved her. She recognised the throwing knife sticking out the henchman's neck. Her calm evaporated and with a soft sob, she threw herself into Francis' arms as he came around to her. For Francis, their embrace could not have been sweeter.

For a moment, it looked like Satan would explode with rage as his face darkened. He looked at Gaspard's body with disgust. Almost as quickly, he brought himself under control, turned and walked over to one of the large windows. It was as if there was suddenly something of interest he needed to look out at.

Earlier that evening Francis had been passing time in his room. As he wondered what the night's event would bring, he was absentmindedly throwing his knives into a board that he had set up at the top of his bed. When Catherine had knocked on his door and called him to the evening meal, he had put the knife that he was about to throw into his pocket. He had forgotten about it until Saint Michael had spread his wings. The Archangel, in his full state of being, had finally focussed Francis on the one, and only one throw, he could make. Looking back he suspected that this was exactly what the Archangel had in mind. By settling Francis' fear and giving him faith in himself, Saint Michael had allowed him to intervene when the great Archangel himself could not.

Catherine used the break in the proceeding to rush out the door to attend to her husband's friend, Delano, and his bleeding arm. Ignoring his foe by the window, the Archangel came over to check on Francis and Marguerite. Francis reluctantly released his hold on her. He turned to the being who, in a more human form, had been his teacher and softly asked, 'Did you know I had a throwing knife?'

'Not exactly. We Angels can see potential, parallel, future outcomes. One outcome that I could see was Gaspard dead and Marguerite alive and you playing some role. There was another one that did not end so happily. Which outcome actually occurs depends, as it always does, on which of the possible outcomes the people involved invest the greatest emotion. That outcome was simply the one that had the most emotion attached to it, both individually and collectively. I then needed to distract Lucifer so that he did not search the possible outcomes as I did. Had he seen you, he would have turned his man on you. He was not looking as he did not believe there was a threat. He has grown over-confident of late, which means that now he will be much more careful, as must we all.'

Francis felt a little faint. He trembled slightly. He was not sure what was the more unsettling, that he had just killed a man, that he had been able to hold Marguerite, or that he was conversing with a real angel – an Archangel no less! It had only been a few minutes since Satan had walked into the room and total havoc had followed him in. Catherine had quickly bandaged Delano's arm with her scarf. As she walked back into the room, she came up to Francis and took his left hand while Marguerite, on his right, slipped her arm around his waist. Everyone was now on their feet.

'My hero – again!' Catherine squeezed his hand and immediately Francis felt more grounded. Shifting into her caring mode, in her soothing physician's voice she said, 'The full meaning and shock of what you have done will hit you in time. Right now you need to focus, as this night is not yet over.'

XXV TRUE LOVE

Whoever is out of patience is out of possession of their soul.

*Fortitude is the marshal of thought,
the armour of the will, and the fort of reason.*

The turn of events had changed the tone of the room. Saint Michael had his boots back down on the floor and his wings folded behind his back. At his request, The Big Man had removed the body and was wiping up the blood. Lucifer, also with his wings folded, sat quietly on the table, smouldering. He knew that, at least for the moment, he had no real power with these people. Their fear was gone. Nevertheless, his business was not finished.

Francis could not keep his eyes off Satan. The right hand of the fallen angel slowly clenched and unclenched the black leather grip of his long sword. The pommel and elaborate guard of the hilt were a highly polished, glossy black inlaid with more huge, light-stealing black diamonds, as was its scabbard.

Francis had to remind himself of what was happening in this very room, right before his eyes. The being he had known as 'The Duke' was not a man at all. He was the glorious Archangel Michael. He would not have believed it himself if not for the wings and the floating above the floor. And then there was the Devil himself in the room with them! Once his mind had accepted one archangel, it was not so much of a leap to accept the other. As The Big Man closed the door after him, the Archangel spoke.

'Please, everybody return to your seats. It is time for our meeting to begin. We now have the correct numbers.'

Francis was reluctant to step away from Marguerite who still stood beside him, her arm around his waist. Only a night like this could allow such a departure from decorum. In the end it was she, always the stronger, who gently pushed him away. Dr Whitgift had given him a hearty slap on the back. Christian shook his hand, looked him in the eye and said, 'Good throw'. He meant it. Damn him, Francis thought, but he could not help but like him. Slowly everyone returned to their seats.

'As you may know, from time to time selected leaders amongst humankind are given direct instruction. This is done through someone like me appearing to a small group or even to a single person. Sometimes awareness is delivered via a prophet for the masses. Different prophets have been called to different peoples at different times.

'The role of prophets, however, has not worked out quite as might have been hoped. We have noticed that you have a bad habit of forming a religion behind them and then warring with those who do not believe as you do. Often these are simply people who did not meet the prophet. In your failure to engage them, often through your own failing as communicators, you kill them instead. It would appear that it is easier for humans to kill than communicate effectively.'

'May I ask a question, oh great Archangel?' It was the Bishop who spoke up.

'Dispense with the formalities. We are amongst friends – well almost,' he said throwing a side-ways glance at Lucifer who sat, biding his time. This drew a nervous laugh from those in the audience. 'Please call me Michael. I can only answer those questions that you ask, so formulate them carefully. Gaining knowledge is all about getting the question precisely right. Without asking the right question ultimate knowledge, knowledge that could change your lives, will lie out of your reach. I know you will have many questions and my time here is limited.'

'Thank you ... errr, Michael,' even for an enlightened Bishop, it was difficult to address a deity so informally, 'Why is it that we humans would rather kill than communicate?'

'As a race you are inherently insecure. It is not a bad thing. If not you would have nothing to aspire to, there would be nowhere to go. When someone agrees with you, you feel good and righteous. When they disagree with you, especially around deeply held beliefs, your insecurities are triggered. If your beliefs are found wanting, maybe you are not good enough either.

'This is a very uncomfortable feeling for humans. They rid themselves of the feeling by trying to get the other to agree with them. Few, however, have the wit of Cicero or the debating power of Socrates. Violence is failed words. Killing or vanquishing the person who leaves you feeling more insecure not only stops the feeling, but leaves the victor feeling stronger and more secure. Then they meet the next person who disagrees ....

'You often also forget that it is important for any society to have some who do not believe. The non-believers train the believers up to play at a higher level and communicate more effectively. The believers are forced to become more creative and eloquent in their delivery. This process shows the flaws in their beliefs. Beliefs need to evolve as you evolve. If everyone believes, there is something desperately wrong. You should embrace those who challenge you. They are essential to your improvement.'

'So, if God knew that sending prophets would result in so much warring and killing, why did He send them?' The Bishop went on.

'Firstly, I need to say that we see "God" differently from the way you do. It is a force, an energy, The Light, that surrounds us all. It is the ultimate, all-knowing, all-loving sentient being. It is there to be tapped into, or denied. You each have free choice in this matter. The Light does not take decisions. It provides. Whatever you focus on, be it collectively, or individually, it gives to you, good or bad. If it turns out to not be what you wanted after all then this adds to your collective experience. Experience is what you get when you do not get what you want. This is precisely the way you gain wisdom.

'So while you should be very careful what you wish for, rest assured that if you do not receive it in quite the form you wished, you receive it in the form you need. It adds to the growth of your wisdom. Indeed, this is why life must not always work out for you. For this to occur, you would be denied the gift of wisdom.'

'You said that what we focus on will come to us?' Marguerite asked.

'In time, eventually, if you are patient. The process is not as precise as it could be for a very good reason. To bring anything forth in your life you have to imbue it with energy. Just as a great painting cannot come forth unless the painter gives of his or her energy to create it, so it is with all things. The more powerful energy is not that of thought, but that of emotion. If you gently and lovingly wish to have something in your life, the Light will assist you. The more desperate the need, however, the less likely the assistance.'

'Why is that?' Marguerite asked, 'Why should desperation make it less likely?'

'Because patience is the mother of love, the glue of life. Impatience pushes people away. This is a critical point because it is through the people around you that The Light usually delivers its assistance. As your desperation pushes people away, or makes them feel uncomfortable , they become less available for The Light to work through.'

'Does this mean that if we worry about bad things they too are more likely to happen?'

'Yes that can occur, but there is a particular and intended delay in the timing. Most humans want things too quickly. Humans are fickle, today they want something, a week later they want something else.'

'So you are saying we need a delay period to be sure that what we want is really what we want and this also gives us time to move ourselves away from focussing on bad things?' Marguerite clarified .

'Exactly. By providing more slowly than you might like The Light gives you time to correct the process of focussing excessively on negative things that you do not want to give life to.'

'What kind of magic is this process?' Christian queried.

'There is little magic. You have all seen this process at work. As I have mentioned, nearly everything that comes to you, every opportunity, will come to you through another person. Let us say you wish for more wealth. If your lack of wealth causes you to worry and to complain, others will notice this at one level or another and will not be drawn to you. Indeed, they will be repelled away from you. The offers of better paying work, or of buying your merchandise, will not appear.

'If, however, you desire to do work that is meaningful for you and you have a passion for it, your mind will seek ways of preparing you for the opportunity when it presents itself. Others will be drawn to you. Most people, indeed all people who themselves are successful, when they come across passion will want to nurture it. A clever landowner will always hire the man who loves making things grow with a passion over a stronger man who has no passion for his work, no love for his plants.

'In the same way, merchandise crafted from a passion for the work will sell over that not crafted with a love of the work. No, there is little magic, you are just seeing the very nature of how things are brought about. This process is a collective one. The collective is made up of The Light and the people who can make whatever it is you desire, come into existence. Understand the nature of what draws humans to each other, and what repels them from each other, and you will understand the very fabric of the process of manifesting your desires.'

Thinking of her own sons, Catherine offered an example. 'In this way the child who most earnestly desires a horse, and continues to do so over time, will find that a parent, friend or relative will be inspired to make the wish true. The child who simply complains about not having one will not so inspire others?'

'That is precisely how it works,' Michael responded.

Francis could appreciate what the great Angel was speaking of. At Cambridge, the professors who saw his real interest on certain subjects gave him their time, nurturing his knowledge. On the subjects he had less interest in, no matter how well he wanted to do, they were less forthcoming.

'So returning to your question, Bishop, as to why The Light sent the prophets. They say a teacher, will not appear until the student is ready. The fullness of this notion is that, the prophet cannot appear until the students collectively call him or her forth. So it was not "God" who took a decision to send a particular prophet to you – collectively the people made that happen.

'Over time, however, your world will become less religious as people look for a more direct relationship with The Light. If people were to remember the teachings of the Apostle Thomas, they would realise that being spiritual does not require a prophet, let alone a church or a preacher to tell you what to believe or how to be.

'As people become better educated and learn to read, the need for prophets to drive the spread of understanding by word-of-mouth will become less. Writings from different Light-inspired writers will do this. In the years to come, almost every important idea will be written somewhere.

'But even then, like The Light itself, the Church simply serves the people. Too many people do not have the desire to think too carefully on spiritual matters. They leave the Church to order it, simplify it and serve it up to them in a neat package. Like I said, be careful what you wish for.'

The Bishop went on, 'So when you say "we" called this meeting, you do not mean God and you, as I first thought, you mean the "we" here in this room.'

'That is what I mean. This is the collective process – co-creation if you like. Each of you are here because you have been…' he looked at Francis as he said this '… on a quest to know. Again, you only have to look to the word "question" to be reminded. The word is built around the word "quest." The way of the quest is to question. A quest is not so much a physical journey as it is a mind journey. In the physical journey, you start with your first steps. In the mind journey, you start with your first questions. Each of you have earnestly and persistently asked questions that we can help you with. You have asked questions that deserve answers.'

'But if you could see that we would follow the prophets and turn to war, why did you allow us to go down this path?' The Bishop pushed the point.

'First, we can see multiple outcomes. It is not entirely clear which one will dominate until it does. This is your free choice. Second, neither The Light, nor we as Angels, interfere unless we are invited to do so. That is the very essence of your free choice – your first right in either soul or human form. No one has been asking us to stop the prophets. Indeed, any prayers on this matter are typically to return them to lead the people again. We get requests to send Jesus and Mohammed back all the time.'

'If we ask your kind to help and heal illness or avoid tragedy you do not always interfere it would seem. Often it appears that you do not help, even when true believers ask for your help. Why is this?' The Bishop had been pondering this question for some years.

'There are different factors at play in that big question. The first comes back to the idea of co-creation between collaborators in a collective process. The nature of our interference or help is typically through others. Often people ask for help and we bring others to them. Sometimes this could be in the physical form, at other times it could be the help they need in the written word. The real tragedy is when the person asking for the help does not see the person we have sent as our agent. The person asking for the help does not allow the help to be given. Often they look for a greater miracle than is needed.

'Second, through prayer and meditation you can sometimes commune with us directly and we can then assist by giving you increased fortitude – the courage to go on. Then you must apply this fortitude to heal or cope with the tragedy. Too many have thought that once they pray, their work is done.

'And then sometimes people find life too hard. Usually this is so if they have not found meaning or their purpose. They set up their death over time. The person who drinks or eats too much, who has had enough of life, when finally faced with the end, cries for our help. While we can put our help in motion, it is often too late in the play to make a difference. As I said earlier, there is a delay before what you focus on comes to be, but in the final stages, the chosen process is more difficult to stop.

'You also need to know that we come from the perspective that death is not a bad thing. Death is simply another rebirth. While death is sad for those left behind, for the person who dies the rebirth from death is a time to rejoice.

The final factor is that often you chose a particular life to have particular experiences which may include pain, suffering and premature death. These are amongst the most powerful of learning experiences. Part of the learning is to how manage these experiences with dignity. In choosing these experiences willingly, prior to your incarnation, it would be wrong for us to interfere when you ask us to. We know that the asking in this situation is simply because you have forgotten your life choice. We will always, however, remain by your side to guide you through the adversity you have chosen. If you ask, you will never be alone.'

The Bishop had nothing more to say. He was deep in thought. The expression on his face suggested that even for a liberated thinker, it was a major shift for him to enter the new world order that the Angel was laying out for him.

It was the Templar who spoke up this time. 'We all thank you for gracing us this night.' He could not bring himself to refer to the Archangel by his first name. 'Could you tell us what makes a prophet? It would seem they are not the "Sons of God"?'

'Actually they are, just as each of you are the sons and daughters of The Light – that is very much the point. What makes a prophet is that they simply remember more than you do of the existence one has between lives. To understand this I need to talk further on the process of choosing your life.

Your Plato had an excellent understanding of this process, as did Pythagoras before him – he was not just a great mathematician. In Plato's Story of Er, he gave a very accurate account of how this works. He wrote of how souls choose their next life while they remember their previous lives. Having made this choice, souls experience the veil of unknowing. Before their birth, a soul is taken to the River of Forgetfulness. Once they drink of the water, they forget their life between lives. Prophets simply do not drink at this river. They do not forget where they come from.'

'Why is it so important for us to forget?' Marguerite asked, 'It confuses people who often argue that because they cannot remember their past lives they must not have happened.'

'We have watched humans grapple with this point. Unknowing is the beginning of the journey of life, it allows the quest to begin. Forgetting allows you to embrace fully the challenge of the life that you have chosen. Otherwise it would be like finding your way through a maze that you remembered the solution too. You would waste much time before you realised that the maze was a different one. You need to be unencumbered by your preconceptions, your knowledge of all that has gone before.'

'Are you saying that by forgetting our previous solution to the maze, this allows us to come up with a better solution?' Marguerite said.

'And a more creative solution. Humans have a tendency to stick to what they know, what worked before. Forgetting allows you to approach a problem from an entirely new perspective, a new vantage point. Moreover, the baggage of a long past can weigh you down. By forgetting, you have the opportunity to re-invent yourself from a higher place.'

'But what about the learnings and wisdom that one has built up from their experiences in one's past lives – it is all wasted?' The Bishop asked.

'Not at all. You carry forward the experiences and wisdom of past lives not as known memory, but as an energetic awareness. This means you will know certain things and have certain abilities. You will just not remember how you acquired them.'

Catherine, Dr Whitgift, The Templar and several others in the audience nodded at this.

Catherine spoke. 'I must say your words have a strange familiarity to them. Rather than you telling me something new, it feels more as if I am remembering that this is how it all works.'

'That is because you are remembering. I am not telling you anything your soul does not already know. The veil of unknowing was aptly described by Plato. It is just a veil, not a wall. Gently allow yourself to remember and you will recall the principles of what I speak.'

'You have said that we choose lives that will present us with certain challenges that may be confronting and painful. And we choose this existence as the quickest path to evolve, which makes sense, but why evolve at all? You have said that souls all choose to, but why?' It was Marguerite again. She was not backwards in engaging in a debate, even with an Archangel.

Saint Michael smiled. 'Now we get to the heart of it. I have spoken previously about how to find meaning and make sense of your life. You come to this life to find your Daimon – your unique mix of talents, capabilities and interests. Having found it, you then can experience the happiness that comes from this discovery and the expression of this awareness. More correctly, this feeling is called Eudaimonia. By the way Mr Bacon, have you made a record of our recent conversation on this subject and left it with the Librarian for those who wish to read it?'

'Yes I have, Sir ... err Michael.'

'Very good. So, why incarnate at all, why live, why evolve, why dance with your Daimon? The answer is so simple, most do not believe it ....'

'The biggest question has the shortest answer. Just two words ... to enjoy.' He let that sink in.

'The French word "enjoier" means "to give joy to." It comes from "en" to make and "joir" which in turn comes from the Latin word gaudere, which means to rejoice. The fullness of this word means to "make rejoice" and then both give and partake of this joy – much as one might make a wonderful pie and then share it with others.

'To enjoy?' The Turk General intoned to himself as he turned this odd, perplexing idea over in his mind.

'Yes. While it is a key ingredient, along with loving, you cannot dance with your Daimon all of the time. And most of you know that the excessive pursuit of pleasure inevitably leads to unhappiness and a feeling of emptiness. Equally, there are times where you need to deal with the mundanities of day-to-day life. Food needs to be procured and prepared while leaky roofs need to be fixed and crops harvested.

'To enjoy life is about the way you live in the present, moment by moment. It is a way of life. It is about how you choose to live around challenges and problems. While problems are inevitable, normal indeed, they typically sit in the background and only need to be given full attention from time-to-time. To enjoy is about how you live in the never-ending moment, in the gift of the present, around those inevitable problems in the background. It is about living moment by moment in good humour ready to appreciate the little wonders of day-to-day life. The goal is not necessarily to feel intense joy. The goal is just to use these little wonders to lift your mood just a little higher from where it otherwise might be. Use them to remind you not to take life too seriously.'

'The little wonders of life?' It was the General again.

'The wonder of a child's smile, a belly-laugh or a beautiful sunny day, are often overlooked. The Archangel paused and turned again to Francis. 'Do you recall the words of the poem from my anteroom entitled "In the Now"?'

'I do.'

'Would you be so kind as to also write them out and provide them to the Librarian?'

'Yes, Sir.'

'Whereas pleasure can be fleeting, and you can only dance with your Daimon some of the time, enjoyment, as I speak of it, is a way of life. To understand best what I am talking of, think about people who take life too seriously. People who have no sense of playfulness, no sense of humour, no sense of fun. When life is being taken too seriously, you are forgetting that you also came here to enjoy, to rejoice. You are here for fun … *for fun*!

'When you are taking life too seriously, you are living in the past, or worrying about the future, not appreciating the richness of the now, the present. If you do not live in the present, there is nothing to rejoice, the will be little to enjoy. If you do not live in the now, you will find yourself asking the question you have just asked - why live? When you greet your day, your partner or neighbour with joy in your heart to share, appreciation of the small wonders in that moment, all of this will make sense.'

'Is it not also about having new experiences? Did we not come here to have as many varied experiences as possible?' It was Anna of Austria who asked.

'A truth indeed,' Michael responded with a radiant smile. 'Yes, you incarnated primarily to have new experiences. New experiences are what follow from better questions. They make a quest a true quest, but if you have not learnt the art of enjoying and of being fully present in the moment, then you cannot appreciate your new experiences. They will be wasted. If new experiences are the seeds, you need the rain of being present in the now, and the sunshine of enjoyment, to make them grow into fullness.'

'Talk to us of love,' it was Catherine who spoke. 'As we evolve are we more able to access love? Is this what you mean when you talk about why we need to grow and evolve? Am I right in thinking that love is a key part of enjoying life, of living from a perspective of enjoyment?

'Yes, that is a big part of it. Immature souls find themselves more readily distressed by life here. Their time feeling the love from The Light is less frequent. You may connect with this love indirectly through loving and being loved by others, or connect directly with The Light through meditation, in its many forms. The more mature the soul, the more frequently it connects to The Light's love.

Anna from Austria asked the great angel, 'But, how do you define love?'

'In its essence, *True love is the feeling of being accepted without judgement by another who knows you intimately and is committed to nurturing both your personal growth and their own*. You can experience this love in many ways. It may be at the hands of a lifelong partner or a good friend. You may think you feel love in a brief encounter with a stranger. A stranger, however, cannot completely accept you, simply because they do not fully know you.

'Because the feeling is one of acceptance, you can imagine that the better someone knows you, the more powerful the feeling of being loved. Earlier in a relationship, the love remains in doubt because you know that the other does not see the fullness of who you are: strengths and weaknesses, aspirations and fears, capacity to do good and to do otherwise. Over time, over years, the other cannot help but to see the fullness of you.'

'Is that not a conflict, to accept someone just as they are, warts and all, but then want them to grow and change into something more?' Anna queried.

'At first glance it might appear so, but then there is that important word "nurturing." It means that one is not demanding of another's growth. Sun, soil and water do not demand the flower to blossom, but they are there to make it possible. The sun, soil and water are eternally patient. They demand nothing.

'In the same way, in a relationship one needs to be patient and ready to assist when the other desires to grow. Such a desire is inevitable for humans, but their partner must be patient. Again we come to this important word. In this way, patience is one of the greatest virtues. Impatience has the opposite effect. Impatiently pushing someone to grow when they are not ready, will not only fail, it will delay them coming to this desire themselves – sometimes for years.'

'That rings true. I see what you mean by this sense of remembering what I already know. Anna said. 'So how do you nurture this growth?'

'The best way to stimulate personal growth is given in the definition. There is no more powerful way to bring another to grow than to pursue this yourself. When you nurture your own growth, you awaken in those you care about, their desire to do likewise. In the most convincing way, you show that it is okay and important to do this for yourself. This is why nurturing one's own growth is such a critical part of loving.'

'Am I right in saying that this also encourages people to step away from the need to work and appear productive if they see another taking time to nurture themselves?' Dr Whitgift added.

'Yes, work appears to be a solution when often it is a distraction from higher challenges.'

Christian spoke, 'Sir, could I ask you to repeat your definition of love, so that I have it clear please.'

'Certainly, it is worth repeating. *True love is the feeling of being accepted without judgement by another who knows you fully and is committed to nurturing both your personal growth and their own.*'

'There is something else I would like to ask if I may?' It was Anna again.

'Please.'

'In this world we often find ourselves in relationships where we are not loved in this way. To tell someone the importance of a love they may not be able to access, may leave them feeling even more alone and sad.'

As she spoke, Francis heard the pain behind her words. He understood how high-born women were traded like cattle to create bonds between powerful families. They would be sent away from those who loved them into heartless marriages within different cultures.

'I am glad you raised this important point. All humans benefit if they connect with love. A connection has two ends. While it is nice to be on the receiving end, as you say, often this is not to be found. It is certainly not reliable.

'What is reliable, what is under your control, is the giving of true love. At any time you wish, you could find someone to love. Someone to accept without judgement. Someone you can nurture. Rarely do you need to travel far to find another who would benefit from your kindness and nurturance. Connecting from the giving end can be just as rewarding as connecting at the receiving end. Connecting from this end is available to all, reliably.'

'Thank you,' Anna said. 'That is very helpful.'

Michael returned to his topic, 'But there is another part to why you want to grow and expand. Growing itself is fun – it is the most sustainable of all forms of pleasure. The feeling of expansion, of knowing more, of being more capable feels good. This pleasure sustains us. On the other hand, the pleasure of a good meal with Catherine's wonderful wine …'

Catherine accepted the compliment with a smile.

'… just like pleasures of the flesh, can be intense, but they are fleeting, ephemeral, transitory. The feeling of growth is a deeper, longer-lasting happiness. Then, there is the highest form of growth. This form is accompanied by the highest most sustaining feelings of happiness. Mr Bacon, could you enlighten us please?'

Francis was unsure as to how to address the glorious creature smiling down on him, but he did know what he was being asked to talk about. It was so clear to him now. Clear from his time with The Duke, from the accepting, nurturing people he had spent this time with at The Mont. 'Sir, I have found myself wondering if eudaimonia, that feeling one gets when one is doing something meaningful that fits with one's purpose, is a form of the meditation. I think that the feeling is actually because one has opened a direct connection with The Light.'

The Archangel's smile was wondrous. 'By The Light! You have it in one. You are no more aligned with The Light than when you are in the midst of expressing your Daimon – the fullness of who you are. From this vantage point your life, and all its challenges, will make sense.'

Catherine spoke up. 'I see it now, in my work. I have always felt blessed to know how to care for others. Secretly, I have felt guilty about the pleasure it gives me, especially when I am paid for it.'

'That confuses many physicians and others who have found their Daimon and are enjoying their dance together,' Saint Michael said with a chuckle. 'Those of you who have discovered this sacred dance will often feel guilty as you watch those who struggle and cannot join you on the dance floor without their dancing partner. Without the dance there is only drudgery. Work that does not relate to your Daimon will truly be "hard work".'

It was Christian who spoke next. 'So what you are saying is that while pleasures will be fleeting and will not make us happy over time, there are two pursuits that will sustain us. First, there are the feelings that come from the appreciation and expression of our Daimon and this is our individual mix of interests and capabilities. The second thing that will lead to life satisfaction is the personal growth that goes with new experiences and overcoming challenges.'

'Yes and the two are often linked. When you understand how to give expression to your Daimon, the challenges you are then capable of taking on are truly glorious. The truth is that all of your prophets have known the deep rewards of taking on challenges of the highest order. These are the challenges that gave full expression to their Daimon. They came to you to nurture their own growth as much as to help you with yours – remember the definition of True Love. While they often experienced what you might have seen as great persecution and pain, they knew that pain is only in the eye of the beholder and adversity the greatest teacher.'

'You are boring me yet again, Mikey and wasting your breath.' Satan had been sitting patiently, regrouping, but his tone made it clear that his patience was at an end. He slowly stood and turned to address his old foe. 'Humans have been told this and much other knowledge of how best to live, many times over the last couple of thousand years. These drivelling, beetle-brained clotpoles are the slowest learning creatures in the universe. You can give them all our secrets and we could come back in another four hundred years and start all over again. This is why I am not concerned about them knowing how things work, they will forget it soon enough.'

The Devil started to warm to his subject. 'When one group finally gets it into their overly bony craniums, the next generation comes along and says, "Hey old man, what would you know? That might have worked for you but it is all different now." And it starts all over again. It would bore me to tears if I was capable of crying. God knows how you can stay so upbeat about it all,' he said looking at Michael.

Turning back to his audience, 'And yes I prefer the word "God." After all putting the fear of God into people is my favourite pastime. Besides, I designed the symmetry of removing one letter from good and adding one letter to evil to get "God" and "Devil". The spell of spelling is something we on both sides like to play with.'

Turning back to Michael, Satan pushed the point, 'When are you going to get it?! The human race does not bloody learn!!

Lucifer had hit a nerve. Michael knew he was right about the next generation's failure to carry the learnings forward.

Sensing the hesitation, the creature in black turned from his audience and moved to stand in front of his archenemy. His red eyes glowered as he stared into the face of his nemesis. With soft malevolence he whispered, 'Besides Brother, you and I have unsettled business.' The venom dripped from his voice.

'All in good time. I am almost done here.'

'NO!!' The very walls seemed to shake as Lucifer shouted the word out. 'You are not almost done. The bull shite stops now. They need to know the truth. The truth! Is that not a concept dear to your oh-so-large, loving, ever-forgiving, bottomless heart? I presume you are going to tell these narrow-minded simpletons why they need me. If you are going to waste your breath, you should at least waste it on the full truth!'

The Angel of Truth made as if to speak, but the Devil walked in front of him and took centre stage. 'On second thoughts, allow me to explain. You will wax on forever given half a chance.'

'The floor is yours,' Saint Michael said with forced graciousness.

XXVI THE IMPORTANCE OF EVIL

*The momentous thing in human life
is the art of winning the soul to good or evil.*

*The good things which belong
to prosperity are to be wished, but the
good things that belong to adversity are to be admired.*

Francis watched the interchange with fascination. It was as if the Devil was right about something. Something that both archangels knew to be true, that Saint Michael had been holding back on.

Lucifer spoke, 'Listen up you gorebellied, fool-born malt-worms. If it was not for me you would have nothing of worth. He paused to let his point sink in.

He spat the next words out slowly, 'Without me, your most rewarding challenge … your precious personal growth,' he delivered the last two words with dripping sarcasm, 'would not exist. Imagine a world without lust, greed, jealousy and hatred. Imagine a world where everyone is kind and caring with boundless generosity. At first glance it might sound attractive, but look more closely. Why aspire to anything if your generous neighbour will give it to you? How do you learn self-reliance if everyone cares and looks out for you? But most of all, think of the unending, interminable, unrelenting boredom!'

'You ask why souls incarnate? Think about it! They come from The Light where they are surrounded by eternal love, kindness and caring. Why do you think they leave this realm? Let me tell you. It is so uninspiring and boring Goddamnit! And I use that word advisedly. You came here for a challenge, something to triumph over. Guess who is in charge of the day-to-day challenges!

'You feeble-minded minnows have no idea of the value of what I give you and why I am here. I was not cast out. I was bored! I needed to save my soul. Nothing like a decent celestial battle to make life interesting!

'And tell me, who would want to hear a story of a world where everyone was ceaselessly nice to each other? Is this the kind of you tale are drawn to? I have watched you listen to your great storytellers for millennia and I can tell you the answer is No. The epic adventures that are retold are those that feature me and mine.

Francis had never thought of how a life of unending generosity, kindness and caring would be intolerably boring. He thought of Homer's epic tale "Odyssey" from the eighth century BC and how it still fascinated and was retold today. There would be no story to tell, he realised, if it were not for its evil characters.

'You have no idea how boring life was as an angel!! Nor did I want to stay. It is so much more fun down here messing with you lot! Thank your God that you never learn, that your following generations forget. This spiritual amnesia has kept me entertained for centuries. It is like telling an old woman, whose mind has gone, every morning that her favourite son has just died a slow painful death. It is so wonderful to watch the reaction! Talk about fun and enjoyment!

'But here is the point. You puny-minded humans cannot grow and prove yourselves without me and my rather excellent work. There is an art to what I do. The highest form of my art is war – getting entire countries to battle each other on a massive scale. Religious wars are my crowning achievements. There is no heartache like the absolute carnage they create. Just think on it for a moment! How brilliant am I to get religions, based on loving one's neighbour, to kill their neighbour in the name of love? In the name of "God". I think that rather clever.'

The Devil chuckled with obvious delight. For the moment, he seemed to have forgotten about his issues with Michael.

Despite the putdowns and vitriol, Francis, for one, wanted to hear what he had to say. This was a perspective on life that he had not heard before. He was fascinated to see that Saint Michael had taken the seat occupied by the Devil only minutes before. It was as if they were taking turns in some sacred debate. Moreover, it was as if Michael had no great disagreement as Lucifer went on ...

'With a religious war, one can rape the daughters in front of their parents, then rape the mothers and then kill them in front of their husbands. Killing the sons shifts from being a terrible atrocity to a strategic way of ensuring the other side's armies are crippled for years – and all in the name of God! Your God of course, not that of the other side's. Their God is clearly the wrong God. It is bloody genius if I say so myself!'

'You always were the modest one.' Saint Michael threw in from the side.

'Yes, I know what you are thinking: That was what started you and me fighting in the first place! You are probably right, but at least I admit to my pride in myself and in what I do. Look at you and Jesus and Buddha, you all love the feeling of growing, of being guides to the masses. You said it yourself. To love these poor wretches, you have to nurture your own growth. You do it because it makes you feel better, it gives you enjoyment. Humans just happen to benefit from it – or at least they think they benefit from it. That is what you said to these misguided fools sitting before us was it not? And as we know, their children will forget. If they do not, their children's children certainly will.'

Michael did not respond.

Lucifer turned his steely, red gaze over the audience and as it passed over Catherine it left her feeling cold inside.

'I am growing too. I am getting better and better at what I do. I enjoy my growth. But forget wars, although that is me at my best, you all know my work on a daily basis. Succeed at what you want to do and someone will become jealous of you. They can make your life truly miserable if they are good at what they do – if they are good students of mine. There is something to challenge you all in your quests to pursue your purpose. While wars are my crowning glories, jealousy is my pièce de résistance, my finest, most insidious work. Jealousy brings down neighbours, great people, even countries.

'And then I have other emotions to cultivate in humans like hatred, fear, anguish, revenge and aggression. This is my purpose, my passion, my destiny. Without me and my work, your growth and ultimate happiness, as Mikey has so eloquently pointed out to you, would be unattainable.

'You fear failure, you fear pain and you fear death. More often than you realise, you fear success. Look more closely in the looking glass at these times and you might just glimpse me standing at your shoulder.'

'Would I be right in saying someone has to do my job Mikey? I am not sure you would have the stomach for it. You only fight well when it is for someone else. I have often wondered if that is because you do not think enough of yourself,' Lucifer taunted.

Saint Michael just smiled back at his counterpart. He refused to be baited.

The Devil went on. 'Someone has to inspire the small-minded, power-hungry war-mongers. Without my evil there could be no heroism, no great acts of personal sacrifice. Think about it, how could there be any hero if everyone was loving and caring. Who could stand up and be counted if there was nothing to count for? Without my influence, natural disasters like storms, floods, earthquakes and volcanic eruptions were your only opportunities to be heroes.

'As you have learnt to not build on flood plains and build stronger houses and to come in out of the rain – yes I will give you that you are not absolute and total fools – these opportunities are less frequent. When they do come, they are the more simple challenges of life. They pale into insignificance compared to the challenges that true evil can create in your life. Natural disasters are nothing like what I can offer you.

'As I have said, think of your great stories. They need a great villain. A great storm is not enough. The stories most retold are about me, my protégés and our work. You need me to inspire them and give you something meaningful to triumph over.

'In between my wars and the world's natural disasters and diseases, I give you the daily opportunity to find the better person within you. More than once I have given you, and will again give you, seven great gifts:

'I give you lust so that you might find your fidelity.

'I give you greed so that you might discover your capacity for charity.

'I give you gluttony so that you might find temperance.

'I give you sloth so that you might develop diligence.

'I give you wrath so that you might find patience and forgiveness.

'I give you envy so that you might develop your generosity of spirit.

'I give you pride so that you might develop your humility.

'Think deeply on what I am saying. How could you possibly develop the virtues of which I speak without my gifts of sin and temptation in the first place? It is simply not possible for what you most admire to exist without me and my work. It is an essence of life. To lament the presence of evil in your life would be like lamenting the presence of fire. Yes it can burn, destroy and cause suffering, but it is the building block of warmth, light and cooking.' At this point Lucifer turned to face Saint Michael, 'Am I not correct?'

There was a long pause as the Archangel and the ex-Archangel faced-off. The one in black moved his fighting hand to his huge sword.

The emerald green wings twitched as if to flare. With some resignation Michael finally said, 'As unusual as it may seem, on this matter you speak the truth.'

Satisfied, the Angel in black spun on his heel and faced his audience again. 'It is good to finally have the truth outed. I think you can now see how your lives would be significantly poorer without me!'

'Although, let us be clear here,' Michael interrupted, 'we both know that you do not give the temptation of the sins to make people better people. Your hope is to corrupt them.'

'Absolutely,' Satan said with grin, 'I have my work to do and I so love my work!'

Lucifer turned. His eyes drilled straight into Francis causing him to flinch. 'You, young man, owe me. This night you are a hero. Women will admire you. Beyond this, what you have learnt in confronting your own soul in the face of evil has brought you courage and confidence. This admiration would have been much harder to come by, or indeed not come by at all, if you had had no evil to stand up against. You may thank me later. Maybe you should pray to me!' He chuckled at the thought, 'Now that would be a nice change! Maybe you could try something like this:

'Our Lucifer, who outgrew heaven

Hallowed be thy name

Thy Kingdom come

Thy will be done on earth

As you have given

Give us this day our daily challenges

And forgive us our failure

To recognise that without you

Courage and confidence could not be ours

And lead us into temptation

And deliver us more evil

So that we have something worthy to overcome

For ours is the kingdom
The power and the glory
Thanks be to you Lucifer
Amen'

The angel laughed raucously at his version of the Lord's Prayer. Francis could not help but smile. The Turks were laughing out loud. Even The Bishop was chuckling. Satan was enjoying himself. Then he changed horses.

'But there is a greater example of how I give the world heroes, of how I give the world inspirational figures. You, Mikey are my best example!'

'Think on it. If it were not for me, you would not be heralded through Christendom as the greatest hero of all. Our battle and you getting the credit for me leaving that God-boring place you call heaven has made you revered the world over. You owe me more so than anyone!'

Michael thought of pointing out that he had fought Lucifer for all that was good, but realised that, it was not the point. Satan was simply saying that the battle had made him famous, and an inspiration to others, and that was true.

With his own sarcasm, the Archangel replied, 'Remind me to learn your new prayer.'

XXVII ALCHEMY

*The fortune which nobody sees
makes a person happy and unenvied.*

'As one who is at the very centre of the process of causing people pain and suffering, let me share something with you all. Remember I have seen it all. No one is more qualified to speak on this.'

The Devil had more to say. It seemed as if he wanted to teach, just like Saint Michael. Indeed, it was like another level of competition between the two. Here they were competing to see who had the more important knowledge to share. Francis realised that the Archangel and his fallen compatriot had as much in common as they had that was different.

'There are souls that run from me in fear and those that are not at all difficult for me to tempt and corrupt. Then there are those who stand up to me, who resist temptation. Would you like me to tell you how this latter group differ?'

He had their attention. Several could not help themselves but nod. The opportunity to understand evil and how to manage it at its very core was lost on none of them.

'You see when you are scared, having the feeling of fear is not the problem – that is normal. Indeed, it is the fool who has no fear, who does not realise the fullness of his situation. No – it is what you *think and do* next. Do you give into the fear, or do you exercise your free will and act? Do you let your fear feed greater fear, or do you rein it in? Do you surrender to your fear or exercise your ultimate freedom?' Satan paused again. 'Do you even know what your ultimate freedom is?'

He stopped, enjoying the moment. No one spoke up, more from fear of the unwanted attention than anything else. They all understood now that their fear would make them vulnerable to the dark angel's wrath and would rather avoid the test. The role of the subject under discussion – fear – in this very interaction was not lost on Francis. This was definitely not a teacher who suffered fools lightly!

'As much as, at one level, it pains me, I will tell you. No one, but no one – me included – *can make you feel anything, most of all fear*. To be more specific, I can frighten you, but where you then take it is up to you. How do I know this? Well, for a rather long time I have been frightening people, literally millions of them. I have been mastering my craft since before recorded time. I have seen it all. To the same threat, people respond differently. Most become drivelling, milk-livered imbeciles.

'From time to time, I come across someone, who in the face of that same threat, gathers themself and pulls their fear completely back. They look me in the eye and do what needs to be done. And then, there are all positions in between.

'At first, I thought it strange, but then I realised that ultimately you have the freedom as to whether you allow your initial fear to grow or recede. The initial fear is much the same, it is how you then decide to manage it that is all-important.

'How you manage your initial fear is the test of fortitude – another good word. Where a mental fortress is created by one's attitude – hence "fortitude". It is how you choose to think of the fear – whether you decide to feed it or starve it. Then, most importantly, it is how you act that determines how much of a hold it will have over you.

'Many are not even aware that they have this capability. They are the easiest of you to deal with. Those who see me as "putting the fear into them" or any other emotion, like jealousy or hatred, are the easiest to control. They have no idea of their freedom. They have no idea that how they react is up to them. If you think you are imprisoned, then you are as imprisoned as any jail bars could ever make you. Indeed,' Lucifer enunciated each word with care, 'my greatest weapon is the mind of the scared.'

'The ultimate freedom is how you choose to respond in the face of fear. First and foremost, you need to know that how you continue to respond to any emotion you start to feel is not a given. So many of you think that once an emotion is triggered in you, you have no control or influence over it.

'Where you then take your initial emotional response is your ultimate right that no one can take from you. It is the one thing even I respect. As you might imagine, there are few men whom I respect. If anything, there are more women I respect. Men are too used to fighting with their bodies to develop the mindset of the true warrior. Most whimper like lambs when they are maimed, when they cannot fight the only way they know how. Because women rely less on their physical strength and fighting skills, they have learnt to fight more successfully with their minds. They are often more skilled in the art of fortitude.'

'Excuse me err …. Lucifer,' it was The Bishop who spoke, 'why are you prepared to share this with us? Why would you let us know how this works?'

'What is in it for me, you ask? What? You do not believe I am giving you this out of the goodness of my angel heart?' Lucifer laughed. You are The Bishop are you not?'

In that moment The Bishop felt very vulnerable. He was not at all sure where this was going. Nevertheless, he saw no point in trying to hide his identity. He gave a little nod.

'Of course you are. If there is one reason why I am happy to share this with you, it is because I would like to face more worthy adversaries in future. Even down here, my life can get boring at times. Cowards are boring. I look forward to doing battle with any human who can manage their fear when I get fired up.'

'Lucifer, if I may. I would like to finish what we have started to discuss today and then I will give you what I know you came here for.' The Archangel of The Light walked slowly back to stand in front of those gathered. His sword hand rested lightly on the elaborate pommel of his glowing sword.

The Angel in black, paused and turned to face him. Francis watched closely as they stood toe to toe. There was no fear evident on Michael's face. The tension, having decreased in the room as Lucifer had spoken to the gathering, was now back.

'Be my guest,' the black Angel said overly graciously, 'but make haste. You and I still have a score to settle and I grow impatient.' As he spoke, Satan clenched and unclenched his hand around the handle of his sword as if he was anxious to draw it.

Michael ignored the threat. Turning to his audience once more he announced, 'I made a promise some time ago to talk about a process that is as old as time itself. Alchemy.'

The Archangel let the word hang in the air. 'I am going to share with you all a knowledge and practice that is older than we are,' he said, gesturing to the ex-Archangel. 'So, what exactly is alchemy?' Michael asked his audience.

It was Christian who responded. 'Is it not the practice of making gold from simple metals like lead or tin?'

'Yes, this is what is believed. As with so many of your religious teachings, the metaphors have been taken as literal truth. The metaphor is about taking something, apparently of little value, and turning it into something of great value. Riddle me this. What costs you nothing, can never be depleted and the more you give away the richer yours become?'

No one answered.

'Ideas. People waste their time looking for gold or work hard to create wealth, when the resource they seek is available from within. Let me take an example from your recent history – The Templars. At their peak, they had amassed greater wealth than all that held by the Kings and Queens of their time combined. What sat behind their huge wealth? Indeed, we have someone who knows much about the Templars with us.' Turning to the bald-headed man Saint Michael asked, 'Monsieur d'Anjou, would you be so kind as to share with us the ideas that generated the Templars' wealth.'

'It would be my pleasure, Michael.' The Templar seemed to have no trouble addressing the Archangel as if they were old friends. 'Besides they are not secrets. They are there for any students of history.'

'What was the idea that lead to more wealth than people are capable of imagining?'

'Well like most successful ideas, this one was prompted by others coming to us. After we began escorting pilgrims and their belongings to the Holy Land, we were asked by merchants if we would take their goods with us. Then they began asking us to take their gold to purchase goods at the other end. Once it became known that we were transporting gold, we became more of a target than before. We did take heavier losses as greed drove more attacks on the travellers, but in the end, our knights reigned supreme. Merchants were happy to pay us a percentage of their gold if we moved it safely. Nobody was as reliable as we were.

'Eventually, one of the early Templars put up the idea that instead of carrying the gold, we carry a note of promise. So, a merchant travelling from Paris to Jerusalem would deposit his gold with us in Paris and be given the note of promise. When the merchant, or his agent, took the note to our men in Jerusalem, we would give him the gold from our reserves there, knowing that the gold had been deposited with our monks in Paris.

'In this way we had effectively moved gold from Paris to Jerusalem without having to risk it on the journey. As transactions were made in the opposite direction and gold was delivered into our holdings in Jerusalem, we rarely had to move any actual gold at all.

275

We also realised that we were the only trusted organisation that spanned multiple countries. No monarch in Christendom could offer such a service. No other organisation was as trusted or had people in every country in the world. The Promissory Note, as it came to be called, was a simple idea that was the beginning of our real wealth.'

'And how much hard work was involved for the Templars with this new service?' The Archangel asked, clearly knowing the answer.

'Yes, that is the best part. It was much less work actually. It was much harder, indeed deadlier, work defending the gold we had been physically transporting.'

'Did you charge the same money as you were when you were physically moving the gold?'

'Yes, and people were happy to pay it to us. Indeed, with the move to Promissory Notes we had many more people banking their gold with us.'

'In fact, were you not the first organisation to earn a million pounds since this currency was established in the eighth century? And so, your wealth increased as your work demands decreased.'

'That is correct Michael.'

'Listen all. The Templars personify alchemy. Never in the history of the world has such enormous wealth been created,' his voice softened, '… and from what? From something cheaper than even lead or tin! A wealth that was more than most dream of having, was created from nothing but good ideas, from thoughts. They were then mixed with a tincture of something that was necessary to bring forward the wealth. Did anyone hear it?'

'It was trust, Michael,' Catherine said, 'The essence of integrity.'

'Precisely. Jean, tell us more about that word "trust" that you spoke of? How important was that in creating the wealth your organisation amassed?'

'It was Critical. The entire process relied on trust. Without trust there was no business, at least no sustainable business.'

'So how did you build this trust?'

'It was there from the start. People knew that we had an ideal that was higher than creating wealth – the wealth was a by-product of doing a good thing. One of our primary goals was to safeguard people in their pilgrimage. If people could trust us with their wives and children, they could trust us with their gold.'

Michael turned to his audience. 'Never forget that point: wealth is a by-product of trust, of doing a good thing, or of selling a good product for a fair price. For those who see wealth as the primary goal, it will either elude them, or come and then go.'

'But it went further than that,' The Templar added. 'The trust and our values then lead to our greatest material assets. People, who shared our values and appreciated our services, bequeathed their estates to us. Ironically, the idea that led to the creation of Poor Knights of Christ and the Temple of Solomon made we "poor knights" more wealthy than our forefathers could have imagined. We ended up with enough land across Christendom that, had it been in the one place, we would have owned a country the size of France.'

'Thank you Jean. We are most indebted to you for your openness.' Turning back to the room, he went on. 'Most people will say something like, "Ahh, but that opportunity has passed. If only I had been there then, maybe I could have alchemised that idea into gold." Let me assure you that there are always opportunities. As your society evolves, new ideas are needed. Most people let most of the opportunities, begging to be married to a good idea, pass them by.

'A final point on this matter. By what process do we access and create better ideas? … Mr Bacon?'

'By asking better questions, Sir.' Francis answered on cue.

'With respect m'Lord, what about the demise of The Templars?' Dr Whitgift asked. 'With their good ideas and their trust, what went wrong?'

'It is the nature of all things to be created, blossom and then die. Only the length of this cycle can be changed. Few organisations will ever run for as long as the more than two hundred years of The Templars. It is possible, but over time, new and very different ideas are needed. They made the mistake of doing more of what they had been doing. Two centuries later, they needed very different ideas from those they were initially comfortable with. Ideas that answered questions like: How to respond to the jealousy of the powerful Kings who were now very, very indebted to them?

'Typically, the people who run established, successful organisations well, are not of the mindset required to bring new life to them. Two centuries later, The Templars were being run by elders with very different mindsets from the founders. They came from the position of maintaining, not creating. They relaxed into their success – this is the usual danger. The growing threats were not fully recognised. Even if they had recognised the threats created by envy and the indebtedness of monarchs, this would not have been enough.

'Their only hope was to bring in smart young blood, hungry for new opportunities, new ways to operate. But the young have to be prepared to learn the lessons the elders have to teach. From this position, they then adapt the enterprise to their new world. To achieve this mix is very difficult. Lucifer was correct when he said that your young typically dismiss what has gone before as being out of date and irrelevant. For this reason the learned elders are often reluctant to bring them in. So, the Templars' business slowly weakened. Eventually, it weakened to the point where those of the jealousy could act.'

'Nice work of mine that, if I do say so myself,' Lucifer threw in with a laugh. 'As I said jealousy is my pièce de résistance.'

Michael ignored him, 'This is one reason why you have limited life spans. If you lived longer, you, not just your enterprises, would evolve more slowly. Humans are not good at changing established beliefs, despite overwhelming evidence to the contrary. To grow, evolve and allow new thinking you need to have those with the old beliefs die off. New beliefs need fresh, cleared soil to flourish.

'You need the Prince or Princess to take over from the King or Queen. "The King is dead, long live the King," is all about this process. The only question that will determine the new King's success is: How much did he learn from his Father? The best that can be hoped for is that the new reign takes the best of the old learnings, while adapting itself to the new world it finds itself in. Unfortunately, as my old colleague has pointed out, often the baby is thrown out with the bathwater.'

'The greatest learning from history is that men do not learn from history,' Lucifer chimed in with a sneer.

'Perhaps it is. But then, the real power of knowledge, of learning, is not that it gives you the answers you seek. The real power is that it nurtures the capacity to ask better questions that match an evolving world. Have faith that with the right question, the answers will come. Better questions beget better ideas. These ideas will take you to your true prosperity and make your whole life rich. This is true alchemy. Remember, your true wealth will not be gold or currency, it will be the capacity to create it, your capacity to generate the ideas.

'As time is running short for me I cannot speak further on the matter of alchemy, particularly as it relates to wealth. If you would like to understand more on creating wealth, speak with Catherine, or The Templar, both are masters in this matter.'

'Some time ago now, I promised that if this island was built upon, I would bring you the secrets of alchemy. Tonight I have fulfilled that promise. I have, however, one last point I need to share with you before this visit, is done. My fallen brother here,' he said gesturing to Lucifer, 'left out an important point before. He wants the truth out. Let me do so.'

The Lord of the Dark looked up and threw a smouldering, questioning look at his counterpart.

'His power and influence over people comes through playing on their fear, greed and insecurities.'

'I thought I had made that clear,' Lucifer responded, his voice dripping with sarcasm, 'any ten-year-old could understand the point.'

'Maybe, but what every ten-year-old does not know is how to disarm you when confronted by you. That little part you somehow managed to leave out. I am guessing it just slipped your mind.'

Michael turned to the audience before him. 'He has told you to manage your fear. That his greatest weapon is a scared mind. This is true, but he has not told you what you actually do. An important point he neglected to explain. This is why he needs a henchman, because if you do what I am about to tell you he is powerless.

'I warn you. Go no further Michael,' a demonic hiss crept into his low voice.

Saint Michael appeared unperturbed by the obvious threat.

'Whenever you are confronted by the Devil, simply turn your back on him and walk on. Do not run in fear. Harness your fortitude and calmly walk on to do what you need to do. Do this and he will be unable to touch you. This takes all power from him. While it is different between us angels, this works between angels and humans. The same goes for his tools of the temptations such as lust, gluttony, greed and envy. Turning your back as you walk on, to do what is right for you, signals you have managed your emotions and you refuse the temptation targeted at you.

'When he spoke before of managing your emotional response and carefully choosing your next action, this is the ultimate form of this teaching. It is a very old strategy of enormous power. The saying, "to turn your back and walk away," holds magical power. It ...'

The Archangel never got the words out as a roar came from his eternal foe. 'Enough. I have let this foolish charade go on far too long. I have played along while you have wasted my time with these snivelling, ill-begotten maggots. Now you go too far. I may not be able to take my sword to them but with you, it gives me great pleasure. En guard!'

Francis remembered the account of the great celestial battle between these two generals that The Big Man had given him and the children not long after he had arrived. He realised that while humans could turn their back on the Devil and walk away unharmed, an angel could indeed kill another angel. The battle between the army of Michael's angels and that of Lucifer's had taken a significant toll on the angel population.

One moment it was not there, the next, the black sword was out and in Lucifer's hand. The blade was a strange black. Whereas the hilt with its inlaid black diamonds gleamed in the light, the blade did not. It was as if all light was drawn into the metal and none escaped. With similar speed, The Blade of Truth appeared in Michael's hand. Whereas the black sword seemed to suck light, its counterpart seemed to generate light.

Lucifer went straight into the attack.

Once more, their wings were extended. With slight movements, the wings were used to help their balance. Lucifer was fast, light on his feet, a clear match for the Archangel. The blades moved so fast that the eleven pairs of eyes in the room could only see the points of contact. This was because sparks flew from the Sword of Truth as it made contact with its dark equivalent. The spectacle was made stranger by the absence of the usual sound of blade clashing blade. Instead, there was a crackle of sparks, like small lightning strikes, with every contact between the mighty swords.

They paused circling each other, sizing each other up. 'You do not need to do this Lucifer, as we have discussed, there is room for both of us in this world – a need for both the light and the dark.'

'There is undoubtedly a need for me, but you? No. The world can survive quite happily with one less do-gooder. Your end is nigh. By these eleven as my witness, I am here to show the world who is really the greatest, most powerful of all the archangels. The world wants inspirational heroes? Under my rule the world will want for many more heroes. I will give them a need to exist. That ... I can graciously accommodate,' Lucifer cackled at his generosity.

'You never got over your defeat did you?'

'Let us just call that round one shall we? Tonight we finish this.'

Lucifer moved in quickly. In a flurry of attacks, he came at his ancient enemy. He went for his opponent's chest. Michael's quick block pushed Satan's black blade down and to Michael's left. Lucifer let the blade go with the block and then swung it around and up to come in at Michael's neck. The strike was designed to kill. Michael's sword was there glancing the sword away, but it struck him in the top of his left arm. The cut started to bleed, but it was not like human blood, it was like liquid light. While a sword wielded by a human could not hurt an angel, it was a different matter when it came to the sword of another angel.

'You have lost your edge Mikey. Doing good and teaching little boys to play knight have made you soft. You should spend more time fighting your equals! That is where you learn to really fight!' Lucifer mocked.

'We shall see.' Michael responded quietly and evenly.

Lucifer brought the attack again, thrusting and striking first high and then low. Michael's sword was there to parry and block. He stepped backwards, away from the windows, towards the entrance door allowing the ex-Angel to advance.

Francis and Christian could see that, for the first time, the being they had known as The Duke, had a real fight on his hands. The ex-archangel in black pressed the attack. On the defence, Michael was pushed back towards the door and the forward left hand corner of the room.

Francis looked at Christian. Why was Michael allowing himself to be worked into a corner? He had drummed into them never to allow this to happen. Lucifer smiled with confidence as he advanced. He slowed the speed of his thrusts as if he was toying with Michael.

As the Archangel backed up against the wall beside the door, Lucifer lunged with a powerful thrust to the chest. Michael blocked with a backhanded upsweep of the Sword of Truth. Sparks crackled as the lethal weapons smashed together. As their blades crossed in front of them, Michael relaxed his own sword bringing Lucifer closer. His left arm closed around Lucifer's neck and brought him into a clench with their swords flat across their chests. For a moment, neither could harm the other.

Nose to nose, evenly matched in height, the two great angels faced off as close as lovers in an intimate dance.

'Time for you to leave these good people,' Michael said with a smile. A shadow of doubt flitted across Lucifer's face as the Michael brought his left hand around from behind the black-winged Angel's neck. With an explosion of force, using the wall behind him as a backstop, Michael's wings came together propelling him off the wall. At the same time, the back of both his fists drove into Lucifer's chest with the power of a cannon ball fresh from the barrel. With the combined force of Michael's wings springing off the wall and his muscled arms, the ex-Archangel was thrown across the room. The force was such that he exploded a hole in the stone wall beside the window. He disappeared from view.

Christian and Francis exchanged knowing glances as they realised they had just seen one of The Duke's strategies at work – letting one's opponent become overly confident.

Saint Michael turned to speak to those gathered. He knew that he only had a moment. Most sat with their mouths open, agog at the rapid unfolding of events as the two heavenly beings battled for supremacy. It seemed surreal, except for the very real hole in the wall.

The Turks were the first on their feet, as the Archangel spoke, 'This brings our time to an end. My old friend and I have some unfinished business that we need to attend to. Reflect on what we have discussed here this night. Return to your worlds, as I must to mine, and do what you can to care for your fellow travellers in this life. Show them the way of The Quest. The Light knows they could use some guidance. Most of all, teach the children – boy and girl alike – they must remember. Now I must take my leave. My fallen brother will come for me if I do not go to him.'

On cue, a demonic voice, full of rage called from outside under the light of the full moon. 'MICHAEL!!'

The Archangel bowed deeply and graciously to his audience. Bringing his sword vertically in front of him with the blade touching his forehead, he intoned, 'May The Light flow through you all.' He turned and dived out the hole in the wall. As one, the eleven remaining men and women rushed to the windows. Francis went to the Angel-sized hole in the wall.

Five hundred yards away Lucifer was hovering in the air. Moonlight reflected off his shiny black wings. As his enemy came out he yelled, 'Come on. Let me make your existence more interesting. Prepare to lose your wings.'

Michael hovered at the same height. They eyed each other off as they slowly backed away from each other. Lucifer was more wary now. Suddenly, in the same moment, their heads went down and like powerful hunting birds they swooped towards each other at speed, accelerating as they went, their swords out in front. The point of impact was marked by a full lightning strike accompanied by the crackle of thunder. And then there was nothing. The sky was empty. Several, smaller lightning bolts crackled before the sky went quiet. The Archangel and the Fallen One had flipped into the heavenly dimension to continue their eternal battle.

There was silence in the room. All eyes were on the sky that was now empty. It took a moment for their minds to process what they had just seen, let alone the events of the last half hour. The explosion of Lucifer through the wall had brought The Big Man back in to the room. He came up to his wife and Francis. He put an arm around her shoulder obviously relieved to see she was all right. 'Well there is another story to tell,' he said softly, 'you must both fill in the details for me.'

Francis looked over his shoulder as Marguerite's Ladies-in-waiting rushed in. With concerned voices, they hustled her out. She threw a quick glance at Francis and for a moment, their eyes met. Francis was anxious to go after her, but the Templar and Dr Whitgift collared him.

The Templar spoke, 'Mr Bacon, we would like a word.'

'Certainly Sir.'

'We would like you to become a Templar. It is a great honour, as you can only become one of us if two of us sponsor you. This we are prepared to do.'

Despite the honour, Francis was only half-listening, his eyes pulling towards the door. She was gone. He resigned to see her first thing in the morning. She could not refuse to see him after the events of this night. He turned back to the two men …

XXVIII DEAR FRANCIS

Are not the pleasures of the intellect
greater than the pleasures of the affections?

Is not knowledge a true and only natural
pleasure, whereof there is no satiety?

After the events of the night, Francis' sleep was crowded with dreams. He witnessed heavenly battles between the forces of The Dark and The Light. At times Marguerite's serene face would appear – lit like that of an Angel. Then there was a disturbing dream of Gaspard dying with Francis' knife in his throat. It was his red eyes burning into him that awoke him in a sweat. While he did not regret his actions, he appreciated that you did not kill a man without some emotional cost. When he finally got back to sleep, he had a less intense dream.

He was back in the huge library. It was the one from the dream that he had shared with Dr Clost in the coach on their way to The Mont. He was seated in front of the leather-bound book. The quill and the inkpot were beside it. Last time he had run from it in fear with his demon chasing him. This time there was a calmness to the experience. His demon was gone, at least for the moment. The first line was there as before: 'Grant me the gift of insight to know my truest ability.' His attention was on the four new lines below this:

Beware those pursuits that I am good at
That do not serve what is of meaning to me
For in time they shall frustrate and delay me
From my quest and true purposes in this life

While he knew not from whence the words came, he felt them with strong emotion. Francis did not need Dr Clost to interpret the dream or the words. He remembered the physician's advice to note the emotions in the dream. He remembered the peacefulness he felt as he sat in front of the book and how different this was from his last visit to the library. Clearly, he was in a different place after his time at The Mont. This is what personal growth looks and feels like, he thought. Then there was the emotional charge in the words as he read them.

With the late hour and his unsettled rest, he had then overslept. The drama of the night's experience had quickly dissolved as his day had unfolded. He had meant to be up early. He had wanted to write down the words from the book in his dream, but on awakening he had dressed and rushed to Marguerite's quarters. While he had not dared to visit her before, he knew exactly where she resided.

He arrived to find a maid sweeping the floors. He asked if her Lady was in.

'No m'Lord, they left at first light as the tide was soon to come in.'

'NO! Francis cried as he rushed to look out the nearest window. The tide was now well and truly in. There was no way to defeat the Mont's most powerful defence. It had kept entire armies at bay – now it kept him prisoner and apart from Marguerite. No amount of boundless love could prevail against Mother Nature.

Feeling empty, he walked aimlessly back to his little room. The bustling life and colour of the Grand Rue held nothing for him. It was as if his world had turned a lifeless grey.

While he had been at the meeting the night before, a letter had been pushed under his door. It was from the Ambassador. After meeting with The Templar and Dr Whitgift, he had felt dog-tired. He had resolved to read it first thing the next morning.

Through his dejection, he remembered the letter he had put under his pillow. He reached for it and that was when his day went from bad to devastating.

Dear Francis

It is with a heavy heart that I give you these tidings. I barely mentioned to the Queen in a dispatch that I sent the day after I received your letter, that you had an interest in Queen Marguerite. I saw it as of little matter. I have just received an urgent dispatch by return.

I am very sorry to say that, in the most strong terms, she has forbidden you from consorting with Queen Marguerite at any level. As you know, Mary Queen of Scots remains the primary threat to the Queen's reign. These last nine years that she has been under house arrest at her Majesty's pleasure, have caused our Queen much nervousness. No other rival holds a right to the throne as strong as Mary. What you may not know is that Marguerite and Mary grew up sharing the same bedroom suites. From the age of five, with her betrothal to the next King of France, Mary spent thirteen years at the French court. Marguerite spent the first seven years of her life knowing and treating Mary as a big sister! Mary and Marguerite have remained loyal friends with ongoing correspondence. In short, the friend of the enemy of Queen Elizabeth is your enemy.

On this matter she clearly will not be moved. You must also know of the low regard that our Queen holds for Marguerite's mother – the one she refers to as "The Black Queen." In light of these matters, your beloved might as well reside on the moon.

Indeed, our Queen seems quite annoyed by the matter and displeased with both of us. She has now instructed that in due course I am to become Mary's custodian – a chore I do not look forward to.

I fear this is not what you had hoped to hear and for that, I am truly sorry.

When will we see you here at the French court in Paris?

Yours faithfully,
Sir Amyas Paulet

What had he done to deserve this? Francis fell back on his bed and fought to stop the tears from flowing. Francis' mind went back to the words his mother had used in their fateful meeting before he had left England: '... the Black Queen nurtured my greatest enemy.' At the time, he did not know their meaning. Nothing less than the deep, old and pervasive enmity between the English and its French and Scottish neighbours stood between him and Marguerite. Two of England's greatest enemies. Even if he could win her love ... it had no future. It was as if his world, for the second time in only a few months, was caving in on him.

There was a soft knock at the door.

Francis did not want to see anyone. 'Come in.'

The knock came again. He realised he had spoken with so little energy that the person outside had not heard him. Dragging his feet, he walked across and opened the door. It was young Josephine from next door.

'Hello Francis. Madame Catherine asked me to give you this. She had to go to the prison. Someone is very sick. But she said that a waiting-lady left this for you early this morning while you were asleep.'

Francis almost cried out as he realised that Josephine was talking of Marguerite's lady-in-waiting. He just about snatched the letter from her small hand. 'Thank you Josephine, thank you.' He had to stop himself from shutting the door in her face as he turned and opened the missive. Although he had never seen it before, he knew the soft, flowing script could only have come from one, perfectly-shaped, delicate hand.

My Dearest Poet

I am sorry I could not see you before I had to leave. After the events of last night, I am told that I am no longer safe here and must return to court.

Thank you for the sonnet you sent me. Fortunately, Mary was the one to receive it and she passed it over. Your words made my throat close and my heart ache.

And then, there was last night. I think there were three angels in the room last night – with you my Guardian. I long for you to put your arms around me again. You have my heart.

Come to Paris.

M

Francis did not need a third signpost. It was time to return to Paris.

Epilogue

Francis Bacon's own recollections of his trip to France:

'So with much interested, though sometimes apprehensive mind, I made myself ready to accompany Sir Amyas to that sunny land of the south I learned so supremely to love, that afterwards I would have left England and every hope of advancement to remain my whole life there. Nor yet could this be due to the delights of the country by itself, for love of sweet Marguerite, the beautiful young sister of the King, did make it Eden to my innocent heart."

Uncrowned: A story of Queen Elizabeth and the early life of Francis "Bacon"

by CYC Dawbarn, 1913

Afterword - The Backstory
The Parentage Question

This story plays with the idea that Francis Bacon was the son of Queen Elizabeth. Since being asserted by several authors, this has raised some fascinating questions. While there is evidence in favour of the notion, the primary argument against the assertion is how could Queen Elizabeth possibly have hidden a pregnancy? How might it have been orchestrated? If there is an answer, I believe it is not about the 'how'. In matters of the heart, it is always about the 'who'.

When one looks at the people around the Queen at the time, and their close relationships to each other, the 'who' becomes evident and the 'how' follows. In Chapter Two, I outline the close relationships between the Queen and Francis Bacon's purported father and mother, Sir Nicholas and Anne Bacon.

As you have seen, it was a tight knit, inter-related, loyal group in the immediate circle of the Queen. The Queen's most senior advisor, William Cecil, effectively the equivalent of a Prime Minister today, was married to Anne Bacon's sister. They were the keepers of the secret – well practiced at keeping secrets of state with a clear loyalty to each other. Through knowing the relationships between the players in this real life drama of intrigue and secrets, the truth might be allowed out.

In considering the evidence, allow me to start with the following from a letter written by Lady Anne Bacon in 1593. It was sent to her son Anthony and refers to her relationship with Francis. She wrote: "... it is not my meaning to treat him as a ward: Such a word is far from my Motherly feeling for him. I mean to do him good." She is very clear here about the word 'ward' and her next sentence removes any doubt that she might have been using it loosely to refer to a biological son. She is arguing that despite being a 'ward' she has a deep 'motherly' affection for him. While this letter tells us that

Francis was not her biological son, it does not tell us who his mother was.

Several authors have uncovered historical accounts that, together, paint a reasonably complete picture. The six primary writers in this matter are Dr Orville Ward Owen (*Sir Francis Bacon's Cipher Story*, 1893); Parker Woodward (*Tudor Problems,* 1912); CYC Dawbarn MA (*Uncrowned*, 1913); Isabella Nicholls (*The Eldest Son of Queen Elizabeth,* 1913); Amelie Deventer von Kunow (*Francis Bacon, Last of the Tudors*, 1924) and Alfred Dodd (*The Marriage of Elizabeth Tudor,* 1940). While there is significant variation on the quality of the underlying research, references to diplomatic communications and the facts of inheritance, in my mind, carry the most weight in this matter.

Dawbarn's account is of particular interest as it argues that it is "as told in his [Francis Bacon's] secret writings and in other contemporary records of her [Queen Elizabeth's] reign."

While it might seem fantastical to argue that the Virgin Queen actually married and had a child, the more one reads on the subject the less fantastical and more inevitable it seems. Even before one considers the evidence, to think that this gifted, highly-educated, passionate woman with her lust for life would live the celibate life of a nun, in a world where she could choose any man, stretches credulity. History records that this forceful, zesty woman was certainly interested in men with Robert Dudley appearing at the top of the list.

Often the only way we hear the truth about a person is from what is being said about them by their spiteful enemies. Queen Elizabeth's greatest enemy was Mary Queen of Scots. Mary was in constant contact with powerful people in England through letters coded in cipher. (With the likelihood of letters falling into the wrong hands, sensitive communications were either coded or entrusted for verbal delivery by loyal envoys.) At her trial, Mary was found to have the decoding keys for no less than sixty different ciphers. (For not dissimilar reasons, Francis Bacon was also an expert in cipher.)

The first chapter of Dawbarn's book is about a letter from Mary sent to Elizabeth while in her 'protective custody'. In her letter (to be found in Murdin's collection of State Papers) Dawbarn writes (p.5) that Mary clearly takes some delight in sharing with Elizabeth "the wicked slanders that the Countess of Shrewsbury so delights in spreading about her ... Why, she had even told her [Mary] that her Majesty had actually given a promise of marriage to a certain person; and more, before a dame of her chamber; and still more, that there had been intimacies between them usual between husband and wife alone."

So how *did* Elizabeth keep the pregnancy that followed a secret? The short answer is, 'Not very well.' The account in Chapter Two around the public knowledge of her marriage and pregnancy is sourced from these authors. Woodward reported that on 13 August 1560 (five months before Francis was born) Cecil was given the report 'concerning Mother Dowe of Brentwood in Essex, who openly asserted that the Queen was with child by Dudley.' (Lord Robert Dudley, later the Earl of Leicester.) Quite independently, von Kunow tells us that: 'In December 1560, a secret despatch of the Spanish Envoy advises that the Queen is expecting a child by Dudley (Escurial Papers).'

As played out in Chapter Two, Dodd tells us that Throckmorton, the English Ambassador to the French Court, initially sent an envoy to Elizabeth, as he did not trust a lesser, or written, form of communication on this sensitive matter. Dodd goes on to report that subsequently, on '31st December 1560, Throckmorton writes to Cecil certain significant passages which seem to indicate that he had resigned himself to the inevitable, and was making the best of a bad job. His phrases suggest that he was aware that the Queen was married and that he had been informed that the marriage was a secret one which would never be made public.' Dawbarn, Dodd and von Kunow record other communications between the three courts around the issue of the marriage and pregnancy.

As mentioned, most accounts of the men in Elizabeth's life place Dudley at the top of the list of suitors for her heart. He was often by her side. It is of particular note that he began sleeping in nearby chambers as her Master of the Horse within weeks after her ascension in 1558.

Robert Dudley's powerful family enjoyed a long and close relationship with the royals. They had grown up together as children. From when Elizabeth was eight, they shared the same tutors in the royal household at Hatfield (considered a satellite of Cambridge University). Dudley was Elizabeth's intellectual equal, but without her interest in the classics. While his interest was in mathematics and astronomy, he was a gifted and renowned horseman.

They were both in prison in The Tower in 1554. This followed allegations that Elizabeth had been involved in the Wyatt Rebellion to dethrone her older sister, Queen Mary. Elizabeth was aged just 20. Dudley, only a year older, had been imprisoned nine months earlier.

While it is rumoured they married while in the Tower, both expecting to be executed, this appears unlikely. As an example of their close relationship, Dudley later sold some land, before Elizabeth became queen, to help her out of financial difficulty. It is a notable sign of their friendship that Dudley himself was struggling with his own financial problems at the time.

Dudley had hoped that with the death of his wife, allegedly by falling down the stairs in August 1560, he would be free to publicly marry Elizabeth. If Elizabeth did give birth to Francis, she would have been pregnant at the time of Dudley's wife's death. However the timing, following rumours of him trying to poison his wife, proved too dangerous for Elizabeth. Moreover, she was not yet ready to dash the hopes of other potential suitors – especially the political ones.

When Dudley finally gave up on the open ratification of their relationship eighteen years later and remarried, Elizabeth in anger, permanently banished his new wife from court. Nevertheless, upon his death, when Elizabeth was 55, she was openly distraught.

It is curious to note the date in von Kunow's finding in the Dictionary of National Biography, (Volume XVI p. 114): "It is herein recorded that on January 21 1560/1 Queen Elizabeth was secretly married to Robert Dudley in the House of Lord Pembroke before a number of witnesses." This date is the actual day of Francis Bacon's birth. To avoid 'bastard' status it was critical that his parents' marriage, which may have occurred earlier, was not registered after the date of his birth.

As we will see with William Shakespeare, it is with death and the subsequent will and testament that much is declared and the truths outed. Sir Nicholas Bacon was a wealthy man who, as a lawyer by profession, held the most senior legal position in the land. As one would expect, he left a detailed will. In it, Francis received nothing.

Francis was eighteen when Sir Nicholas died. So it was not because he was only recently born that there was no time to write him into Sir Nicholas' will. Nor had his father disowned him. Indeed, they had an excellent relationship. Sir Nicholas clearly expected that as he was a ward, another would provide for Francis. That is precisely what happened – although not to the degree that Francis had hoped.

As a footnote to this exploration I include the following excerpt from the book 'Who Wrote Shakespeare?' by John F. Michell. I include it simply because of the link the building provides between Robert Dudley (the Earl of Leicester), Queen Elizabeth and Francis Bacon. As it turns out, in my research I visited this very building and attended a meeting held by the Bacon Society there. Afterwards I interviewed some senior members of the society about the mysteries around Francis Bacon. The excerpt comes from page 151 in the chapter on Francis Bacon's candidacy as Shakespeare:

'Then there is the strange matter of the inscription in Canonbury Tower, Islington, where Bacon lived for several years. The medieval tower once belonged to John Dudley, the Earl of Leicester's father. Queen Elizabeth used to stay there in a room known as the Queen's lodge... In the 1930s something else was discovered to encourage the belief that Bacon was Elizabeth's rightful heir. While the ancient, grimy walls of the top room in the tower were being cleaned, an inscription was uncovered above the door lintel. It was a list of English sovereigns from William the Conqueror to King Charles. Their Latin names are given in correct order up to Elizabeth and then follows: SVCCEDIT FR -- -- JACOBUS. The letters following FR had been thoroughly obliterated by gouging with a chisel. The apparent meaning is that King James succeeded or took the place of FR-----, possibly Francis, the Philosopher-King who could never openly claim his throne.'

Before we leave the parentage question, keep in the mind this point as you read the next section. Dudley, who Elizabeth later made the Earl of Leicester, became an outstanding patron of the Arts, literature and the theatre. Leicester's Men, as his acting company was known, were the forerunners of The Lord Chamberlain's Men, the acting company of William Shakespeare. Dudley's was the first major company in Elizabethan theatre of its time, establishing the pattern for the companies that would follow. It was the first to be awarded a royal patent and the first to occupy one of the new public theatres on a permanent basis.

THE SHAKESPEARE AUTHORSHIP QUESTION
Hiding Authorship is Easy, Hiding Genius Impossible

As outlined in the foreword, I wrote this book to elaborate and detail the process and challenges of finding meaning and thereby pursuing one's purpose in life. I was inspired to finally put pen to paper after visiting the magical Mont St Michel in early 2007. The authorship of Shakespeare's works was the last thing on my mind. At the time, I had two teenage children grappling with study and career decisions. Equally, in working with so many patients over the last two decades, I found that a lack of meaning and purpose would often underlie people's misery.

The reality is that life is intrinsically meaningless until you make it otherwise. Hence, the subject that inspired this book. When I chose the historical figure of Francis Bacon as the sixteen-year-old protagonist of this book, I had no idea how many worms were to be found in this proverbial can.

In researching this book, I visited, among other places, Francis Bacon's home town of St Albans. An early Roman city, from the time of Jesus, it sports the oldest pub in the UK dating back to before 1000AD. I was able to walk the back yard of Sir Nicholas Bacon's house (now in ruins) in which the young Francis would have played as a child from the age of seven.

The magnificent Cathedral and Abbey Church of Francis Bacon's residential town of St Albans is not only one of the oldest (early foundations laid in 793AD with the current buildings begun in 1077) but one of the largest in the land (at 550 feet, or 170 metres, it is longer than Westminster Abbey). Both the pub and the Abbey were well established in the time of Francis Bacon. As there is little written about Francis Bacon's role in the editing of the Bible, I put this to the minister in attendance at the Cathedral. His response? 'He was the most learned man of the time, and as the senior advisor to King James, it would make sense.'

There was another reason as to why this would more than make sense. Francis Bacon, as Lord Chancellor, was also the most senior lawyer in the land. The King would have wanted to ensure that the 'rules' he had given to those who had worked on the Bible had been adhered to. These rules were essentially about the King being positioned right next to God, as the head of the Church.

The more I read about Francis Bacon the more intrigued and impressed I became – intrigued by the complex richness of his life and impressed by his remarkable mind. A true genius is rare – but the more I read about him, the more I could see what Alexander Pope had meant when he said "Lord Bacon was the greatest genius that England, or perhaps any country, ever produced." I was even more interested in what Bacon's detractors had to say about him. When an enemy begrudgingly offers praise, one has to take it seriously! A great detractor was Lord Thomas Babington Macaulay, who said of Bacon: "He had the most exquisitely constructed intellect that has ever been bestowed on any of the children of men."

Early in my research on him, I came across the arguments that Francis Bacon was Shakespeare. I dismissed them to focus on how it was that this man, became not just Lord Chancellor, the head of the judicial system, but also became one of the most influential people in science and in history generally.

It was not until I was reading *Uncrowned* by CYC Dawbarn, that I was forced to confront the question of Bacon being the author of Shakespeare's works. Dawbarn's book, based on Francis Bacon's personal account, was about his right to the throne as the son of Queen Elizabeth and Lord Leicester ('Dudley'). While I was not entirely convinced about this proposition, I was devouring all that I could find on Francis Bacon. Throughout the book there were off-hand references to 'his plays'. I was already aware that Queen Marguerite (de Valois) had enthralled Francis Bacon from his time at the King's court in France. I had already written the chapters of their meeting with this knowledge in mind.

I was taken aback when Dawbarn started to matter of factly talk about how Romeo and Juliet was simply a play recounting Bacon's desire for Marguerite that could never be. Dawbarn's book was not about the controversy around the authorship of Shakespeare's plays, it was focussed on another controversy altogether – his parentage. It approached 'his plays' as an obvious truth. It was as if, to those in the know, there was no debate.

Having researched the captivating Marguerite I realised how, in real life, the problems and politics facing Francis and Marguerite in reality were so much greater than those of the warring merchant families of the famed play. Like it or not, I was now in the middle of the authorship debate.

My approach to this debate has been to study closely the lives of not just Francis Bacon, but also the man who most assume to be William Shakespeare who came from Stratford. To avoid confusion, I will refer to him by the name he used – William Shaksper. (When it comes to the spelling of the name of the man from Stratford, the most notable fact is his own variation in spelling his own name. Even as late as 1604, as a witness to a legal matter, he shakily signed his name to the deposition as 'Willm Shaksp' or possibly 'Willm Shaksper'.)

As we will come to, I have also looked at the life of Edward de Vere, Earl of Oxford, who is seen as the other frontrunner for the authorship candidacy. Accordingly, the supporters of each man's candidacy are called Stratfordians, Baconians and Oxfordians.

As I mentioned in the Foreword, my approach has been to look at the internal consistency between these men's formative years and the content and genius to be found in the plays.

My research has left me understanding the authorship question in the following way: Francis Bacon was the gifted wordsmith behind the plays and sonnets. He collaborated with other poets of the day, most notably Ben Jonson, Christopher Marlowe and possibly even

Edward de Vere. Shaksper very probably brought to the final stages of any collaboration an understanding of stage direction and of how to relate to the common man.

As Frances Yates discusses in the book, *Theatre of the World* (1969), it was known that Francis Bacon often met with colleagues at Gray's Inn to not only discuss politics and philosophy, but to actually try out various theatrical scenes that he admitted writing. I suspect that these men had no doubt as to who the author behind Shakespeare's works really was.

Ben Jonson, as well as being a recognised poet who would have made valuable contributions, was the go-between who linked the other two. It is worth remembering that when the complete works of Shakespeare were published in the First Folio, Ben Jonson wrote the introduction – he was clearly at the centre of the mystery.

Allow me to flesh out how I came to this understanding. I will start with the anonymity question, elaborate the psychological signature evidence and then finish on Ben Jonson.

WHY THE ANONYMITY?

People invariably ask, 'Why would Francis Bacon not openly admit his authorship of the plays if he was Shakespeare?' To understand this issue we need to realise that plays and their authors in sixteenth century London were not even vaguely valued, let alone respected, as they are now. While poetry or plays could be performed privately for friends and family, a true aristocrat would never write works for the public. If they did so it would never be under their own name – it simply was not the done thing.

The world of playwrights and actors was regarded with complete disdain and disrespect. When Francis Bacon was eleven years old, parliament passed the Vagrancy Act of 1572. It declared that all common actors who were not under the patronage of an honourable personage would be 'deemed rogues, vagabonds and sturdy beggars.'

An actor, not so associated, purely as a result of his profession, was to be stripped to the waist and whipped until his 'body be bloody'.

Equally, public theatres were considered meeting places for thieves, whore-mongers, con-men and women of ill-repute. High-ranking persons would not sully their name by writing for such an audience. Moreover, for any high-born person to write for the public, was equally disreputable. While Francis Bacon was not technically of noble-birth, he lived at the very top of this world in the direct service of both Queen Elizabeth and then King James.

He was employed as Queen's Counsel and, because of his skill with words, he was often called upon by Her Majesty to write various documents such as the 'Declaration of the Practices and Treasons attempted and committed by Robert late Earle of Essex and his Complices, against her Majestie and her Kingdoms.'

This created another reason for why Francis Bacon needed to keep his authorship secret. His plays often parodied people and situations at court. In those days, honour was protected much more preciously than it is now. Worse than his plays landing him in court for slander, he was at greater risk of being challenged to a duel. Francis Bacon was many things, but he was not a physical man. His tools of battle were his tongue and his quill. (For the purposes of storytelling, his skill at knife throwing at Mont St Michel, was fictionalised.)

Francis Bacon's other risk was the dreaded rack. To explain this I need to recognise another key resource. I think it unlikely that any living person has collected more information and has a better grasp of the unique man that was Francis Bacon than Lawrence Gerald. Gerald hails from the San Francisco Bay Area and for the last twenty-five years has been collating information on Francis Bacon and posting it on his comprehensive website, www.sirbacon.org.

I had read that the play Richard II had triggered the wrath of Queen Elizabeth. I had also read that the house, owned by the man from Stratford-on-Avon, known to the world as William Shakespeare, was linked to Francis Bacon. I had not realised how this fitted together until I came across the following, quite independently, on Lawrence Gerald's website:

"Edward Johnson writes that Wil Shaksper asked to be given a house at Stratford after he was packed off to Stratford as a safeguard when Queen Elizabeth became infuriated over Richard II because the play renounced the divine right of kings. In 1597, the Queen sought to discover the author with the intention of bringing him to the rack.

In 1598, a new edition of Richard II appeared with the name "William Shake-speare" on the title page. (The pseudonym Shake-speare relates to the Greek goddess Pallas Athena, with her spear, the divine symbol of wisdom and power and the patroness of learning.) Shaksper was given 1000 pounds and New Place (which formerly belonged to Lady Anne Russell, who was Francis Bacon's aunt) and told to lie low, which he did until after Queen Elizabeth's death.

Bacon knew Will Shaksper at the theatre and in his dilemma came to an arrangement to use his name as the author, even though Bacon had used the signature William Shakespeare before he had ever heard of the actor. Bacon wished to be certain that Shaksper was going to keep his part of the bargain, so New Place was not formally transferred to Shaksper until some years afterwards."

As a final note on the anonymity issue, Shakespeare's sonnets declare love and admiration for a female and then at times for a male suggesting the author was bisexual. This could be an embarrassment for a well-known, respected, (and later married) author. Francis Bacon married Alice Barnham. By all accounts, it was not a particularly close relationship and it remained childless. It was repeatedly rumoured that Francis Bacon was bisexual. While not the most socially helpful personal attribute, in this context it actually supports his candidacy for the authorship.

Of all these reasons, the paramount one was that if you wanted respect at the highest level of the English aristocracy then you did not want to be openly associated with the gutter-world of the theatre. Unlike well-endowed nobles, such as Edward de Vere, Francis Bacon's prosperity depended entirely upon the respect and patronage of others for his career advancement. Remember he was not technically of noble birth and Sir Nicholas Bacon had not provided for him. Initially, he wanted the respect of his peers. Later in life, he simply wanted the financial support to be able to explore and write on the ways to better advance humankind.

THE EARLY LIFE OF WILLIAM SHAKSPER

The authorship debate is a heated one. The possibility that William Shaksper, a poorly educated, low-bred man could come from obscurity and become the greatest writer of all time is incredibly seductive – an inspiration to all. Why let go of such a wonderful story?! Fantasy is fun, but not inspirational and not instructive. Stories of real people are truly inspirational. Moreover, understanding a great person's journey to their achievements can be truly instructive for those of us interested in personal growth.

There are two kinds of evidence, or facts, to be considered on the authorship question. First there are the known historical data, dates and written accounts for example, and how they fit together. Second, there is the psychological science of how the human mind works – my area of expertise. The first has been discussed at length by many writers and will be reviewed briefly. The human mind, and what I call the 'psychological signature' of a polymath, is the focus of this discussion. (Revisit the Foreword for the discussion of polymath.)

Psychologists or psychiatrists, like myself, are not the only ones qualified to debate this from the perspective of a psychological signature. Great writers, philosophers and thinkers are natural psychologists whose persuasive power comes from an innate and intimate understanding of how the human mind works. Minds like those of Mark Twain, TS Elliot, Dickens and Nietzsche have looked at this question. Each of them concluded that William Shaksper from Stratford clearly could never have been the author of the plays attributed to him.

In the book *Mortality,* the author, Christopher Hitchins, writes of Nietzsche's preoccupation with this matter such that, 'In the course of his mental decline, he became convinced that the most important possible cultural feat would be to prove that the plays of Shakespeare had been written by Bacon.' Hitchins portrays this as an insurmountable task.

The author of Shakespeare's works was more than a gifted linguist with an extraordinary vocabulary. He had vast knowledge of ancient and modern texts that had not yet been translated in to English.

Contrast the education of Francis Bacon with what is known about William Shaksper. Remember that Francis Bacon was raised by an unusually well-educated woman and his lessons were mostly conducted in Latin. I did not mention it in the story (as it had not yet occurred), but Francis Bacon also attended the University of Poitiers in France.

Accounting for William Shaksper's formative years can be done quite succinctly because almost nothing is known about them! There is actually no evidence of the man from Stratford having ever received an education. There are no school records and no accounts of people saying they attended school with him. It is presumed that the man from Stratford got his formal education by attending the grammar school in this small farming village of fifteen hundred people. A village that was so illiterate that thirteen of the nineteen men who governed the town, including Shaksper's father, a leather goods maker, could not sign their name and had to make their 'mark' instead. William's father, John, was a town alderman until he had to resign due to financial hardship (and subsequent lawsuits) when William was around twelve years old.

Even less is known about Shaksper's mother, a local girl in this rural, largely illiterate province. Contrast this intellectual environment to Francis Bacon's.

People do not realise that there are almost no records even of Shaksper's adult life. As Shaksper had a tendency towards suing people, the only reliable, written records of his life are lawsuits against others. There are no letters, diaries or manuscripts ... not a single note by his hand. At the age of eighteen when applying to marry, his name was spelt 'Shaxpere.' The next day it was recorded as 'Shagspere'. This would seem to indicate that by the end of his schooling, he did not know the spelling of his own surname. It suggests that the persons who recorded his name on these different occasions were guessing, without guidance from their owner, as to its spelling, based on the phonetics he offered.

Finally, given the depth of understanding of the law reflected in both the plays and the sonnets, the Stratfordians argue that Shaksper 'must' have spent time reading law. (Recall the sonnet Francis Bacon sends to the Ambassador for his feedback that was embedded with law metaphors – this is Shakespeare's Sonnet 46.) There is no evidence to support this notion at all. There are no accounts of any kind that Shaksper studied law and, as we will see in the next section, no books were found in his library to support the notion that he read law in his own time (despite his readiness to take people to court from time to time).

It must be assumed Shaksper studied law, because if it was not, it would immediately disprove Shaksper's claim to the Shakespeare throne. Of all the contenders for this throne, Francis Bacon remains, without dispute, the foremost legal mind of all the candidates.

THE WILL

The totality of Shaksper from Stratford's proven writings are six signatures on various documents. Three of these are on the pages of his will. Not only are they written in shaky handwriting but, in each one his name is spelt differently! Most people who write frequently tend to develop stable, consistent signatures, not so William Shaksper. His will is important for another reason.

Of all the evidence about his literary life, the most telling is his death in 1616. The man who died in Stratford left a very detailed last will and testament. It detailed his sword, his plate and a 'broad silver gilt bole'. His wife was to be given his 'second best bed' and its sheets and pillows. He provided for small bequests to allow three friends, who had been his co-owners in two theatres, to buy rings to remember him by.

Back then, one of the most valued assets of the educated and the literary was their library. Books were so treasured that often specific books, like specific items, would be left to certain people – just as Shaksper had done with his memorial rings and his 'second best bed.' Books were considered to be of greater, or at least equal value to bowls and beds. So what of his books and his precious manuscripts?

Note that the greatest and first compendium of all of Shakespeare's plays, the First Folio, would not be printed for another seven years i.e. until 1623. Indeed, there were more than a dozen plays by Shakespeare yet to see the light of day at the time of death of the man from Stratford. Moreover, existing plays would include new additions e.g. the beautiful passage added to Part II of *Henry VI*.

So how did Shaksper's will deal with the trappings and tools of his literary trade when there were all these valuable plays awaiting publication? Simply, it did not. While bowls and beds rated highly, there was no mention of a book to be left to anyone. No mention of a manuscript, finished or incomplete. No record of literary property of any kind. No instructions as to how any publication of his great plays should be handled. With well over a dozen great plays allegedly finished but unpublished, not one ranks a mention. Plays had a value. They could be sold to theatres –as Shaksper knew better than most!

The author of Shakespeare's works had sourced information from a veritable library of books in Greek, Latin, Italian and French that had never been translated into English. The man who died in Stratford either owned no books at all, or if he did, they were of no value to him. This was, to all observers, not the last testament and will of a celebrated and respected poet and playwright with a passion for words.

The greatest and most internationally celebrated literary figure of his time, Mark Twain, wrote a dissertation on the authorship debate. Mark Twain notes that the man thought to be a great playwright was, in reality, a businessman of the theatre. He was known to be somewhat penny pinching, quick to sue those who owed him money. I cannot resist but quote Mark Twain's own words (Is Shakespeare Dead? 1909) on the matter of the man from Stratford's will and the lack of mention of anything literary.

"If Shakespeare had owned a dog: we know he would have mentioned it in his will. If a good dog, Susanna would have got it; if an inferior one his wife would have got a dower interest in it. I wish he had had a dog, just so we could see how painstakingly he would have divided that dog among the family, in his careful business way."

There is, however, a bigger argument than the will. Anyone who wishes to hold an opinion in this debate should read Mark Twain's full account. Twain was the first to explicate the psychological signature issue. He expertly explains how an author can only write convincingly about matters of which they have a deep knowledge.

Then Mark Twain spends some time on the circumstances of Shaksper's death. Twain draws a comparison to the huge public interest in his own, lesser life (by his own comparison), the town he was from and the people who knew him. (He was more qualified than most on this topic, having had the interesting experience of reading misinformed media reports of his own demise – to which he famously responded with, 'The report of my death was an exaggeration.')

By highlighting the facts, Twain makes it exceedingly difficult for any thinking person to believe that the real Shakespeare died in Stratford. Dying as purportedly the most celebrated playwright in history in 1616, no one cared. Despite his poetry and plays being in high favour for around a quarter of a century, there was no funeral service, no tributes, no public mourning or eulogies, indeed no notice taken by anyone. Not a single word was written by anybody, let alone his theatre or literary contemporaries.

The volume of the *Annals* published for Stratford for 1616 made no mention of Shakespeare, or Shaksper, even though the man from Stratford was personally known to its author, William Camden. In great contrast when Francis Bacon died in 1626, there was a massive public response, especially from his peers. Eulogies and tributes poured in, not only from England, but the continent as well. No less than thirty-two eulogies were subsequently published in Latin. How often are eulogies collected and published!

In short, the resounding lack of reaction to the death of the man from Stratford told the truth of who he was. In Mark Twain's words, the man from Stratford *"had no prominence while he lived, and none until he had been dead two or three generations. The Plays enjoyed high fame from the beginning ..."*

Earlier, I made the observation that Dawbarn wrote about Francis Bacon being the author of the plays as if it was common knowledge to those in the know. It appears to be equally common knowledge in Stratford that Shaksper was not the famed playwright. His will is consistent with this assertion.

Shakespeare's death would be like George Lucas dying around half way through making his eleven Star Trek movies or Steven

Spielberg dying at the peak of his career after giving the world E.T., Back to the Future and Schindler's List. Shakespeare's death should have been acknowledged at some level in his home town, at least by the author of the Annals that knew him personally. While it was not the done thing for a person of standing to be recognised as a playwright, there was no obstacle to celebrating a commoner who was apparently highly gifted.

In a letter by Tobie Matthew to Francis Bacon, in 1623, written from France, he casually mentions this matter of identity as not uncommon knowledge: 'The most prodigious wit, that ever I knew of my nation, and of this side of the sea, is of your Lordship's name, though he be known by another.'

When Henry James wrote that he was 'haunted by the conviction that the divine William is the biggest and most successful fraud ever practiced on a patient world,' he did so with good reason.

The facts around the death of the man from Stratford are compelling, especially the lack of interest in his death. However, I would suggest that the man from Stratford was not Shakespeare for a very different reason. This reason may not satisfy people who hunger for black and white evidence, but to psychotherapists, or the great writers who are natural psychologists, with their understanding of the human mind, it is the more convincing argument.

THE PSYCHOLOGICAL SIGNATURE

Let me turn fully now to the psychological signature issue as introduced by Mark Twain. A psychological signature has three parts – nature, nurture and relationships. They make up a unique representation of each of us as individuals.

In this context, nature refers to one's inherent intellectual capability. In the case of whoever wrote Shakespeare, they were born an unqualified genius. We have already touched on this issue and shall return to what I call the 'Genius Argument' as the final point in this dissertation.

Nurture refers to one's formative experiences. As a psychotherapist, I have spent over two decades piecing together people's life stories and formative experiences. As mentioned in the Foreword, as a therapist one explores these experiences until they give up a certain level of internal consistency – the point at which even odd adult behaviour becomes understandable.

With this perspective in mind, you can nearly always see the influence of formative years on adult thinking, words and actions. Indeed, an understandable relationship to one's formative years must be there, just as surely as the sun will rise tomorrow. Whoever wrote Shakespeare's plays must have had experiences in keeping with being: a) a precocious intellect, b) intimate with life at court and c) highly educated and capable of reading the classics in Latin and Greek and d) widely travelled.

Third, we have relationships. By understanding the relationships between the key players in any intrigue, valuable insights around the real story are given up. Simply understanding allegiances, as we saw in the parentage question, provides much information.

Let us turn our focus to the issue of nurture and formative experiences.

The 'author-ity' of the author comes by virtue of learning and experience. In Mark Twain's words: *For experience is an author's most valuable asset; experience is the thing that puts the muscle and the breath and the warm blood into the book he writes.*

Authors cannot help but write about what shaped them – the indelible imprint of their formative years. After twenty years at sea, a ship's captain has no difficulty reading the signs of a storm approaching from over the horizon. To the trained and experienced psychotherapist, with similarly extensive experience, it becomes patently evident which earlier life events are consistent with which later thoughts, words and deeds.

What any writer knows is that you cannot write with passion, complexity and authority about matters that you have not experienced firsthand. The famed writer, Ralph Waldo Emerson on the man from Stratford's life, wrote that 'the best poet led an obscure and profane life.' He went on, 'I cannot marry this fact to his verse. Other admirable men have led lives in some sort of keeping with their thought; but this man, in wide contrast.' (Emerson: Essays and Lectures, 1983)

I believe that Emerson is struggling with a 'psychological signature' that was forged.

I was first published eighteen years ago. I had tried to be published before and many times since. I have been regularly published in one field or another from scientific peer-reviewed journals to parenting and women's magazines on a range of subjects. What has become clear to me is that, beyond the obvious requirement of capable and engaging written expression, it is very difficult to bring to rich life a subject that you do not know well. Editors can identify this from a mile away. A successful author is an authority on their subject matter by virtue of learning and experience.

As we have seen, a defining characteristic of Shakespeare's plays and sonnets is their deep understanding of the law. Some of the points of law dealt with complex legal issues still being codified in the justice system at the time. Even if Shaksper had taken the time to read up on this most complex subject, it is unlikely he could write about it with an ease that brought it to life and demonstrated a deep understanding of its intricacies. (While Edward de Vere did attend Gray's Inn, he never worked in or contributed to the legal profession.)

Equally, many of Shakespeare's plays are set in the life of monarchs, at their courts. We would expect the author to have an intimate knowledge of life at court. You have just read the story of how young Francis Bacon grew up ...

Plays by the man from Stratford should contain traces of life in rural Stratford where he spent all of his formative years. They should at least touch on the life event, at the age of twenty-four, of joining a touring company of actors that had played briefly in Stratford, leaving behind a wife and three children and moving to the dirty, uncaring and exciting city of London. This was undoubtedly the greatest culture shift of his life.

This point is well elaborated by Howard Bridgewater a Barrister who wrote *Evidence: Connecting Sir Francis Bacon with "Shakespeare"* (Baconiana, 1949). On this point he says:

> *"If, therefore, we thought that the butcher's apprentice of Stratford-on-Avon had written the plays attributed to him we should expect to find at least one reference to that village in one or other of them. But it is not mentioned in any single Play. This omission is surprising only to those who still cherish the traditional belief as to their authorship. What we* [who know Francis Bacon to be the author] *expect to find is reference to such places as St. Albans, Francis Bacon's country seat, to Gray's Inn; of which he was so prominent a member, and to York Place, where he was born. Needless to say we find allusions to all these places. St. Albans, although at the time "Shakespeare" was written was a village of no more importance than Stratford-on-Avon, is mentioned in the Plays no less than 23 times."*

Bridgewater, with the logic of a barrister in court, goes on to argue Bacon's case. Specifically that:

1. That the Plays contain references to events and places unlikely to have been referred to by any other writer of his time;

2. That thoughts and expressions identical with those in the Plays occur throughout his [Bacon's] acknowledged works;

3. That tricks of style are common both to his acknowledged writings and to the Plays; and

4. That even some errors peculiar to [Bacon] are repeated in "Shakespeare."

The last point is particularly telling. Bridgewater is not the only one to argue these points. Many authors have identified parallels between Bacon and Shakespeare's. A good summary is that written by Edwin Reed in 1998 entitled *'Bacon and Shakespeare Parallelisms'*.

Shakespeare's *Love's Labour's Lost* was one of his earlier plays, dated to the early 1590s. It refers to life in the court of King Henri of Navarre (Marguerite's husband). Professor Abel Lefranc, though not arguing for the authorship of Francis Bacon, has made a very special study of this play. He highlights how extraordinarily faithful the author is, even in the smallest details, to historical truth and to local colour. Professor Lefranc goes onto say:

> *"That the author of Love's Labour's Lost knew and had visited the Court of Navarre is apparent, if only we can agree to study the play without any preconceived hypothesis ... in order to justify the theory of its composition by Shakespeare, the player at the outset of his dramatic career ... every incident in the life of the Stratford player, prove the impossibility of his being the author of such a work."* (Sous le Masque de William Shakespeare by Abel Lefranc. Paris, Payot et Cie; translation from Vol II, p.p. 33-34, 1919.)

When *Love's Labour's Lost* was written, the 'Stratford player' had only left his hometown a few years earlier, touring England with the travelling acting company. While it is theoretically possible, there is no evidence to suggest that he travelled the hundred miles to London from Stratford via the small kingdom in the Pyrenees between France and Spain.

Lefranc has pointed out that the writer of the play had, *"virtually impeccable and absolutely amazing acquaintance with aspects of France and Navarre of the period that could have been known only to a very limited number of people."* Love's Labour's Lost was about the visit of Queen Marguerite to the court of her estranged husband. We would expect Francis Bacon to take a very keen interest in events involving the subject of his infatuation. (In all probability, his affection for her was ultimately unconsummated.)

Less well known is the fact that Francis' dearest brother Anthony, with whom he maintained a close correspondence, resided at the Court of Navarre between 1585 and 1590. Accordingly, given the pivotal importance of this play, Lefranc, unaware of Francis Bacon's abiding interest in Queen Marguerite, and of Anthony's presence at court, opts for William Stanley, the Earl of Derby, as the author of Shakespeare's works.

THE OXFORDIAN CANDIDACY

As mentioned, Edward de Vere, The Earl of Oxford is considered to be the other frontrunner for the authorship of Shakespeare's works. In essence, it is based on the psychological signature argument. The content and setting of Shakespeare's plays indicates an author who travelled widely, was highly educated and who was very familiar with life at court. Indeed, de Vere and Bacon grew up in the very same world, walking the same hallowed halls of Lord Cecil Burghley's mansion, Cambridge and Gray's Inn. Although they were not close friends, they were well known to each other.

The arguments against Shaksper and for Francis Bacon can be largely applied to de Vere. In the same way, when one reads the arguments for de Vere over Shaksper, they largely apply to Francis Bacon. This point that they lived in the same circles, seems to have been overlooked by the proponents of de Vere. They make the point, quite correctly, that to write plays about life at court that are so accurate and alive, the author must have been there. It has also been argued (as it has for Francis Bacon) that Shakespeare's plays reflected certain events in de Vere's life. As each man was familiar with the events in each other's life, this argues for either man – though it does exclude the man from Stratford.

More importantly, it is argued that de Vere received the education that Shakespeare must have received as he was tutored in Lord Burghley's (William Cecil's) great house with access to his massive library. Francis, however, not only grew up being tutored in the Burghley house from a much younger age, he had the brilliant Anne Bacon as his mother! At the same age de Vere was grieving for his father and heading off to Lord Burghley's house, a young Francis was heading off to Cambridge University!

To see a fuller argument for Oxford, read the 2005 book *Players* by Bertram Fields. Fields is not aware of Francis Bacon's full history, so when he says that 'reportedly Shakespeare revised some of the biblical verses' he was absolutely correct. As he goes onto assert this, he says that even if Shakespeare did contribute to the Bible, 'it doesn't tell us who he was.' It does if you know of Francis Bacon's role in editing the Bible (as mentioned in the Foreword). I recently came across independent confirmation of this role as I read Isabella Nicholls' book on Francis Bacon (see The Parentage Question).

And then there is the issue of de Vere's wealth. Sonnet 111, as Bertram Fields admits, is a problem for the noble born and the extremely-well-provided-for Earl of Oxford, for in it Shakespeare laments how he was not provided for in life and had to work for a living:

> *That did not better for my life provide*
> *Than public means which public manners breeds.*

This clearly was not Oxford, who was of the Tudor dynasty, making him the nation's greatest and most respected peer. He started life with a huge inheritance (which he then proceeded to diminish). Francis Bacon, unlike the other four sons, as we have seen, was not left anything in Sir Nicholas Bacon's will. He clearly believed that providing for Francis Bacon was not his responsibility. Again, truth is declared through death and the resulting will.

Bertram Fields goes on to overlook Sonnet 111 as he argues that the author was primarily Edward de Vere with input from Francis Bacon, William Shaksper and the other contenders such as Christopher Marlow and William Stanley. Being what might be called a 'groupist', Fields appeases all camps and makes no enemies.

For completion, obviously the man from Stratford, who was born into the working class, would not be lamenting 'public means which public manners breed'. To do so would be to betray his working class values. Moreover, such a statement would be a betrayal of his very heritage, parents, extended family and friends. The sonnets, by their very nature, are more directly autobiographical than plays which need to serve the greater purpose of the construct of the play itself.

Yet again, the greatest point of fact against Oxford comes, as it did for the man from Stratford, with death. Oxford died in 1604. In 1608 and 1609, three new plays were published, *King Lear, Troilus and Cressida* and *Pericles. Othello* arrived in 1622. A year later, the First Folio of Shakespeare's complete works was published with eighteen plays that had never before been published.

Remember, William Shaksper died in 1616. Francis Bacon lived until 1626.

It has been argued that Oxford simply wrote the plays prior to his death, made no mention of them in his will and then persons unknown organised for their completion, and or release, at these irregular intervals. This argument, despite the massive Machiavellian mental gymnastics involved, might have prevailed except for a few points of fact.

If *Othello* had been written prior to 1604 and then presented for publication in 1622, whomever was rummaging through Oxford's belongings, found another version a year later. This version, published in the First Folio, had 160 new lines along with other amendments. It is possible that two versions were uncovered a year apart, in the order that they were written, but it stretches credulity.

Unfortunately, the proponents of Oxford cannot run this argument when it comes to Richard III. Six editions of this play evolved from 1597 to 1622. In the First Folio edition of 1623 there were 193 fresh lines with hundreds of minor amendments. Admittedly, the person rummaging through Oxford's attic could have been finding the new editions in turn. Mind you, this now suggests they were hidden in such a way that they could only be found sequentially. This makes no sense. An author refining subsequent editions would typically keep the versions together, with the latest to the fore. However, there is one problem that puts an end to the Oxford debate.

Twelve printer's errors are identified, as having been carried over from the Quarto of the sixth edition of Richard III into its final edition in the Folio. ('Quarto' refers to a smaller book size and format than 'folio' which was the largest format of the time.) These twelve errors mean that the author must have been working from the published text of 1622. This would require either Oxford's (or the man from Stratford's) ghost to be able to hold a quill. Otherwise, we bring in another author who completed Oxford's plays without any editorial input or overseeing from the primary author. This might be an easier argument if not for the following from the Cambridge editors of the First Folio who say:

> *"The passages which in the Quarto are complete and consecutive, are amplified in the Folio, the expanded text being quite in the manner of Shakespeare. The Folio, too, contains passages not in the Quarto, which though not necessary to the sense, yet harmonize so well, in the sense and tone, with the context, that we can have no hesitation in attributing them to the author himself."*

The creative mental gymnastics required to reconcile a very dead Oxford with these facts, can be replaced with a much simpler explanation: Francis Bacon was alive and doing what he had been doing for the past few decades. Indeed, the fact that the editors go out of their way to make the point that the new additions are by the same author is rather intriguing. It is as if they want to send the message that the author is still alive.

As a final note on the de Vere candidacy, much simpler reasoning leads me to believe that he was not Shakespeare. It comes back to the psychological signature of these candidates. Francis Bacon was a genius who influenced the world. Edward de Vere was not – unless you assume that he is Shakespeare. Francis Bacon was lauded for his brilliance in court, in parliament and in his writings. Oxford was not.

JT Looney was one of the first to argue that the man from Stratford was not Shakespeare and proposed that it was de Vere. *The Oxford Companion to Shakespeare* edited by Michael Dobson and Stanley Wells (2001) makes the following point on the Oxfordian theory: "Looney offered no explanation as to why or how de Vere should have published mediocre work under his own name, and masterpieces under Shakespeare's." This statement goes to the essence of what I call the 'genius argument'.

Actually, Edward de Vere does appear in Michael Hart's book *The 100: A Ranking of the Most Influential Persons in History* (2000) that I mentioned in the Foreword. He comes in, very impressively, at position 31. Not mind you, for anything that he had done in his own life, but simply because Hart is an Oxfordian who believes that de Vere was Shakespeare and Shakespeare deserves position 31. He makes no mention of Francis Bacon's candidacy for the authorship. I would suggest that Francis Bacon appears twice in the one list. This is precisely what one would expect from a genius using a nom de plume – a 'literary double'.

The recognition of Bacon's genius as a true polymath – that is ongoing today – relies entirely on his masterpieces outside of the Shakespearian collection. Hiding Authorship is easy, hiding genius impossible.

For a readily accessible list of Francis Bacon's incredible array of publications on a huge range of topics simply search Francis Bacon on Wikipedia and refer to his Bibliography.

How did Mark Twain see Francis Bacon? He wrote:

"It is evident that he had each and every one of the mental gifts and each and every one of the acquirements that are so prodigally displayed in the Plays and Poems, and in much higher and richer degree than any other man of his time or of any previous time. He was a genius without a mate, a prodigy not mateable. There was only one of him; the planet could not produce two of him at one birth, nor in one age."

I believe that one of the reasons why de Vere is seen by many as a preferential candidate to Francis Bacon is to do with the latter's fall from grace. In 1621 as Lord Chancellor, Francis Bacon pleaded guilty to accepting bribes. Like so much in Francis Bacon's life, this event is surrounded by mystery and intrigue. It is true that Francis Bacon was not a master of his finances. It is also true that it was not an unusual practice to accept gifts to supplement what was not a particularly high income in this role. He pled guilty, was discharged from office and was fined and jailed. A few days later, somewhat irregularly, he was freed by royal pardon and his fine was cancelled by King James.

It is a long story, but the essence of it is that it was King James who had the conflict of interest and was at risk of being outed for corruption. Francis Bacon took the fall on his behalf. I cannot be sure, but certainly the documented leniency by the King fits this argument. The full story is on the www.thewayofthequest.com website for those who are interested.

It is ironic that his fall from grace and enforced retirement gave Francis Bacon the time to work on the First Folio, which came out two years later, and several other of his most important works. In his dedicatory epistle to Bishop Andrews, prefixed to that Shakespearean *'Dialogue Touching an Holy War,'* written in 1622, he gives an explicit account of what he saw as his purpose at that point in his life. He compares his fortunes to those of Seneca, like himself, a learned poet, moralist, statesman and philosopher, who, being banished into a solitary island, "spent his time in writing books of excellent argument and use for all ages." Having determined, as he says, "(whereunto I was otherwise inclined) to spend my time wholly in writing; and to put forth that poor talent, or half talent, or what it is, that God hath given me, not as heretofore to particular exchanges, but to banks and mounts of perpetuity, which will not break."

Which brings us back to Ben Jonson.

RELATIONSHIPS - THE BEN JONSON FACTOR

As is often the case in a mystery, the truth is best elucidated by understanding the 'who' and their relationships and loyalties to each other. As I have suggested, the go-between for Francis Bacon and William Shaksper was Ben Jonson who knew both men. Francis Bacon used the actor's knowledge of what worked for the audiences of his time to add bawdier action and less sophisticated humour to the plays. While he did not have Bacon's sheer brilliance and literary gifts, Shaksper knew his audience and his craft – it was a marriage made in heaven.

Bertram Fields unwittingly provides an important piece of the jigsaw that I had not come across before. He tells us that in 1620, Ben Jonson went to live with Francis Bacon at Gorhamsbury. Ben Jonson is the most important player in this fine mystery. He was the one who wrote the introduction to the First Folio. No other person can be identified so closely with the greatest, most comprehensive publication of Shakespeare's works. It was published three years after he moved in with Francis Bacon. Preparing the manuscripts for this publication would have been a major undertaking. Not only were old plays revised, but new ones written (all by hand) and finalised. It would probably take say … three years!

Ben Jonson, living with Francis Bacon and writing the introduction to the First Folio, clearly knew the truth of its authorship. Bertram Fields points out that prior to the publication of the First Folio, Jonson had 'extraordinary praise of Bacon.' He was on record as saying about Francis Bacon: 'He who hath filled up all numbers, and performed that in our tongue which may be compared or preferred either to insolent Greece or haughty Rome ... so that he may be named and stand as the mark and acme of our language.' (The Merriam-Webster dictionary defines 'acme' as 'one that represents perfection of the thing expressed.')

In the introduction to the First Folio, Ben Jonson described its author as 'the greatest writer of ancient or modern time ... leave thee alone for the comparison of all that insolent Greece or haughty Rome sent forth.' Fields described Ben Jonson 'as an extraordinarily articulate writer with a large vocabulary.' Such a wordsmith would not have had difficulty finding different words and turns of phrase for different men, so why would he use the very same words for two allegedly very different men? I would suggest that the need to never crossed his mind – why would he need to when they were the same man?

Ben Jonson is the key player here. It has been argued that these very words of Ben Jonson's support the argument that the Folio was written by the man from Stratford, for Ben Jonson knew the truth. Indeed, he did. So why did he misdirect the truth? For the very same reason he had been doing it for decades. After all, the author was still alive and well, nothing had changed.

Each of the three was necessary for the thinly disguised ploy to be sustained for so long. There was stronger motivation to hide the identity of the true author, than there was to argue that it was the man from Stratford. Certainly no one of the period wasted time with the notion that the man from Stratford was the brains behind the greatest and most loved plays of their time.

As I have explained, I did not write this book to debate of the authorship question. Having studied this fascinating matter at length, I felt compelled to write about it, and elaborate this Backstory, from a viewpoint than I had not seen articulated previously with all the evidence in the one place. While Mark Twain's argument in particular, articulates beautifully the issues of the psychological signature, he did not know of the Ben Jonson factor. He is in good company. No writers on the authorship debate have focussed on the importance of Ben Jonson and Francis Bacon living together in the period before the publication of the First Folio. I believe it is the key to this wonderful conundrum.

As I come to close on this fine mystery, allow me to share with you the words of John Michell, the author of "Who Wrote Shakespeare?" Michell sits on the fence as to who he believes it was, but then he does not have the benefit of all you have just read. In particular, he is not aware of the Ben Jonson factor. The closest he comes to assuming a position is the following:

> "There was one man at the time with the learning, imagination, cunning and position in affairs to create the state myth and organise cultural support for it. Francis Bacon was theatrically inclined and dwelt among mysteries ... He knew everyone's secrets and created secrets of his own. If the confusion of clues in the Authorship puzzle was the work of some ingenious puzzle-maker, Bacon was the expert in the field."

Supporters of the Stratfordian and Oxfordian schools undertake monumental, historical machinations, presuppositions and mental gymnastics to explain how long dead authors revise, edit and publish their plays. Most of all, they must work very hard to explain how their genius remained otherwise hidden to the world.

As they argue, I think of Ben Jonson and Francis Bacon beavering away at Gorhamsbury in the months before the First Folio is published. I see these two great literary minds bantering backwards and forth as they share cups of tea, vigorously debating grammatical and stylistic issues as they get on with the task of finalising the greatest publication of plays in the history of the world. They slap their legs with laughter as Ben Jonson reads the introduction he has drafted about the man from Stratford saying, "Do you think they will work it out? Should I not be more obscure?"

Francis Bacon responds, "Do not worry my old friend, for those who do not already know, I think it will be a long time before they think too deeply about it. They just want to enjoy a hearty, rollicking, good play."

***

Also by Dr Blair-West
Published in every English speaking country in the
World - now translated into Dutch and Chinese

For More Visit
www.thewayofthequest.com
www.dr.blair-west.com

www.ingramcontent.com/pod-product-compliance
Lightning Source LLC
Chambersburg PA
CBHW022104150426
43195CB00008B/260